Foundations of Criminal and Civil Law in Canada

SECOND EDITION

Nora Rock and Valerie Hoag

2006

EMOND MONTGOMERY PUBLICATIONS

TORONTO, CANADA

Emond Montgomery Publications Limited
60 Shaftesbury Avenue
Toronto ON M4T 1A3
http://www.emp.ca

Printed in Canada.

We acknowledge the financial support of the
Government of Canada through the
Book Publishing Industry Development Program
(BPIDP) for our publishing activities.

The events and characters depicted in this book are
fictitious. Any similarity to actual persons, living or
dead, is purely coincidental.

Acquisitions editor
Peggy Buchan

Marketing manager
Christine Davidson

Copy editor
Anita Levin

Supervising editor
Jim Lyons, WordsWorth Communications

Production editor and typesetter
Cindy Fujimoto, WordsWorth Communications

Proofreader
David Handelsman, WordsWorth Communications

Indexer
Paula Pike, WordsWorth Communications

Cover designer
Susan Darrach, Darrach Design

Library and Archives Canada Cataloguing in Publication

Rock, Nora, 1968-

    Foundations of criminal and civil law in Canada / Nora Rock,
Valerie Hoag. — 2nd ed.

Includes index.

ISBN 978-1-55239-159-4

    1. Law — Canada — Textbooks.   I. Hoag, Valerie   II. Title.

KE444.R62 2005   349.71   C2005-904847-6
KF385.ZA2R62 2005

Contents

APPENDIXES

PART I

Introduction to the Law: Function and Structure

CHAPTER 1

Introduction

Chapter Objectives

After completing this chapter, you should be able to:

- Describe the various functions of law in society.
- List at least three stages in the life cycle of a law.
- Describe the origins of and differences between common law and statute law.
- Describe the relationship between common law and statute law.
- Understand the distinction between substantive and procedural law.

This book is designed to provide an introductory overview of Canadian law. Although it will not make readers experts in any of the many specific areas of the law, it will provide an understanding of how the Canadian legal system is structured and how the law changes as society changes.

Why Make Laws?

All societies in all parts of the world govern themselves according to what can be described as codes of law. In order for the members of a group to live together peaceably and to govern their affairs efficiently, the group must develop, communicate, and observe certain norms of organized and predictable behaviour. As a group of members living together grows larger, the potential for conflict and the need for organization increase. In response to these changes, the group's code of behavioural norms — or laws — increases in complexity and in formality.

Religious and Secular Laws

Not all codes of behavioural norms resemble "laws" as we typically recognize them. Some groups identify their rules as being part of their religion, given to them by a god or gods. Some groups live by rules that are never explicitly spoken. Consider, for example, a high school clique, membership in which depends on "being cool" — either students are cool (understand the unspoken rules and govern themselves accordingly) or are not (haven't cracked the admission code).

In some societies, codes of religious rules actually evolve into laws for governing society (sometimes called "civil laws"); in other societies, a separate civil code emerges and evolves parallel to the religious code — hence the distinction between religious laws and secular laws. For many Canadians, secular laws have come to assume much greater importance than religious laws for governing behaviour, but aspects of the parallel systems remain. For example, a modern Jewish (or Christian, or Muslim, and so on) wedding ceremony incorporates the solemnization of both religious and secular contracts, each with different provisions and implications. The Ontario government is currently considering whether religious law, such as sharia (Islamic law), should be applied under the *Arbitration Act, 1991*.[1] As well, most nations have deliberately separated religious and secular laws.

Of course, many codes of social rules coexist with religious and secular laws — that is, every school, every family, and even every friendship has its own code.

The Life Cycle of Laws

Because of the many codes that everyone uses to govern their lives, most people are already familiar with, whether they realize it or not, the "life cycle" of rules. For example, they know that rules are born when they are proposed by a member and adopted by the group, and that rules often evolve to accommodate changes in the group's composition or circumstances. Rules also become increasingly complex. As a group's membership expands, rules that were once either unspoken or communicated orally may become **codified** or formalized — that is, written down in an organized way for easier dissemination. As social circumstances change, rules go through the processes of amendment and reform whereby some rules are revised and others are replaced because they no longer meet the needs of the society.

Civil or secular laws (simply "laws" from here on) follow a similar life cycle, which may include some or all of the following stages:

1. introduction,
2. debate and discussion,
3. adoption,
4. evolution,
5. codification,
6. **amendment**, and
7. reform/**repeal**.

Laws are valuable to a society only insofar as they meet that society's existing needs and deal adequately with the variety of circumstances that its members may experience. When a law stops meeting the needs of or taking into account the circumstances of the society, it must evolve or be amended.

This need to respond to change and to be flexible is the reason that all of our laws cannot simply be written down in one comprehensive (albeit lengthy!) and final code for everyone's reference. It is also the reason that lawyers are needed to keep track of the myriad intricacies of the law, courts are needed to settle disputes that arise over interpreting those intricacies, and a legislature is needed to create new laws to handle emerging issues. Basically, the judicial and legislative systems

codify
formalize a law or rule by incorporating it (usually in print form) into an existing or new code

amend
change a law or rule

repeal
terminate the application of a statute or statutory provision

are the mechanisms by which laws are formulated, designed, and interpreted in a consistent and orderly way.

Sources of Law: Common Law and Statute Law

Our legal system in Canada has two sources of law: common law and statute law. Statutes are made by the federal and provincial levels of government. Laws passed by the third level of government — the municipal level — are called bylaws. Each of these levels passes laws through the life cycle described in the preceding section. The other source of law in Canada (in all provinces and territories except Quebec[2]) is common law, or case law, where the courts make law by judicial decisions.

COMMON LAW

The role of the **common law** in our legal system is a direct result of our history as a British colony; we have inherited the common law as part of our law-making system. The common law is the body of judicial decisions made by courts in England and in Canada that establishes legal rules and principles dealing with specific issues. The common law has evolved over many years and reflects changes in society.

The use of common law to guide judicial decision-making is based on the concept of **precedent**. A precedent is a judicial decision on a particular legal issue that sets the law for the same or similar cases that follow. The courts in these later cases will apply the precedent and make the same or a similar decision, thereby maintaining the legal principle of the precedent. The body of law — these cases — makes up part of the common law.

The advantage of the common law system is that it provides consistency across decisions and predictability. Parties to a case will consider the decisions made in previous, similar decisions, and the parties should be able to predict what the result in their particular court case may be, barring any unforeseen developments. For example, a person charged with driving while impaired may want to challenge the manner in which the Breathalyzer test was conducted. This person, with the assistance of a lawyer, can review the large body of cases that already have considered this issue to determine whether there is a valid argument to be made to the court.

One advantage that the common law system has over statute law is its ability to respond to changes in society and to particular fact situations. The recent change to the common law definition of marriage is a good example of the flexibility of precedent. Previously, the common law definition of marriage prohibited people of the same sex from marrying each other. Various court decisions had supported that prohibition. However, societal views appear to have changed over the past 10 to 15 years. In the summer of 2003, the Ontario Court of Appeal considered decisions made by other courts (cases) to help it decide whether the definition of marriage should be changed to include same-sex couples. The Ontario Court of Appeal decided that it would be discriminatory not to change the definition of marriage to include same-sex couples. This decision became the law in Ontario and applies to any other cases in lower courts involving this issue. The decision was **binding** in Ontario.

common law
a legal rule or a body of legal principles, established through judicial decisions, that deals with a particular legal issue or subject area

precedent
a court decision that influences or binds future decisions on the same issue or similar facts

binding
in common law, the determinative quality of a legal decision on future decisions (assuming similar facts) if it was decided in a court of superior jurisdiction

Courts of appeal in other provinces heard cases regarding whether the common law definition of marriage should be changed. The Ontario Court of Appeal decision acted as a precedent and it was persuasive to the other provincial courts of appeal. They came to the same decision although they were not required to because the Ontario decision was not binding on them. The combined force of these decisions across Canada (and a decision from the Supreme Court of Canada) helped persuade the federal government to proceed with legislation in Parliament to change the definition officially. The *Civil Marriage Act*[3] came into effect in July 2005, allowing people of the same sex to marry each other. Prior to its enactment, the statute was hotly debated both within and outside Parliament, demonstrating that the courts and the legislature may not always agree on what the law should be.

STATUTE LAW

statute law
legal provisions, in codified form, that are developed and adopted by the parliamentary and legislative process

Governments make **statute law**, whether federal, provincial, or municipal (by-laws). Typically, the governing party in Parliament or the provincial legislature will introduce a bill — a piece of legislation — designed to address an issue or a procedure. For example, the Ontario government introduced a bill to address the issue of vicious attacks by dogs. The government chose to amend or change existing legislation by adding provisions dealing with specific breeds and by imposing liability on the owner if one of those breeds attacks a person.

This method of changing the law may be more time-consuming than having a court create a new precedent because of the democratic process of debate and review that is an important part of our parliamentary process. However, once the statute has been passed and becomes law, there is stability and consistency in that "the letter of the law" has been published and is available for all to read. For example, drivers of automobiles should know that there is legislation that prohibits speeding, careless driving, and "running a stop sign." The requirements for safe driving are not up to an individual's whim, but are codified by statute, and are enforced accordingly.

Statutes may also reflect government policy objectives, for example, mandating fair treatment of all employees in the workplace regardless of race, sex, creed, or religion, by passing a human rights code. Having a statute that prohibits discrimination in the workplace on the basis of a prohibited ground sends a message to all employers about the government's expectations and places them at risk of being investigated and penalized for violations. A statute is a more effective and efficient way of regulating behaviour than leaving the issue to a judge to determine and monitor on a case-by-case basis.

Similarly, if a statute no longer reflects the government's policy objectives (if the government changes after an election) or if a statute is no longer in step with societal values, then the government may decide to repeal the statute and the statute is no longer in force.

THE RELATIONSHIP BETWEEN COMMON LAW AND STATUTE LAW

As we have just discussed, common law and statute law come from different sources and each has advantages and disadvantages in terms of advancing the state of the law. The two systems do not operate independently of each other, however; the nature of the relationship could be likened to a "chicken and egg" question — which comes first? Both influence each other and both have the capacity to change each other. In using the same-sex marriage example, the courts redefined the common law definition of marriage, and Parliament followed suit.

The tension between common law and statute law comes from two competing concepts: rule of law and parliamentary supremacy. Rule of law means that no one is above the law, including governments, so that if a government passes an "illegal" law or a statute that was contrary to its authority, the courts can strike down that law, effectively cancelling or revoking it. On the other hand, parliamentary supremacy means that Parliament makes the laws, not the courts. Occasionally, the tension between these two concepts is covered by the media, usually at election time or after a controversial court decision. However, both concepts are fundamental to our legal system and directly inherited from the British legal system.

A great deal of statute law has resulted from the government's decision to codify the case law on a particular legal issue. The government may make this decision because it believes that the common law rules are appropriate and worthy of entrenchment in statute, or because it disagrees with the common law rules that have developed on a certain legal issue and wants to ensure that changes are made. Once the legislation is passed, common law will evolve because the courts will be called upon to interpret and apply the new statute. For example, the first time a dog owner who has been charged with a provincial offence because his or her dog attacks someone decides to fight the charge, the court will be required to interpret and to apply the new law. The decision by the court will have an impact on both the common law and the statute.

The *Criminal Code*,[4] for example, provides a statutory framework of rules that are **considered** by case law. Therefore, law enforcement students cannot simply carry around a pocket *Criminal Code* and be confident that all the law they need to know is contained in its pages. Much of the detail they will need to know to do their job properly can be found only in the common law — in the rules (and police practices) that develop out of the *Criminal Code* sections through daily judicial interpretation and reinterpretation of the words used in the Code.

considered
applied or interpreted in a court case; refers to statutory provisions

While criminal law has the *Criminal Code* as its statutory framework, many other areas of law, such as contracts and torts, are based almost completely in common law, with some specific subtopics the subject of statutes. Contract and tort law are covered in chapter 10. For example, family law statutes and landlord and tenant statutes, discussed in chapters 11 and 12, demonstrate the implementation of government policy objectives and the influence of societal values in changing the common law.

Substantive Versus Procedural Law

Another distinction that law enforcement students should be aware of is the difference between **substantive law** and **procedural law**. Substantive law describes the type of conduct that is acceptable and unacceptable. Procedural law describes the process to be followed when there is a violation of substantive law.

Colleges have codes of student conduct that cover cheating. Cheating, as described in its various forms in a college's code of conduct, is the substantive law. If

substantive law
law that addresses the substance or factual content of a legal issue

procedural law
law that establishes the process by which substantive issues will be addressed

a student violates the prohibition against cheating, there is also a prescribed process whereby members of faculty and/or administration conduct an investigation and render a decision, in which a penalty may be assessed. This process is the procedural law and includes such matters as what forms are used, what the student is expected to do, and whether the student can appeal.

In criminal law, the *Criminal Code* contains both substantive law ("Every one commits robbery who ...") and procedural law ("A judge ... may ... release an appellant ..."). The *Criminal Code* tells us what the offences are and what happens if an offence is committed. Both aspects of the *Criminal Code* are explored further in later chapters.

In civil law, there are statutes and cases that describe the substantive aspects of civil claims, such as liability for injuries suffered in a motor vehicle accident or in a slip-and-fall accident on an icy sidewalk. The injured party will be guided by the rules of civil procedure that describe requirements such as the documents to be served and filed and the time limits that must be met. Some of these requirements will be discussed later.

It is important for the law enforcement student to understand that procedural law is as important to respect as substantive law. Procedural law provides the "same rules" for all participants in the process to follow. Failure to follow the procedural law can be very serious for law enforcement officers, law clerks, paralegals, and other participants, as will be discussed in more detail later.

KEY TERMS

amend

binding

codify

common law

considered

persuasive

precedent

procedural law

repeal

statute law

substantive law

NOTES

1. *Arbitration Act, 1991*, SO 1991, c. 17.
2. Quebec's legal system is somewhat different. Quebec has a *Civil Code* — a general code of provincial law that addresses a wise range of legal issues that, in other provinces, are covered primarily by case law.
3. *Civil Marriage Act*, SC 2005, c. 33.
4. *Criminal Code*, RSC 1985, c. C-46, as amended.

EXERCISES

Multiple Choice

1. Statute law offers the following advantage(s) over case law:
   a. it allows easier public access to the state of the law
   b. it can provide policy directions to specific groups to follow
   c. it addresses all possible fact situations
   d. a and b
   e. all of the above

2. Some laws are described as procedural because they
   a. regulate the performance of complex scientific procedures
   b. are less important than substantive laws
   c. prescribe the process by which justice is to be achieved
   d. can be applied only by courts of superior jurisdiction
   e. none of the above

3. The life cycle of a law includes the following stages:
   a. introduction, amendment, citation, repeal
   b. introduction, debate, codification, citation, statute, substantiation
   c. adoption, evolution, termination, repeal, substantiation
   d. introduction, debate and discussion, adoption, evolution, codification, amendment, reform/repeal
   e. introduction, debate and discussion, adoption, repeal, evolution, codification, amendment

4. Common law is
   a. the set of laws that are common, everyday occurrences
   b. a body of legal principles established through court decisions
   c. a set of statutes passed by Parliament
   d. a body of cases established through court decisions and codified as statutes
   e. the set of bylaws passed by a municipal government

5. Substantive law
   a. describes an expectation of behaviour or responses
   b. is designed to govern the way the law is brought to bear on a dispute
   c. is a body of legal principles established through the judicial process
   d. is a body of statutes passed by Parliament
   e. is also called civil or secular law

True or False?

_____ 1. Converting a common law rule into statutory form ensures that it will no longer evolve in response to court decisions.

_____ 2. All criminal law is statute law because it is contained in the *Criminal Code*.

_____ 3. Religious laws no longer apply in the common law world.

_____ 4. Religious laws are not interpreted or applied by Canadian legal courts.

_____ 5. Procedural law governs the way substantive law is brought to bear on a dispute.

Short Answer

1. Based on your understanding of this chapter, draft a definition of the word "law."

2. This chapter describes many of the practical advantages of statute law. What are the advantages of case law?

3. The *Charter of Rights and Freedoms*, part of Canada's constitution, was drafted broadly, with the expectation that its provisions would be interpreted by case law. Why do you think the drafters chose to be vague about such important legal issues?

CHAPTER 2

Statute Law: Function, Jurisdiction, and Structure

Chapter Objectives

After completing this chapter, you should be able to:

- Explain the concept of jurisdiction with respect to lawmaking.
- List the principal levels of lawmaking jurisdiction in Canada.
- Describe the function of the constitution in establishing lawmaking jurisdiction.
- Describe, in general terms, the scope of provincial and federal jurisdiction.
- Explain how to locate a statute.
- Describe the typical structure of a statute.
- Describe the function of regulations.

The Concept of Lawmaking Jurisdiction

As explained in chapter 1, statute law (legislation) is the formal, written law enacted by governments. Canada has three principal levels of government — federal, provincial, and municipal — and each level has a specific lawmaking **jurisdiction**, or sphere of appropriate legislative action, reserved to it.

In countries with a federal system of government (a system that contains a number of semi-autonomous units), these levels are a common way of organizing legislative responsibility. However, the degree of control given to the smaller government units varies widely from federation to federation. As a general rule, the central government in a federation tends to reserve to itself jurisdiction over very important issues or issues of national importance, including serious crime, national security, immigration, and trade. Issues of daily life, such as employment and family law, are assigned to the smaller government units. In Canada, a comparatively large degree of legislative responsibility is delegated to the provinces — that is, there are

jurisdiction
authority to make law, either by governments or by courts

many more provincial statutes, and accompanying regulations, than there are federal ones.

A coherent organizational scheme for assigning jurisdiction is important because it prevents legislative overlap while ensuring that all of the issues that need to be addressed are covered somewhere. An organizational scheme also allows for shared governmental responsibility, including financial responsibility, for administering the legal system. Decisions about which level of government has jurisdiction over a particular issue are often the subject of political tension in a federation. While the smaller government units often prefer to have the power to decide a particular issue, having that power usually means being responsible for the cost of its administration.

How Is Legislative Jurisdiction Assigned?

cite
describe or refer to, orally
or in writing, a legislative
provision or legal decision

In Canada, as in many federations, legislative jurisdiction has been established by the constitution. The constitution is considered to be the law that creates, or "constitutes," a nation. It is a basic plan for the government of a major political unit, in our case Canada. Canada was created in 1867 by an act passed by the British Parliament **cited** now as the *Constitution Act, 1867*,[1] previously known as the *British North America Act, 1867*. In 1982, the British Parliament passed the *Canada Act, 1982*,[2] which contained the *Constitution Act, 1982*.[3] The *Constitution Act, 1982* was passed by our Parliament. The *Constitution Act, 1982* includes the *Constitution Act, 1867* and the *Canadian Charter of Rights and Freedoms*. The passage of these pieces of legislation by both the British and Canadian parliaments meant that Canada officially had a constitution and that the constitution was completely Canadian. The *Constitution Act, 1982* states that it, and therefore the Charter, is the supreme law in Canada. No single government, federal or provincial, can change the constitution.

One of the most important tasks performed by any constitution is the assignment of legislative jurisdiction. In the case of the *Constitution Act, 1867*, this assignment is made by ss. 91 and 92, which read, in part, as follows:

> 91. It shall be lawful for the Queen, by and with the Advice and Consent of the Senate and House of Commons, to make laws for the Peace, Order and Good Government of Canada, in relation to all Matters not coming within the Classes of Subjects by this Act assigned exclusively to the Legislatures of the Provinces; and for greater Certainty, but not so as to restrict the Generality of the foregoing Terms of this Section, it is hereby declared that (notwithstanding anything in this Act) the exclusive Legislative Authority of the Parliament of Canada extends to all Matters coming within the Classes of Subjects next herein-after enumerated; that is to say,
>
> 1A. The Public Debt and Property.
> 2. The Regulation of Trade and Commerce.
> 2A. Unemployment Insurance.
> 3. The raising of Money by any Mode or System of Taxation.
> 4. The borrowing of Money on the Public Credit.
> 5. Postal Service.
> 6. The Census and Statistics.

7. Militia, Military and Naval Service, and Defence.
8. The fixing of and providing for the Salaries and Allowances of Civil and other Officers of the Government of Canada.
9. Beacons, Buoys, Lighthouses, and Sable Island.
10. Navigation and Shipping.
11. Quarantine and the Establishment and Maintenance of Marine Hospitals.
12. Sea Coast and Inland Fisheries.
13. Ferries between a Province and any British or Foreign Country or between Two Provinces.
14. Currency and Coinage.
15. Banking, Incorporation of Banks, and the Issue of Paper Money.
16. Savings Banks.
17. Weights and Measures.
18. Bills of Exchange and Promissory Notes.
19. Interest.
20. Legal Tender.
21. Bankruptcy and Insolvency.
22. Patents of Invention and Discovery.
23. Copyrights.
24. Indians, and Lands reserved for the Indians.
25. Naturalization and Aliens.
26. Marriage and Divorce.
27. The Criminal Law, except the Constitution of Courts of Criminal Jurisdiction, but including the Procedure in Criminal Matters.
28. The Establishment, Maintenance, and Management of Penitentiaries.
29. Such Classes of Subjects as are expressly excepted in the Enumeration of the Classes of Subjects by this Act assigned exclusively to the Legislatures of the Provinces.

And any Matter coming within any of the Classes of Subjects enumerated in this Section shall not be deemed to come within the Class of Matters of a local or private Nature comprised in the Enumeration of the Classes of Subjects by this Act assigned exclusively to the Legislatures of the Provinces.

92. In each Province, the Legislature may exclusively make Laws in relation to Matters coming within the Classes of Subjects next herein-after enumerated; that is to say,

1. Repealed.
2. Direct Taxation within the Province in order to the raising of a Revenue for Provincial Purposes.
3. The borrowing of Money on the sole Credit of the Province.
4. The Establishment and Tenure of all Provincial Offices and the Appointment and Payment of Provincial Officers.
5. The Management and Sale of the Public Lands belonging to the Province and of the Timber and Wood thereon.
6. The Establishment, Maintenance, and Management of Public and Reformatory Prisons in and for the Province.
7. The Establishment, Maintenance, and Management of Hospitals, Asylums, Charities, and Eleemosynary Institutions in and for the Province, other than Marine Hospitals.

8. Municipal Institutions in the Province.
9. Shop, Saloon, Tavern, Auctioneer, and other Licenses in order to the raising of a Revenue for Provincial, Local, or Municipal Purposes.
10. Local Works and Undertakings other than such as are of the following Classes:
    a. Lines of Steam or other Ships, Railways, Canals, Telegraphs, and other Works and Undertakings connecting the Province with any other or others of the Provinces, or extending beyond the Limits of the Province
    b. Lines of Steam Ships between the Province and any British or Foreign Country
    c. Such Works as, although wholly situate within the Province, are before or after their Execution declared by the Parliament of Canada to be for the general Advantage of Canada or for the Advantage of Two or more of the Provinces.
11. The Incorporation of Companies with Provincial Objects.
12. The Solemnization of Marriage in the Province.
13. Property and Civil Rights in the Province.
14. The Administration of Justice in the Province, including the Constitution, Maintenance, and Organization of Provincial Courts, both of Civil and of Criminal Jurisdiction, and including Procedure in Civil Matters in those Courts.
15. The Imposition of Punishment by Fine, Penalty, or Imprisonment for enforcing any Law of the Province made in relation to any Matter coming within any of the Classes of Subjects enumerated in this Section.
16. Generally all Matters of a merely local or private Nature in the Province.

Considering the hundreds of statutes currently in force in Canada, the relative simplicity of the foregoing jurisdiction plan is surprising. Because the plan was created in 1867, many of the issues that are currently the subject of legislation had not even been contemplated by the constitutional drafters (consider, for example, legislation designed to regulate telecommunications). How, then, do the provinces and the federal government determine which has jurisdiction over new or unique issues? The answer: by analogy. When an issue that requires legislation comes up, it is compared with the matters specifically addressed in the jurisdiction sections of the constitution (ss. 91 and 92), and it is then assigned to either the provinces or the federal government based on where the issue seems to fit based on the intentions behind the original division of powers. In many cases, this is an easy decision and is a matter of agreement between the levels of government; when the decision is more contentious, the courts are called on to interpret the application of the constitution to the new issue. For example, charge cards, such as Visa or MasterCard, are regulated by federal law, even though charge cards did not exist in 1867. The business of charge cards is handled by banks and therefore, by analogy, it makes sense to have charge cards fall under federal jurisdiction.

To help clarify how the division of powers works in practice, here are two lists of statute names. The statutes in the first list are federal statutes, and the statutes in the second list are provincial statutes:

Federal statutes (passed by the Parliament of Canada):

- the *Criminal Code*[4]

- the *Immigration and Refugee Protection Act*[5]

- the *Fisheries Act*[6]
- the *Oceans Act*[7]

Provincial statutes (passed by provincial legislatures):

- the *Family Law Act*[8] (Ontario)
- the *Workers' Compensation Act*[9] (Alberta)
- the *Human Tissue Gift Act*[10] (British Columbia)
- the *Freedom of Information and Protection of Privacy Act*[11] (Ontario)

Municipal Jurisdiction

Sections 91 and 92 of the constitution, reproduced above, include scant mention of municipal jurisdiction. However, certain legal issues in Canada are addressed by municipalities (cities and towns). You will notice that specific items in s. 92 of the constitution refer to municipal matters (see items, 8, 9, and 10) and thus the provinces have jurisdiction over municipalities. Laws passed by municipalities are called bylaws, and usually deal with issues of a very local nature, such as parking, waste collection, and community services. Municipalities hold the authority to regulate these issues by delegation (passing down of responsibility) from the provinces. Although many issues considered part of municipal jurisdiction may seem minor in comparison with national concerns, the smooth management of a large municipality is an incredibly complicated task and can give rise to an enormous number of bylaws. Municipal law is a very complicated discipline and, apart from this brief mention, is beyond the scope of this text.

Researching Statute Law

THE CRIMINAL CODE

The statute that police consult most often is the *Criminal Code*. The most current version of this statute is cited as RSC 1985, c. C-46 (the significance of the elements of this citation will be discussed below). Because it is one of the most frequently consulted Canadian statutes, the *Criminal Code* is often published by commercial publishers in pocket and annotated (with commentary) editions, many of which contain the text of other related statutes, such as the *Youth Criminal Justice Act*,[12] the *Canada Evidence Act*,[13] and others creating criminal or quasi-criminal offences. These editions will typically include, as well, the text of the *Charter of Rights and Freedoms*. A current, commercially published edition of the *Criminal Code* will serve most research needs, but because such Codes are usually published only once a year, new provisions or amendments may not be included in the edition. To be absolutely sure that information is up to date (to prepare for a court appearance, for example), one needs to update, or "note up," research results by consulting an official source for the legislation, as described below.

OTHER STATUTES

Although the *Criminal Code* figures prominently in legal research, there will be occasions to apply or be familiar with other statutes that have a quasi-criminal component. (Many of these statutes will be discussed in a course on provincial offences.)

Because these other statutes are not as commonly applied by police officers, usually no convenient pocket edition is available. Finding these statutes requires performing basic legal research in the same way that a lawyer or paralegal does — either in a traditional law library, or on a computer. There are a number of computerized databases, including government websites (which contain cases, statutes, and regulations), CanLII (supported by LexUM and maintained by the University of Montreal), commercial online resources such as LexisNexis/QuickLaw and eCarswell, and CD-ROM products.

IS THE LEGAL PROBLEM COVERED BY A STATUTE?

In some cases, it may be necessary to research a legal problem without even knowing whether the problem is covered by a statute (remember, a great deal of Canadian law is case law, as explained in chapter 1). In such a case, the first step might simply be to describe the problem to a more experienced colleague or to a law librarian, who may be able to identify the relevant statute.

A statute may also be identified by performing a search based on keywords suggested by the problem. For example, if the problem deals with a tenant who claims to have been locked out of his or her apartment by the landlord, the search for the relevant statute might be based on the word "landlord." (A search based on the words "locked out" may be less productive; it is a good idea to identify as many potential keywords as possible.)

Electronic Sources

An electronic source for legal research, such as a database or website, will likely have a search function that allows searches by keyword. The kinds of documents generated by such a source will depend on the type of source, but if there is a statute governing the problem, there is a good chance that it will be found in this way. As with any website, the user should make sure that the site contains accurate and current information.

Two sources available on CD-ROM are the *Canada Statute Service* (Aurora, ON: Canada Law Book, quarterly) and the Statutes of Ontario published by the Ontario provincial government twice a year. The federal government and most provincial governments maintain websites that include the full text of statutes.

Paper Sources

Legal research can also be done in a law library using paper sources. The librarian can identify any encyclopedic sources that may be available. The most common ones are *The Canadian Abridgment* (Toronto: Carswell), a huge, multivolume legal encyclopedia that is searchable in many different ways (it is a good idea to ask a librarian how best to use it), or *The Canadian Encyclopedic Digest* (Toronto: Carswell), another large encyclopedia that is organized primarily by subject-matter topics. The *Digest* has regional editions, so the appropriate one for the region can be used.

Although these encyclopedias may look daunting, a keyword search will often very quickly reveal the name of a statute (or a case) dealing with the particular legal problem. In the case of the above lockout example, a search under "landlord" will almost certainly lead to a provincial landlord and tenant statute. All of the provinces have one of these.

USING THE CITATION TO FIND THE STATUTE

A reference to a statute will also likely provide the statute's **citation** — a list of letters and numbers following the statute name that represent that statute's "address" for the purpose of research.

A federal statute's citation looks like this:

- *Criminal Code*, RSC 1985, c. C-46; or
- *Immigration and Refugee Protection Act*, SC 2001, c. 27.

A provincial statute's citation looks like this:

- *Provincial Offences Act*, RSO 1990, c. P.33; or
- *Labour Relations Act*, SO 1995, c. 1.

A statute's citation is designed to direct the reader to the most current official print source of the legislation. Each Canadian legislature, federal or provincial, publishes a print collection of its statutes. This collection includes new volumes, printed in each year, containing all new legislation passed by the legislature. As well, the statutes are available on official government websites. Previously, the practice had been to publish a collection of statutes, with any changes or revisions, periodically. For example, Ontario published its revised statutes every 10 years. Because of public accessibility to government websites and the ability to provide current versions of statutes online, governments have ceased to publish consolidated collections of statutes. Ontario's last set of revised statutes was in 1990; the federal government's was published in 1985. Because of this system of revisions, the volumes marked Revised Statutes contain *all* of the statutes of that jurisdiction in force at that time; the more recent volumes, marked simply Statutes, contain only the statutes that were passed *after* the last revision was published. For example, Statutes of Canada 2005 contains only statutes passed in 2005.

The two or three letters that immediately follow the statute name in the citation identify whether it is in the Revised Statutes or in the Statutes: "RSC 1985" means Revised Statutes of Canada, 1985 Revision, while "SC 1994" means Statutes of Canada, 1994. The same is true for provincial legislation: "RSO 1990" means Revised Statutes of Ontario, 1990 Revision, and "SO 1995" means Statutes of Ontario, 1995. (The abbreviations differ for other provinces. For example, "RSA" means Revised Statutes of Alberta. (See appendix A for a list of abbreviations.) This part of the citation, then, identifies which volume contains that statute.

The rest of the citation is a chapter reference (indicated by lowercase "c.") — it tells where in the volume to look for the statute. Revised statutes are usually catalogued or cited by a combination of the first letter of the statute and the numerical position under that letter. For example, the *Criminal Code* is "c. C-46." Statutes that have been passed since the last revision of statutes for that government are numbered consecutively for the year that the statutes were passed.

citation
an expression, in standard form, of the bibliographical information for locating a case or legislative document

Finally, if the statute is very recent — it was passed into law after the release of the last annual volume of statutes — a print version must be searched for in a different kind of publication called the *Canada Gazette* at the federal level, and often called a "bills service" at the provincial level. These are published frequently while Parliament is in session and contain both the official text of just-released statutes and also updates on the status of **bills** that are before Parliament but that have not yet been passed. Unofficial versions of the text of brand-new statutes can be found on the website of the relevant level of government; be sure to check how current the revisions are.

bill
a document created for the purpose of parliamentary review of a proposed statute; usually a statute in draft form that has yet to be adopted as law

UPDATING A STATUTE

While the citation directs researchers to the statute, this is never the end of the process. Most statutes, not only "busy" ones like the *Criminal Code*, are updated occasionally by Parliament through the process of amendment, which involves passing new substatutes that make changes to the main statute. These amending statutes may be found in the Statute volumes following the most recent Revised Statutes volumes. The revisions are incorporated into the statutes on the government websites. If you do not have access to the Internet and you need to find out whether a statute has been amended, you need to check a publication called a statute citator, which is usually updated monthly. A legal librarian can help with using this source. Federal statutes are listed in the *Canada Statute Citator* (Aurora, ON: Canada Law Book). There are also provincial statute citators.

Reading a Statute: Basic Principles of Statutory Organization

Having found a statute, a researcher needs a plan of attack for reading it, especially if it is long. A few statutes — especially longer ones — are published with tables of contents and even indexes, but most are not. Fortunately, most are organized according to a standard pattern, which may include the following features:

1. *Long title* Usually, "An Act respecting ... (the subject matter of the statute)." The long title is rarely used to refer to the statute.

2. *Short title* The name by which the statute is commonly known, which may be provided at the beginning or at the end of the statute. If a short title is provided, it is the only way the statute may be properly cited.

3. ***Preamble*** An introduction, made up of one or more provisions, that sets out the objectives and guiding philosophy of the statute. The preamble can often provide some interesting insights into the sociopolitical context of the statute. It is also an official component of the statute for interpreting and enforcing the statute.

preamble
an introduction, made up of one or more provisions, that sets out the objectives and guiding philosophy of a statute

4. *Introductory provisions* These often include a list of defined terms, a description of the scope of application of the statute, and details about how the statute will be administered.

5. *Body of the statute* The sections in this part deal with the substantive issues covered by the legislation. In a long statute, the body may be divided into a number of parts, each of which deals with an aspect of the statute. Provisions dealing with the same aspect are grouped together in the same part of the statute. Where a statute imposes penalties for breach of its terms, these provisions are often found near the end of the body or near the end of individual parts.

6. ***"Housekeeping" provisions*** These provisions, found at the end of some statutes, deal with administrative issues, such as the timing of coming into force of individual provisions.

"housekeeping" provisions
provisions found at the end of some statutes that deal with such administrative issues as the timing of coming into force of individual provisions

Briefly skimming a statute before beginning to actually read it may help to identify sections that are most likely to contain the information sought, especially if the statute contains shoulder notes — brief references in the margins that describe the content of the provisions. Shoulder notes are not officially part of the statute, but are meant to help readers access the different provisions. Headings are helpful for the same purpose.

Regulations

Many statutes are accompanied by a type of subordinate legislation known as regulations, particularly where the subject matter being covered is of a technical nature. Unlike statutes, regulations are not passed by Parliament or provincial legislatures. They are prepared and published by administrative officials (department or ministry staff), under the authority of the relevant statute, to deal with the technical issues. Regulations tend to be very practical and can include lists, schedules, diagrams, forms, and charts. The rules of various levels of courts are generally published in the form of regulations.

The information contained in regulations is just as important as that found in the primary legislation. It is often even more current because regulations do not require the formalities of the legislative process to be created — they can and do change frequently. This flexibility is one of the reasons they are used. For example, Ontario's *Employment Standards Act*[14] has numerous regulations, including one describing minimum wages to be paid. If a statute has regulations made under it, the regulations will be found published in their own volumes, separate from the statute, and will be revised according to the same schedule as the statute itself. However, regulations cannot exist on their own without a parent statute. For a regulation to lawfully exist, the statute must include a provision that designates regulation-making authority. If no such provision exists, no regulations can be drafted. Regulations are available online on government websites. For example, in Ontario, statutes and regulations are available on e-Laws at http://www.e-laws.gov.on.ca.

KEY TERMS

bill   "housekeeping" provisions

citation   jurisdiction

cite   preamble

NOTES

1. *Constitution Act, 1867*, 30 & 31 Vict., c. 3 (UK).

2. *Canada Act, 1982* (UK), 1982, c. 11.

3. *Constitution Act, 1982*, RSC 1985, app. II, no. 44.

4. *Criminal Code*, RSC 1985, c. C-46, as amended.

5. *Immigration and Refugee Protection Act*, SC 2001, c. 27.

6. *Fisheries Act*, RSC 1985, c. F-14.

7. *Oceans Act*, SC 1996, c. 31.

8. *Family Law Act*, RSO 1990, c. F.3.

9. *Workers' Compensation Act*, RSA 1984, c. W-15, as amended.

10. *Human Tissue Gift Act*, RSBC 1996, c. 211.

11. *Freedom of Information and Protection of Privacy Act*, RSO 1990, c. F.31.

12. *Youth Criminal Justice Act*, SC 2002, c. 1.

13. *Canada Evidence Act*, RSC 1985, c. C-5.

14. *Employment Standards Act*, RSO 1990, c. E.4.

EXERCISES

Multiple Choice

1. Legislative jurisdiction over a particular subject matter is determined

    a. by the courts

    b. by the constitution

    c. by analogy

    d. on a first-come, first-served basis

    e. a, b, or c

2. If you suspect that the statute you are seeking was passed within the last 12 months, you could look for it

    a. in the most recent Statutes volume

    b. on the Internet

    c. in the *Canada Gazette* or a provincial bills service

    d. any or all of the above

    e. b or c

3. The preamble of a statute
   a. deals with substantive issues covered by the legislation
   b. deals with administrative issues
   c. sets out the objectives and guiding philosophy of the statute
   d. lists housekeeping provisions
   e. gives the long title of the statute

4. The abbreviation "RSC 1985" stands for
   a. Revised Substantive Code, 1985 Revision
   b. Revised Statute Constitution, 1985 Revision
   c. Revised Statute Citations, 1985 Revision
   d. Revised Statutes of Constitution, 1985 Revision
   e. Revised Statutes of Canada, 1985 Revision

5. A bill
   a. is a draft statute that is being considered by Parliament
   b. is a statute that has just been passed by Parliament
   c. is a provision of a new statute
   d. is a statute that is in the process of being amended
   e. is a substatute of an existing statute

True or False?

_____ 1. If a provincial statute is currently in force, you will always be able to find it in the Revised Statutes of the relevant province.

_____ 2. All statutes have accompanying regulations.

_____ 3. Canada's constitution was actually passed as a statute of the British government.

_____ 4. Diagrams, schedules, and charts are common features of regulations.

_____ 5. A commercially published edition of the *Criminal Code* is an official statutory source.

Short Answer

1. Based on these statute names and considering the division of powers set out by the constitution, which level of government passed each of these statutes?
   a. *Workplace Safety and Insurance Act*
   b. *Bank Act*
   c. *Meat Inspection Act*
   d. *Highway Traffic Act*
   e. *Broadcasting Act*
   f. *Business Corporations Act*

2. You are a police officer who receives a telephone complaint from a citizen who is irritated by the loud flapping of his neighbour's Confederate flag. The large flag is mounted prominently above the neighbour's front door. The complainant also believes that the flag is a racist symbol because of its connection to the historical practice of black slavery in the American South. As a black Canadian, the complainant feels that as well as being a source of noise pollution, flying this flag in a suburban Ontario neighbourhood is a form of racial harassment.

   Identify and locate legislation that deals with the issues (noise, flag-flying, racist symbols) raised by this complaint. Is the flag-flying neighbour guilty of any offence in your jurisdiction?

CHAPTER 3

Common Law and the Concept of Legal Precedent

Chapter Objectives

After completing this chapter, you should be able to:

- Explain the process by which a body of common law develops to resolve a legal issue.
- Explain the concept of legal precedent.
- Describe the application of precedent to a novel legal issue.
- Describe the various levels of court in Canada and how they determine the value of cases as precedents.
- Explain how to locate a body of case law.
- Explain how to locate an individual case.
- Prepare a case brief.

How Common Law Works

Chapter 1 introduced the common law system and explained that the judgments — usually judges' written **reasons for decision** — produced by individual court cases act as links in a chain of legal principles that make up various areas of law. But how does this work in practice? How does everyone keep track of the current state of the law and the direction in which it is growing?

reasons for decision
the written expression of a legal decision; some decisions include reasons from more than one judge or justice

HOW A LINK IS ADDED TO THE LEGAL CHAIN

It may help to explain that every new court judgment is only a *potential* link in the common law chain. In reality, many judgments are left out of the chain because

- they don't really add anything new to the state of the law;

- they serve only to apply existing law to a novel set of facts without changing the existing law;

- in retrospect, the decision that was reached is considered by future decision makers to be wrong and is explicitly **overruled** (rejected);

- the decision is for some reason unpopular, and while not actually overruled, it is ignored by future decision makers; or

- the decision is superseded by a decision of a higher court within the system of precedent.

overruled
rejected or contradicted in a decision of a court of higher jurisdiction

The decision about whether a court decision will earn a place in the chain of the law is made through the process of citation. In presenting their arguments to the court, the parties in a case — usually plaintiff and defendant, or Crown and defence in criminal cases — support their conclusions by relying on prior decisions in the legal chain. A party (usually through a lawyer) typically makes a point and then *supports* that point by citing an **authority** — that is, by mentioning a previous case in which the same point was accepted by the judge. If the judge in the new case accepts the cited authority and mentions it in his or her judgment, the case has been "cited with approval" and lives on as part of the law.

authority
a previously decided case that supports a particular position or conclusion about a question of law

Often, only a few words of a case, often described as the ***ratio decidendi*** (reasons for decision) or simply *ratio*, live on in this way. In many instances, a frequently cited *ratio* will take the form of a rule or test that can be successfully applied to fact situations that differ from the facts in the original case. Very strong *ratios* can live on for hundreds of years in this way and become as familiar as proverbs to the lawyers and judges specializing in a particular area of law.

ratio decidendi
Latin for "reasons for decision," but often used to describe the few words or phrases that form the most essential part of a legal decision for precedent purposes

In some cases, a party can't find an authority that fits its situation precisely. In these cases, the lawyer must suggest an entirely new principle, or propose an extension or modification of the principle set out in the pre-existing case that comes closest. If this new principle or extension of an existing principle is accepted by the judge and forms the basis for a judgment in that party's favour, a new link in the chain of common law has been made. If the new judgment, in turn, is cited by a future judge, the place of this newborn link in the chain of law is thereby secured.

HOW A LINK IS BROKEN

A new link in the legal chain is a fragile thing. After all, the link earned its place through the actions of only a few people — the lawyer who suggested it, the judge who accepted it, and possibly another one or two lawyers or judges who cited it. Whether the new link will be popular in the wider legal community has yet to be tested.

The test comes when a new case arises in which it would make sense for the new link to be applied. The lawyers in this new case, if they have done their research thoroughly, will come across the new link in the printed or online reports of case law (these will be discussed later in this chapter). If a party likes the link and it supports their position, they will cite it. If they don't like it, they will either argue that their own situation is so different from the situation in issue when the link case was decided that the link case should not be applied to their case (this is called "distinguishing" the link case), or they will argue that the link case was decided incorrectly and should not be followed by the judge in the present case. It will be up to the judge to decide whether the link is binding on the case. In theory, if a link in the legal chain has addressed the same issue as that before the present court, it is a binding precedent and a judge cannot ignore it. He or she *must* acknowledge it as law and apply it to the new situation.

There are two important points to remember when considering whether a link is binding or not. First, the link must be from within the same territorial jurisdiction as the case in question. For example, a decision from a court in British Columbia is not binding on a court in Ontario, and vice versa. Second, a link forged in a court of inferior (lower) jurisdiction need not be followed by a higher court, either on appeal of the same case or in a totally new case. The court of higher jurisdiction has the power to reject the decision of a lower court, knocking it right out of the chain of law. A case that is "knocked out" in this manner is said to be overruled and should not thereafter be applied by any other court. Both points will be expanded upon in the remainder of this chapter.

The Role of Jurisdiction in the System of Legal Precedent

As explained above, judges are not free to decide cases in any way that they want. They are bound by the system of legal precedent, which forbids them to ignore principles that have been added to the chain of the common law. However, the binding nature of legal precedents (existing links) is limited by the level of jurisdiction in which those links were formed.

If we think of the levels of court as the rungs of a ladder, starting with small claims courts at the bottom, rising through the trial courts and provincial courts of appeal, and ending at the Supreme Court of Canada at the top, the binding power of an individual decision becomes clear: the judge of a court is bound by the decisions of all courts within the province that are at a higher level and by the decisions of the Supreme Court of Canada. So, for example, all courts in the country except the Supreme Court of Canada are bound by the decisions of the Supreme Court of Canada; all courts in a specific province, except the province's court of appeal and the Supreme Court of Canada, are bound by the decisions of the province's court of appeal, and so on.

LEVELS OF COURT IN CANADA

The concept of jurisdiction was introduced in the context of statute-making authority in the legislative system in chapter 2. Jurisdiction also has a role to play in the judicial system, but here jurisdiction is quite different. While legislative jurisdiction is designed to facilitate the ordinary administration of government business and to reduce overlap in the subject matter of what is being legislated, judicial jurisdiction serves different functions. In the system of judicial jurisdiction, with the exception of certain special courts and tribunals designed to deal with specific types of cases (such as the federal Tax Court of Canada and the Family Court branch of Ontario's Superior Court of Justice), subject matter does not matter. Instead, the system is designed to sort cases based on how far along they are on the road to resolution and

whether the parties deserve the opportunity to make use of the system and its resources to appeal decisions that they feel are not satisfactory.

To understand the role of jurisdiction in the judicial system, it is important to
know something about the judicial structure.

Trial Courts

Each province has at least two levels of court: trial courts and appeal courts. Trial
courts are divided into various divisions based on the subject matter of the disputes
brought before the courts or the money value of the disputes. For example, the
Ontario court system has separate courts for small claims (where the amount of
damages claimed by the plaintiff falls below a certain maximum), for criminal law
matters, for youth justice matters, and for family matters. In some counties, courts
are further subdivided, with specialized courts reserved for, for example, specialized commercial transactions. In Ontario, not all of these trial courts are at the
same level. In some limited situations, a plaintiff can appeal a decision of a low-
level trial court to a higher-level trial court; for example, decisions of a judge in the
Small Claims Court may be appealed to a judge of the Ontario Superior Court of
Justice.

Appeal Courts

appeal
a review or challenge of a
legal decision in a court of
higher jurisdiction

Each province has a court of appeal that represents the highest level of court in the
province. Decisions made in trial courts can be **appealed** (challenged) by a party
to the court of appeal, where the decision will be reconsidered. (The rules regarding the right to appeal are more complicated in the criminal law context and will be
discussed in chapter 9.) If the appeal is allowed, the lower-court decision will be
reversed. If the appeal is denied, the lower-court decision will be preserved. In
terms of precedent, courts must give greater persuasive weight to an appeal court
decision than to a trial court decision.

The Supreme Court of Canada

leave to appeal
permission to file an
appeal

The Supreme Court of Canada is the highest-level court in the country. It decides
only a limited number of cases every year, and there is no automatic right to appeal
a civil (non-criminal) case to this court. There is an automatic right of appeal in certain criminal matters. Otherwise, only parties with cases of national importance
and general public interest are granted **leave to appeal** to the Supreme Court of
Canada, and a decision rendered here creates a precedent that supersedes all
lower-level judgments in all jurisdictions — it is the final word.

Because of the role of jurisdiction in creating precedents, a party or lawyer
trying to argue a point of law in any level of court will strive to support his or her
argument with authorities from the highest possible level of court, an important
consideration to keep in mind when doing legal research.

How To Find a Body of Case Law

Throughout this chapter we have been using the analogy of a "chain" of law, but most legal writers describe a legal issue or subject area as a "body of law." This section explains how to find a body of law, or **case law**, that addresses a particular issue.

First, if the issue has a statutory connection and the relevant statute is already known (from using the instructions in chapter 2), the first place to look for cases is under the statute. Cases that elaborate on a statutory provision can be found in legal encyclopedic sources, such as the *Canadian Abridgment* (Toronto: Carswell). Encyclopedic sources include a section that lists statutes considered — that is, references within cases to statutory material. Some frequently applied statutes, such as the *Criminal Code*, are published in **annotated** form, which means they are available in an edition that contains references to relevant cases, and even summaries of the cases, below the statute provisions themselves.

With no statute to start from, the researcher must perform a subject-matter or keyword search, either in an online database of cases or in an encyclopedic paper source such as the *Canadian Encyclopedic Digest* (Toronto: Carswell) in a library. The researcher searches under keywords that he or she has identified to find a reference to an applicable case.

case law
previously decided court cases, as described in written reasons for judgment

annotate
supplement published statutes by giving references to cases that have considered the application of statutory provisions

How To Locate a Specific Case

Once a reference to a body of law dealing with a particular issue is found, the researcher will come across references to individual cases (usually the most important ones) within that body of law. These cases are referred to by the names of the parties. The name of a case, which is made up of the names of the two parties, is known as the "style of cause." In criminal law cases, one of the parties is always the Crown. The Crown is identified in a case name by the initial "R" (for "*Regina*," which is Latin for "the Queen"), so the style of cause of criminal law cases is typically "*R v. Somebody*" and is indexed under the name Somebody.

The style of cause is immediately followed by the case citation, a letter and number code that serves as an "address" for the case in the law library. Most case citations refer to a case reporting service — a set of volumes published by a commercial publisher. Not every case is reported. What gets published depends on the decisions of the editorial board and what it views as the case reporter's mandate. Case reporters choose the cases they report based on particular criteria:

- Jurisdictional reporters, like the *Ontario Reports*, report significant or major cases decided in a certain geographical jurisdiction.

- Court-specific reporters, like the *Supreme Court Reports*, report cases decided in a particular court.

- Subject-specific reporters, like *Canadian Criminal Cases*, report cases that deal with a particular area of law.

Most case citations contain the following elements:

- the style of cause — for example, *R v. Ford*;
- a year in round or square brackets — for example, (1982) or [1982] — which is either the year in which the case was decided (round brackets), or the year of the reporter volume in which it is reported (square brackets);
- a number that represents the volume number of the series of case reports in which the case is reported — for example, 65;
- letters that represent the initials of the case reports in which the case is reported — for example, CCC for *Canadian Criminal Cases* (see appendix A). These initials may be followed by a series number if the case reporter has been published in more than one series. For example, "(2d)" means "second series";
- the page number in the case reporter where the case can be found — for example, 392; and
- in parentheses, a short form of the name of the court from which the decision comes — for example, Alta. QB for Alberta Queen's Bench, OCA for Ontario Court of Appeal, or SCC for Supreme Court of Canada — if the court is not obvious from the name of the reporter.

The above examples become the following case citation:

- *R v. Ford* (1982), 65 CCC (2d) 392 (SCC).

This means that the case of *R v. Ford*, which was decided by the Supreme Court of Canada in 1982, can be found in volume 65 of the second series of *Canadian Criminal Cases* at page 392.

Two or more different citations may be given for the same case, which means it is reported in more than one place. For example, *R v. Ford* can also be found at

- [1982] 1 SCR 231 (in the *Supreme Court Reports*), and
- (1982), 133 DLR (3d) 567 (in the *Dominion Law Reports,* third series).

Figuring out what the initials for the name of the case reporter stand for can be a challenge. See appendix A for a list of abbreviations. Most encyclopedic sources provide a list of case reporter abbreviations. A law librarian can help find a name that isn't listed. Practising with a few different cases helps make the process clear.

How To Read and Summarize a Case

Although some terms and phrases are unique to legal writing, legal judgments are usually quite readable and interesting. Most judges strive to present their judgments according to a logical organization, often providing a general statement of the facts, followed by an expression (sometimes even a list) of the issues to be decided, and finally, the decision itself, with an explanation of the legal principle or doctrine on which it is based.

Being able to grasp the meaning of a particular case often depends on how heavily the decision is influenced by earlier decisions (precedents) that the researcher may not have read. Where a case deals with issues that have a long common law history, the researcher may need to seek out and read earlier cases in the chain of reasoning to put that particular case into context. On the other hand, where a case is, for example, the first case decided under a particular statutory provision that has already been looked up and read, it may make perfect sense. Remember that cases build on each other, so grasping them may require more searching.

The length of legal judgments varies enormously. Some are a page or two long, others can be over 100 pages, with decisions (sometimes conflicting) by more than one judge. Figuring out how to distill what's important — the *ratio decidendi* — from several pages of text is an essential research skill that is developed through practice. While a written judgment may provide a detailed history of the facts of the particular case — the legal precedents, tests, and rules influencing the decision — the most important part of the judgment is the part that describes the reason for the judge's final decision. This section may be only a sentence or two long; it may be as simple as "Applying the common law test to the facts, I find that ..." in cases where the common law rules are simply applied, or it may be much more complex when the existing common law rule is changed, expanded, or amended in some way. This statement will live on as part of the development of the common law, and it will have a binding effect on subsequent cases.

To get a feel for how to isolate the *ratio* of a case, try this exercise:

1. Choose a case to read by locating a citation under an interesting *Criminal Code*[1] provision — *not* by reading the description of the case in an annotated Code.

2. Find the case on the library shelf and flip past the **headnote** — the summary that precedes the full text of the case. (This is not an official part of the judgment but is prepared by the editors of the case reporter.)

3. Read the case from beginning to end.

4. Read the headnote and consider how the case has been summarized. Which points did the editor seem to feel were most important? Do you agree?

5. Finally, read the even shorter summary of the case in an annotated *Criminal Code*.

headnote
an unofficial summary of reasons for decision that may precede the full text of a published case in a commercial case reporter

The above process can help a person gain a basic understanding of how to reduce a legal decision to its most concise form. But remember: shorter is not always better. To understand a complicated legal issue *fully*, it often helps to review the full decision so that the result can be put into its factual context.

Preparing a Simple Case Brief

case brief
a summary of a legal
judgment prepared for
research purposes

Someone who will be reading multiple cases in the course of researching an issue may find that reading notes are needed to help him or her remember what is learned along the way. A particularly effective way to prepare reading notes is to write a **case brief** for each case. A simple plan for a case brief follows, but for personal use any model that best suits the researcher's needs is fine.

A basic case brief may contain the following:

1. the full name (style of cause) and citation for the case, including the court in which it was decided;
2. the names of all the parties to the decision;
3. the names of all the judges who wrote the judgment(s);
4. a short summary of the key facts and issues of the case;
5. the decision and concise reasons for it;
6. the verbatim, or word-for-word, wording of any new legal rule or test that was formulated by the decision;
7. any facts or details that make the case of particular interest to the researcher — for example, any facts that are particularly similar to or different from those of the fact situation that is being researched; and
8. any other information that the researcher wants to remember later.

For an example of a simple case brief, see appendix B.

KEY TERMS

annotate	headnote
appeal	leave to appeal
authority	overruled
case brief	*ratio decidendi*
case law	reasons for decision

NOTE

1. *Criminal Code*, RSC 1985, c. C-46, as amended.

EXERCISES

Multiple Choice

1. Despite the principle of legal precedent, case law continues to evolve because

   a. no two fact situations are exactly the same

   b. legislative provisions can intervene to change the course of the common law

   c. the reasons for and effect of a particular decision may be interpreted and applied differently in different courts

   d. a and c

   e. all of the above

2. When considering the application of a current *Criminal Code* provision, it is important to review any court cases decided under the provision because

   a. the provision may have been overruled by a court

   b. the provision may have been held not to apply to the current fact situation

   c. other *Criminal Code* provisions may also apply to the fact situation

   d. doing so may give the researcher insights into the meaning of ambiguous words in the provision

   e. all of the above

3. A full case citation *does not* provide information about

   a. the year in which the case was decided or the year of the reporter volume

   b. the judge who wrote the reasons for the decision

   c. the case reporter in which the case is reported

   d. the level of court in which the case was decided

   e. the names of the parties to the case

4. The judge of a court is bound by the decisions of

   a. all courts within his or her province

   b. only the court of appeal of his or her province

   c. all courts within his or her province that are at a higher level

   d. all courts within his or her province that are at a higher level and the Supreme Court of Canada

   e. only the Supreme Court of Canada

5. The style of cause of a case

   a. gives the names of the parties to the case

   b. cites the case reporter in which the case can be found

   c. gives the date of the case

   d. indicates the court in which the case was tried

   e. indicates the province in which the case was tried

True or False?

_____ 1. A statutory rule is the product of the cooperation of many different people (including politicians, lobby groups, and legal drafters), but a common law rule can be created by a single judge.

_____ 2. A precedent created by the Supreme Court of Canada can never be changed.

_____ 3. When a party cannot find an authority that fits its situation precisely, the party's lawyer may propose a new principle.

_____ 4. The cases described in the annotations to a *Criminal Code* provision typically demonstrate the application of that statutory provision to particular fact situations.

_____ 5. Given an identical fact situation, a judge of the Ontario Superior Court of Justice must decide a legal issue in the same way that the issue was previously decided in the Ontario Court of Appeal.

Short Answer

Choose a case mentioned in your annotated *Criminal Code*. Locate the full text of the decision in the library, read the case, and prepare a short case brief. How does your case affect or illustrate the application of the provision under which it was decided?

PART II

Introduction to Constitutional Law

The Canadian Charter of Rights and Freedoms: Introduction and Selected Provisions

Chapter Objectives

After completing this chapter, you should be able to:

- Describe the origin of the *Canadian Charter of Rights and Freedoms*.
- Explain the function of the Charter and its application to government law and action.
- Describe how Charter rights are enforced.
- Describe the application of the fundamental freedoms described in s. 2 of the Charter.
- Understand the nature of the democratic rights guaranteed by s. 3 of the Charter.
- Understand the nature of the mobility rights guaranteed by s. 6 of the Charter.
- Explain the scope and application of the equality rights guaranteed by s. 15 of the Charter.

Introduction

The ***Canadian Charter of Rights and Freedoms***[1] (see appendix C) plays a very important role in enforcing the quasi-criminal law and criminal law, and law enforcement officers cannot properly carry out their responsibilities without a solid understanding of how the Charter works and the rights that it protects.

Canadian Charter of Rights and Freedoms
the constitutional document that sets out the rights and freedoms enjoyed by all people of Canada

The Charter is not a statute: it is part I of the constitution of Canada, the *Constitution Act, 1982*. The Charter's 34 provisions form the first part of the Act. It is, therefore, part of the law that is above all other laws in the country. If any law passed in Canada or in any of the provinces or territories contravenes the terms of the Charter, that law may be declared unconstitutional and of no force and effect by a court of competent jurisdiction. Any action of an agent or representative of any level of government that contravenes any right or freedom protected in the Charter may attract a remedy under s. 24 of the Charter.

The proclamation of the Charter in 1982 marked the culmination of a complicated initiative to entrench, under constitutional legislation, certain rights and freedoms that the government felt should be guaranteed to *all* people in Canada. The Charter was designed to help accomplish one of the most important constitutional functions — to express the fundamental values and principles of our society.

The provisions of the Charter were the subject of spirited consultation between the federal government and the provinces because, unlike other human rights legislation, the provisions have the force of constitutional law. This means that if other laws — even pre-existing laws — are proven to be inconsistent with a provision, the Charter takes precedence and the offending legislation is rendered invalid, sometimes called **struck down**.

struck down
made null or void; applies to laws that are found to infringe on individual rights and freedoms

Application of the Charter

Section 32 provides for the Charter's application to all matters under the authority of the Parliament of Canada and provincial parliaments. This means, for practical purposes, that

- the government (federal, provincial, or otherwise) cannot pass legislation or enforce existing law that is contrary to the provisions of the Charter, and

- neither the government nor its agents, which include a very wide range of officials (including police officers), can take any administrative, judicial, or other kind of action, whether legislatively based or not, that is contrary to the provisions of the Charter.

The precise scope of the Charter's application has been a matter of debate and litigation. Although it is clear that the Charter applies to the content and effects of government law and to the nature and effects of government action, it has sometimes been difficult to define what is meant by "government" action. Many organizations, undertakings, and regulated industries in Canada have some connection to government; there have been many cases argued that turn on whether the actions of a quasi-governmental organization is government action. Unregulated private activity within a province is not intended to be subject to the Charter. For example, the courts have found that a hospital regulation requiring physicians to retire at age 65 was not government law or administration subject to review under the Charter. Even though the hospital's regulations needed to be approved by the minister of health before they could be passed, they were still considered to be part of the hospital's internal management regime — and thus private activity.[2]

Limits on Charter Rights

The rights guaranteed by the Charter are important but are not without limits. Some rights-granting provisions contain an internal limitation. For example, s. 7 guarantees the right to "life, liberty, and security of the person and the right not to be deprived thereof *except in accordance with the principles of fundamental justice*" (emphasis added). The content of "the principles of fundamental justice" has been a matter of judicial consideration (it has been interpreted by case law), and legal tests have evolved to determine whether a particular violation of a s. 7 right will be deemed to be in accordance with the principles of fundamental justice.

There is also a more general limitation on the guarantee of Charter rights, expressed in s. 1:

> 1. The *Canadian Charter of Rights and Freedoms* guarantees the rights and freedoms set out in it subject only to such reasonable limits prescribed by law as can be demonstrably justified in a free and democratic society.

Because of s. 1, although a piece of government law or a government action may be proven to violate a right or freedom guaranteed under the Charter, the law or action may be upheld (it will not be invalidated or give rise to a remedy) if the government can show that the apparent Charter violation constitutes "a reasonable limit prescribed by law as can be demonstrably justified in a free and democratic society." The reasonableness of such a limit is currently determined by the application of a two-part legal test called the *Oakes* test (because it originated in the decision in *R v. Oakes*).[3] The *Oakes* test is a common law rule and has been expressed in many ways in different cases. In general, it requires that the Crown prove

1. a "pressing and substantial objective" underlying the law or government action that imposes the limitation; and

2. that the law and its effect on rights are proportionate to the interest or objective being protected, which means that the law does not infringe on people's rights to a degree not warranted by the importance of the goal that the law is supposed to accomplish. This second arm of the test has, through common law, developed into a three-part test in and of itself:

   a. there must be a rational connection between the objective and the means by which it is sought to be achieved,

   b. the law must result in a minimal impairment of the right(s) sought to be limited, and

   c. there must be a proportionality between the effects of the limitation on rights and the importance of the government objective.

How Charter Rights Are Enforced: Charter Challenges

Charter challenges are simply legal arguments, made by a party in the course of litigation, that assert the violation of a Charter right. Charter challenges require a multistep process.

First, a person who is claiming that one or more of his or her Charter rights has been violated must prove the violation, and must prove that it happened by the operation of law or by government action.

Once proof of a violation has been established, the burden falls to the government to prove that the right in question can be limited in accordance with the law (and why).

As explained above, some limits on Charter rights are expressed within the Charter's rights-granting sections themselves (see, for example, s. 7). In a case dealing with one of these limited rights, the Crown will first try to prove that circumstances exist to support the limitation of the right in the particular case. If the Crown fails in this, or if the right is not subject to an internal limitation, the Crown must try to prove that the limitation sought is "demonstrably justified in a free and democratic society," according to the wording of s. 1. This part of s. 1 is sometimes called the "saving provision" because it can be relied upon to "save" a law that would otherwise be found to impose an unacceptable limit on a Charter right.

Remedies for Breach of a Charter Right

When alleging a breach of a Charter right, a person can choose one of two routes to a remedy. For breaches involving unconstitutional action (for example, when police conduct an illegal search to find evidence of a crime), the person who was subject to the search will usually make a claim for a remedy that "the court considers appropriate and just in the circumstances" under s. 24 of the Charter.

The court can choose from a broad range of remedies available under this section. One remedy provides for excluding from use at trial evidence obtained in a manner that infringed a person's Charter rights (see s. 24(2)). In other words, because the evidence was obtained in a manner that is in breach of the Charter, the judge may rule it inadmissible at trial, meaning the Crown cannot use it to attempt to secure a conviction of the person.

When a person has alleged that a law (including common law) is unconstitutional, appropriate remedies may include court-ordered amendment of legislation to remove the offending section or a declaration that the legislation is of no force and effect. These remedies can be requested under s. 52(1) of the *Constitution Act, 1982*.

Overview of Selected Sections

Part III of this text, and in particular chapter 6, provides a discussion of some of the individual Charter rights that have particular application to the criminal law. The full scope of "criminal law" rights include:

- s. 7 — the right to life, liberty, and security of the person;
- s. 8 — the right to be free from unreasonable search or seizure;
- s. 9 — the right not to be arbitrarily detained or imprisoned;
- s. 10 — procedural rights upon arrest or detention;
- s. 11 — procedural rights in the course of a criminal prosecution;
- s. 12 — the right not to be subjected to cruel or unusual treatment or punishment;
- s. 13 — certain rights against self-incrimination; and
- s. 14 — the right to an interpreter in a trial.

This chapter will focus instead on the rights that arise outside the context of a criminal prosecution.

SECTION 2: FUNDAMENTAL FREEDOMS

Section 2 is designed to guarantee rights often associated with democratic values and self-expression. It provides that

2. Everyone has the following fundamental freedoms:

   (a) freedom of conscience and religion;

   (b) freedom of thought, belief, opinion and expression, including freedom of the press and other media of communication;

   (c) freedom of peaceful assembly; and

   (d) freedom of association.

Charter challenges that have arisen under this section have been based on such issues as

- the right of businesses to operate on Sundays (and to require employees to work on that day);
- the reciting of prayers of particular religions in public schools;
- controversial historical teachings (such as in the case of teachers who teach an account of the Holocaust that contradicts the factual events that occurred);
- restrictions on advertising (such as advertising tobacco products or advertising that is directed at young children);
- hate speech, racist propaganda, and the assembly/association rights of racist groups; and
- "obscenity" and the regulation of sexually explicit art, literature, and film (including expressions of homosexuality).

As you might imagine, litigation under this section is often politically and morally charged, and involves the court in a difficult struggle to balance majority and minority opinions. Canada prides itself on being a free and democratic country in which individual opinions, however controversial, can flourish, but our government must balance this value against the need to protect society's more vulnerable members.

SECTION 3: DEMOCRATIC RIGHTS

Section 3 of the Charter establishes the right to vote or to be elected:

> 3. Every citizen of Canada has the right to vote in an election of members of the House of Commons or of a legislative assembly and to be qualified for membership therein.

As discussed in chapter 12, this guarantee of the right to vote is supported by provincial employment standards legislation, which allows for short-term leave from work for the purpose of voting.

Charter challenges have been brought by prison inmates who were denied the right to vote because of their incarceration. The decisions have made it clear that inmates are entitled to vote in federal and provincial elections. Restrictions on their voting have been held not to be "reasonable limits" on the inmates' rights for the purpose of s. 1 of the Charter, and policies preventing inmates from voting are unconstitutional.

Note that although many Charter rights are guaranteed to people who live in Canada regardless of citizenship, the wording of s. 3 makes it clear that the right to vote is guaranteed to every *citizen* of Canada — that is, citizenship is a prerequisite to the eligibility to vote in most elections.

SECTION 6: MOBILITY RIGHTS

Section 6 of the Charter is designed to address some of the special challenges of a federal system of government by guaranteeing mobility rights.

> 6(1) Every citizen of Canada has the right to enter, remain in, and leave Canada.
>
> (2) Every citizen of Canada and every person who has the status of a permanent resident of Canada has the right
>
> > (a) to move and take up residence in any province; and
> >
> > (b) to pursue the gaining of a livelihood in any province.
>
> (3) The rights specified in subsection (2) are subject to
>
> > (a) any laws or practices of general application in force in a province other than those that discriminate among persons primarily on the basis of province of present or previous residence; and
> >
> > (b) any laws providing for reasonable residency requirements as a qualification for the receipt of publicly provided social services.
>
> (4) Subsections (2) and (3) do not preclude any law, program or activity that has as its object the amelioration in a province of conditions of individuals in that province who are socially or economically disadvantaged if the rate of employment in that province is below the rate of employment in Canada.

The rights guaranteed by this section are qualified by several internal limitations of the kind described above. These limitations reflect the practical use, for many purposes, of residency requirements to control access to certain government programs. Population patterns in Canada, which tend to be characterized by heavy population in southern urban areas and lighter population in northern regions, pose many challenges for provinces, and issues relating to restrictions on place of practice for certain professionals (such as doctors) have been the subject of Charter challenges.

SECTION 15: EQUALITY RIGHTS

Section 15 protects the rights of people to equal treatment under the law regardless of their own intrinsic differences. It provides that

> 15(1) Every individual is equal before and under the law and has the right to the equal protection and benefit of the law without discrimination and, in particular, without discrimination based on race, national or ethnic origin, colour, religion, sex, age or mental or physical disability.
>
> (2) Subsection (1) does not preclude any law, program or activity that has as its object the amelioration of the conditions of disadvantaged individuals or groups including those that are disadvantaged because of race, national or ethnic origin, colour, religion, sex, age or mental or physical disability.

Despite the general wording of this section, Canadian courts have taken a relatively narrow approach to interpreting equality rights, allowing only those discrimination claims based on the grounds specifically listed in s. 15 or on grounds that can be shown to be *analogous* to those grounds.

Many legal tests for establishing discrimination have been developed by the courts and are applied when new cases arise.

Courts applying the **formal equality** test have defined discrimination by reference to equality (and inequality) of opportunity. For example, a government program might violate s. 15, according to this test, if it extends small-business assistance only to urban, and not rural, small-business owners.

formal equality
a measure of equality based on equality or inequality of opportunity

The **substantive equality** test has been used to prescribe a finding of discrimination wherever there is an inequality of outcome. This test, which involves the examination of adverse effects discrimination, allows the courts to look more closely at laws or government actions that appear, on their face, to be objective but that cause unfair results. For example, one plaintiff successfully argued that the British Columbia health care system, while on its face providing equal benefits to hearing people and deaf people, actually discriminated against deaf people because a lack of funding for sign language interpreters within the system reduced access to health services for deaf people.[4]

substantive equality
a measure of equality based on equality or inequality of outcomes, regardless of opportunity

Approaches to equality issues will no doubt continue to evolve along with changing social values.

KEY TERMS

Canadian Charter of Rights and Freedoms

formal equality

struck down

substantive equality

NOTES

1. *Canadian Charter of Rights and Freedoms*, part I of the *Constitution Act, 1982*, RSC 1985, app. II, no. 44.

2. *Stoffman v. Vancouver General Hospital*, [1990] 3 SCR 483.

3. *R v. Oakes*, [1986] 1 SCR 103.

4. *Eldridge v. British Columbia (Attorney General)*, [1997] 3 SCR 624.

EXERCISES

Multiple Choice

1. To be a "reasonable limit prescribed by law as can be demonstrably justified in a free and democratic society," a limit on a Charter right must

   a. further a pressing and substantial government objective

   b. be rationally connected to the government objective

   c. minimally impair the right that would otherwise be guaranteed

   d. be in proportion to the objective that is sought to be achieved

   e. all of the above

2. A person alleging the violation of a Charter right must always prove that

   a. he or she is a member of a disadvantaged group in society

   b. he or she is a Canadian citizen

   c. there is no internal limitation on the right asserted

   d. the violation was the result of government action or government law

   e. all of the above

3. A person who has succeeded in proving a Charter violation may be entitled to a remedy

   a. under s. 34

   b. under s. 52

   c. under s. 15

   d. in the form of the exclusion of illegally obtained evidence

   e. b or d

4. The Charter is

   a. part of Canada's constitution

   b. a statute

   c. part of the law that is above all other laws in Canada

   d. designed to entrench certain fundamental rights and freedoms

   e. a, c, and d

5. Once a violation of a Charter right is established, the burden of proving that this right can be legally limited falls on

   a. the victim of the violation

   b. the government

   c. the Supreme Court of Canada

   d. the judge

   e. the jury

True or False?

_____ 1. To argue discrimination under the Charter, a complainant must base his or her claim on one of the types of discrimination specifically listed in s. 15.

_____ 2. As constitutional legislation, the provisions of the Charter take precedence over all other legislation, whether federal or provincial.

_____ 3. Section 6 of the Charter guarantees Canadians the right to work and earn a living.

_____ 4. All of the rights prescribed by the Charter are subject to the "reasonable limits" described in s. 1.

_____ 5. Only legislation — not common law — can be challenged under the Charter.

_____ 6. Business transactions between private individuals are governed by the Charter.

_____ 7. Sexual orientation is a prohibited ground of discrimination under s. 15 of the Charter.

_____ 8. Prison inmates are entitled to vote in federal elections.

Short Answer

1. The results of certain challenges under the Charter have made it clear that the right to self-expression guaranteed in s. 2 does not include the right to engage in "hate speech."

   a. What do you think would have been the greatest challenges for the parties arguing for this limitation and for the courts in coming to this conclusion?

b. Are there any pitfalls for a society that decides to limit hate speech? If so, what would these be?

2. A busy, expensive restaurant in a fashionable neighbourhood is decorated with several stylized sculptures of what appears to be female genitalia. The sculptures are the work of the restaurant's owner, an amateur sculptor. After receiving two complaints from patrons, one in February 2005 and another in May of that same year, police charge the restaurateur with the offence of corrupting morals under s. 163 of the *Criminal Code*, and order that the artwork be removed. Section 163 reads in part as follows:

163(2) Every one commits an offence who knowingly, without lawful justification or excuse,

(a) sells, exposes to public view or has in his possession for such a purpose any obscene written matter, picture, model, phonograph record or other thing whatever;

(b) publicly exhibits a disgusting object or an indecent show; ...

(3) No person shall be convicted of an offence under this section if the public good was served by the acts that are alleged to constitute the offence and if the acts alleged did not extend beyond what served the public good.

The police allege that the sculptures are either "obscene matter" or "disgusting objects." The restaurant's owner argues that they are tasteful objets d'art, and that the charge constitutes an infringement of his Charter-guaranteed freedom of self-expression.

a. Who is right? Why?

b. What will the restaurant's owner have to prove to establish a violation of
    his rights? What kind of evidence do you imagine he would need to
    gather?

c. If the owner is successful, what remedy or remedies will he likely seek?
    Under which section(s) of the Charter?

Basic Principles of Criminal Law and Procedure

CHAPTER 5

The Criminal Code and the Structure of Criminal Offences

Chapter Objectives

After completing this chapter, you should be able to:

- Identify the different types of statutes that create offences.
- Describe the basic structure of the *Criminal Code*.
- Understand the differences between federal criminal offences and provincial quasi-criminal offences.
- Explain the difference between *actus reus* and *mens rea*.
- Describe the different levels of intent.
- Understand how absolute and strict liability offences differ from specific and general liability offences.
- Explain the various ways in which people not directly involved in committing an offence can still be convicted for their role in the offence.

Creating Offences

As discussed in chapters 2 and 4, our constitution divides the power to make laws between the federal and provincial governments. This means that the legislatures of both levels of government can create statutes that make it illegal to commit certain acts, as long as the subject matter of these acts falls into the legislature's jurisdiction. For example, the constitution gives the provinces jurisdiction over the establishment and management of hospitals in the province (s. 92(7)). This has been extended, through interpretation, to mean that provinces have legislative jurisdiction over the public health care system in each province. Because of this, a law restricting the use of restraints on a mentally ill patient would be found in a provincial statute — the *Mental Health Act* (Ontario).[1]

While the *Criminal Code*[2] (a federal statute) is by far the best known of the offence-creating statutes, there are many laws at both levels of government that prohibit certain acts and create punishments for those who commit such acts. At the provincial level, quasi-criminal statutes such as the Ontario *Highway Traffic Act*[3] are designed to support the enforcement of activities that fall within provincial responsibility under the constitution. At the federal level, offence-creating statutes other than the *Criminal Code* are typically created to govern subject areas for which the government has a discrete enforcement mission, strategy, scheme, or philosophy. Examples of such subject-specific statutes include the *Controlled Drugs and Substances Act*,[4] and the *Crimes Against Humanity and War Crimes Act*.[5]

Offence-creating statutes not only prohibit certain acts; many also make certain acts mandatory. For example, Ontario's *Compulsory Automobile Insurance Act*[6] requires those who own and operate motor vehicles on public highways to have liability insurance on their vehicles and to carry evidence of such insurance in the vehicles at all times.

This chapter introduces the concept of offence-creating statutes and sets out a useful guide to the most important offence-creating statute: the *Criminal Code*. The chapter then discusses the topic of **offences** in greater detail.

offence

an act or omission that breaks a law and leads to punishment; a crime codified in a statute such as the *Criminal Code*

The Criminal Code

Criminal law is a subject matter that is federal in some aspects and provincial in others. Under our constitution, the federal government has jurisdiction over the creation of criminal law, while the provinces have jurisdiction over the administration and enforcement of criminal law. All criminal laws are enacted by the Parliament of Canada and are codified in the Canadian *Criminal Code*, which creates the offences, sets the rules of procedure for criminal matters, and establishes guidelines for sentencing. The provincial court system then administers the criminal procedure according to the *Criminal Code*.

Criminal law is detailed and complex. The *Criminal Code* is constantly being revised by the federal Parliament. At the same time, dozens of court cases that affect the common law (non-codified) aspects of the criminal law are decided every year. To assist readers in managing these constant changes, commercial editions of the *Criminal Code* include a comprehensive index that helps people become familiar with the legislation and the offences it creates. Some annotated versions of the Code also include an **offence grid** that gives a helpful summary of the offences and their penalties.

offence grid

a feature of some annotated versions of the *Criminal Code* that provides, in chart form, a summary of the elements, punishment, and other aspects of different offences

The annotated versions of the Code (for example, *Martin's Annual Criminal Code* published by Canada Law Book) often also include the text of the *Canadian Charter of Rights and Freedoms*,[7] as well as other major federal criminal law or offence-creating statutes: the *Canada Evidence Act*,[8] the *Controlled Drugs and Substances Act*, the *Crimes Against Humanity and War Crimes Act*, and the *Youth Criminal Justice Act*.[9]

BASIC STRUCTURE OF THE CODE

It is easy to become lost in the maze that is the *Criminal Code*. Even without annotations, it is a long statute with 849 numbered sections, many of which have numerous subsections. To make navigation easier, publications of the Code generally include
a detailed table of contents and index.

The Code is divided into 33 parts, each numbered with a Roman numeral. A
quick scan of the table of contents provides a clear idea of how these divisions work.

Parts II through XIII either create offences or deal with subtypes of offences
(such as attempts and conspiracies to commit offences). The name of each section helps the reader determine under which part an offence falls; for example,
Firearms and Other Weapons (part III) deals with how the use of a gun affects an
offence or an offender, and Offences Against Rights of Property (part IX) deals with
issues such as theft and robbery.

Parts XIV through XXVII are procedural in nature. They set out the rules for
how offences are to be investigated, prosecuted, tried, and, if necessary, appealed.
Parts XIX, XX, and XXVII establish the different types of offences (indictable, summary conviction, and hybrid offences, which will be discussed in more detail later
in this chapter and in chapter 8) and the procedures that go with them. Part XXIII
deals with sentencing, while part XXI covers appeals of indictable offences (see
chapter 9).

Part XX.1 is a fairly new part of the Code that sets out new rules for accused
persons suffering from mental disorders. Part XXIV deals with dangerous offenders.

The final part, XXVIII, contains the various forms used in investigating and trying criminal offences.

HOW TO READ THE CODE — AN EXAMPLE

The Code contains cross-references that, to be properly understood, require the
reader to move back and forth through the text. The simplest way to use the Code
is to begin with the offence being considered, and then to work outward. For example, if the facts suggest that the appropriate charge may be attempted murder,
the first place to look is in the index under "murder," which gives a number of subcategories, including attempted murder.

Not surprisingly, attempted murder falls under part VIII, Offences Against the
Person and Reputation. Section 239 defines the offence itself, along with the potential sentence for the offence:

> 239. Every person who attempts by any means to commit murder is guilty of
> an indictable offence and liable
>
>> (a) where a firearm is used in the commission of the offence, to impris-
>> onment for life and to a minimum punishment of imprisonment for a term of
>> four years; and
>>
>> (b) in any other case, to imprisonment for life.

A reader who is familiar with the Code will realize that four terms included in the
definition of attempted murder are dealt with in more detail elsewhere in the Code:
"attempts," "murder," "indictable offence," and "firearm." To understand the
offence of attempted murder, the reader must also consider the precise terms used
to describe it.

The next step is to review the meaning of "attempts." The Code deals with attempts, conspiracies, and accessories in part XIII. This turns out to be something of a dead end, however, because part XIII indicates that attempted murder is one of the few "attempt" offences that is covered in a separate section of the Code. Since the Code doesn't define the word "attempt," a definition must be found in the common law — in the cases about attempted murder that have been decided under s. 239. The 1986 case of *R v. Marshall*[10] established that an attempt means "to do anything, by any means, to carry out the intent of causing the death of a human being."

If the offence is the attempt to commit a murder, it is also necessary to understand exactly what murder is. The Code deals with the offence of murder in a number of sections, beginning at s. 229. This section defines murder initially as "culpable homicide," which means further research must be done to discover the meaning of both "culpable" and "homicide."

The next term in the definition of attempted murder is "indictable offence." The Code discusses the procedure for trying indictable offences in parts XIX and XX.

The final term that requires further investigation is "firearm," since attempting murder with a firearm carries a potentially more serious punishment than does attempting murder without one. Part III of the Code, Firearms and Other Weapons, explains what is meant by firearm in the offence of attempted murder and what constitutes use of a firearm in committing an offence.

Once a researcher has a good understanding of the offence, he or she may want to move on to review the procedures for trying an indictable offence such as attempted murder, the principles and procedures for **sentencing** for such an offence, and maybe even the process for **appealing** a conviction. All of these matters are discussed in the Code. The researcher will also need to take into account the principles of the Charter (discussed in chapter 4), because the protection of an accused's Charter rights permeates every aspect of Canadian criminal procedure.

A later section of this chapter discusses the structure and elements of offences in more detail.

Quasi-Criminal and Regulatory Offences

The *Criminal Code* and its related federal statutes are not the only laws that create offences. The constitution gives the provinces (and, by delegation, the municipal governments that are created by the provinces) the power to make laws in a number of areas, and many of these laws include offences of their own. Such provincial or municipal offences are often called **quasi-criminal** offences.

These offences are usually punished by a penalty (such as a fine or term of imprisonment) or a forfeiture (the loss of a driver's licence, for example). Provincial offences often require a lower level of **intent** than do *Criminal Code* offences, and provincial offences usually attract less serious penalties.

For example, to obtain a conviction, the Crown prosecutor must prove that a person charged with the *Criminal Code* offence of attempted murder intended to cause the death of her victim, and if a conviction is obtained, the punishment could be imprisonment for life. The Crown prosecutor dealing with a driver who is

sentence
the punishment imposed on a person convicted of an offence

appeal
the review or challenge of a legal decision in a court of higher jurisdiction

quasi-criminal
similar in nature to offences listed in the *Criminal Code,* but under provincial or municipal jurisdiction

intent
the mental element of an offence; see also *mens rea*

charged with the provincial offence of failure to stop at a red light, contrary to the Ontario *Highway Traffic Act*[11] (provincial legislation), does not have to prove that the person *intended* to disobey the light, simply that he disobeyed it. If convicted of the provincial offence, the driver will not have a criminal record but will receive a fine and demerit points on his driver's licence.

What Is an Offence?

Defining the word "offence" is not easy. In simple terms, an offence is an **act** or **omission** that violates a law and from which some form of punishment follows.

Police officers are responsible for enforcing laws of all kinds, not just those created under the criminal law. Enforcing the law involves not only preventing the commission of offences, but also investigating offences that have already been committed. The investigation of offences requires law enforcement officers to collect **evidence** that will support a **conviction**. The collection of appropriate evidence, in turn, requires an understanding of the elements of the offence in question, as defined by the offence-creating statute and the common law.

Chapter 6 discusses the investigation of offences in more detail. This section introduces the elements of an offence, so that you can better determine what evidence is required and which facts must be proven to support a conviction in court. While this chapter focuses primarily on *Criminal Code* offences, the discussion that follows also applies, for the most part, to offences created by other legislation.

act
something done or committed

omission
a failure to do something that is required by statute or by common law

evidence
oral or physical proof of the truth of an allegation

conviction
a guilty verdict, where an accused is found, beyond a reasonable doubt, to have committed an offence

Classification of Offences

Our criminal justice system classifies *Criminal Code* offences into three categories according to their seriousness and the procedure used to deal with the accused — the person charged with the offence — in court: summary conviction, indictable, and hybrid offences.

In general, **summary conviction offences** are less serious offences that carry light penalties. Any charge tried by summary conviction is tried in the provincial court before a judge alone. (In Ontario, the provincial court is called the Ontario Court of Justice. The names of the courts vary across provinces, but the general structure and appeal route are the same.) No preliminary hearing is held.

Indictable offences are more serious crimes that usually carry stiffer penalties. Any charge tried as an indictable offence is tried, according to the election (choice) of the accused, in the provincial court before a judge alone, in the superior court of the province (in Ontario, the Superior Court of Justice) before a judge alone, or in the superior court of the province before a judge and a jury. In most cases, the accused has the right to a preliminary hearing as well.

Hybrid offences are a combination of the first two. The section of the Code that creates a hybrid offence gives the prosecution the option of electing to treat the offence as a summary conviction offence (and thus subject to lesser penalties) or as an indictable offence (and thus subject to stiffer penalties).

Chapter 7 discusses elections and preliminary hearings in more detail.

summary conviction offence
a less serious crime that carries a light penalty; the accused is tried in the Ontario Court of Justice without the benefit of a jury or a preliminary hearing

indictable offence
a serious crime that attracts more serious penalties and that is prosecuted using the more formal of two possible sets of criminal procedures

hybrid offence
a crime that allows the prosecution to elect to proceed by way of summary conviction or by way of indictment

Parts of a Criminal Code Section

In general, each offence is dealt with in an independent section of the *Criminal Code*. Each section is made up of three parts:

substantive part (of an offence)
the part of a section of the *Criminal Code* that identifies the actual elements of the offence created

procedural part (of an offence)
the part of a section of the *Criminal Code* that identifies the type of offence created by indicating the procedure by which an offender will be tried — indictable, summary conviction, or hybrid offence

penalty part (of an offence)
the part of a section of the *Criminal Code* that sets out the maximum or minimum punishment, or both, for the particular offence

- the **substantive part**, which describes the offence itself;
- the **procedural part**, indicating whether the offence is an indictable, summary conviction, or hybrid offence, which identifies the way in which the offence will be dealt with in court; and
- the **penalty part**, which sets out the maximum or minimum (or both) punishment that may be imposed on anyone convicted of committing the offence.

The offence of attempted murder under s. 239 of the Code provides a good example of the three parts of an offence section:

> 239. Every person who attempts by any means to commit murder is guilty of an indictable offence and liable:
>
>> (a) where a firearm is used in the commission of the offence, to imprisonment for life and to a minimum punishment of imprisonment for a term of four years; and
>>
>> (b) in any other case, to imprisonment for life.

The substantive part of the section is "Every person who attempts by any means to commit murder." The addition of the words "where a firearm is used" creates a second, related offence.

The words "is guilty of an indictable offence" make up the procedural part of the section, setting out the procedure by which the offence will be dealt with in court.

The penalty part of the section is actually divided in two, according to whether a firearm is used: "and liable (a) ... to imprisonment for life and to a minimum punishment of imprisonment for a term of four years; and (b) in any other case, to imprisonment for life."

The following discussion relates almost exclusively to the substantive part of offences. Chapter 8 covers the procedural part in detail, while chapter 9 focuses on the penalty aspect.

element
a part of an offence that must be proven

oral testimony
evidence provided verbally by witnesses

physical evidence
proof of the truth of an allegation in the form of actual objects (for example, a gun, bloody clothes, photographs)

Substantive Part of an Offence

The substantive part of the offence section is the part that describes the actions or omissions that constitute the offence. In some cases, a particular mental state — for example, intent, recklessness, or negligence — is also described here. These actions, omissions, and/or mental states are called the **elements** of the offence. These elements must be proven in court through **oral testimony**, **physical evidence**, or both. For most offences, a finding of guilt depends on proving two separate kinds of elements:

- the objective component — the ***actus reus*** — which is the physical act or omission involved in committing the offence; and

- the subjective component — called the ***mens rea*** — which is the state of mind, or level of intention, attributed to the accused, that establishes his or her fault in committing the physical act(s) or omission(s).

For example, in the case of assault and battery (s. 265 of the *Criminal Code*), physically striking the victim is the *actus reus* and intending to strike is the *mens rea*.

Perhaps the easiest way to understand the substantive part of an offence is to think of it as a math equation: *actus reus* + *mens rea* = offence. Both the *actus reus* and the *mens rea* may involve more than one element as well, making the equation more complex.

Using the example of attempted murder, the *actus reus* of the offence involves an effort to end another person's life that fails: effort + failure = *actus reus*. If a firearm is added to the equation (effort + failure + firearm), the offender is subject to the more severe punishment set out in penalty part (a) of the offence. The *mens rea* of the offence of attempted murder is the intention to end another person's life. If the offender simply wants to injure the victim, he or she does not have the required mental state to be guilty of attempted murder (though he or she may be guilty of a lesser offence, such as assault). The offender must intend to kill the victim for attempted murder to be proven.

Therefore, to secure a conviction of a person accused of attempted murder with a firearm under s. 239 of the *Criminal Code*, the police must provide convincing proof (evidence) supporting each element of the offence equation: effort + failure + firearm + intention to end the life of the victim = conviction.

actus reus
Latin for "criminal act"; the objective element of an offence, which may be an act, an omission, or a state of being

mens rea
Latin for "guilty mind"; the subjective element of an offence that describes the state of mind or required intention necessary of the accused

Actus Reus

The objective element, or *actus reus*, of an offence can be a state of being, an omission, or an act. To establish the *actus reus* of a *Criminal Code* offence, the relevant Code section must be considered in its entirety. If the police and the prosecution fail to prove any required element of the *actus reus*, they fail to prove the specific offence and the accused may be acquitted (not convicted). If, for example, the police cannot provide convincing evidence that the accused made some sort of effort to kill the victim (even if the accused carried a firearm and intended to kill the victim), the accused will be acquitted of the offence of attempted murder.

INCLUDED OFFENCES

As you can see from the structure of the Attempted Murder section of the *Criminal Code*, new offences can be created or greater penalties can be imposed with the addition of a single new element to the *actus reus*. Effort + failure + intent to kill = attempted murder, which has no minimum penalty (so a judge could find a person guilty of the offence but sentence him or her to only one day in jail). Adding a firearm to the equation (effort + failure + firearm + intent to kill) makes the penalty potentially more severe: a minimum of four years' imprisonment.

Separate *Criminal Code* offences can build on each other to reflect crimes of differing severity. Assault with a weapon (s. 267(a)) and assault causing bodily harm (s. 267(b)) build on the offence of simple assault (s. 266) by adding either a circumstance (the use of a weapon) or a consequence (bodily harm). This scheme makes it possible for less serious offences to be **included** in more serious ones.

included offence
a less serious offence that might be proven even when the more serious offence charged is not

This has important practical implications for law enforcement officers. If a person is charged with assault causing bodily harm (striking another + injuries caused + intention to strike), but there is insufficient evidence to prove that the actions of the accused caused injuries to the victim, the accused may still be convicted of simple assault (striking another + intention to strike). The police are not required to charge the accused with both offences, because simple assault is considered to be included in assault causing bodily harm. Note, however, that if the police and prosecution fail to prove that the accused struck the victim, then the accused cannot be convicted of either offence.

STATE-OF-BEING OFFENCES

possession
ownership based on rights acquired or conferred through physical occupancy or control

consent
the informed, voluntary approval by one party of the actions of another

Most state-of-being offences are offences of **possession**: of weapons, of controlled drugs, of break-in tools, and so on. The *actus reus* for such an offence is simply the fact of being in possession and control of the particular item. This is where the *mens rea* becomes especially important: legal "possession" generally requires knowledge on the part of the accused as to what he or she possessed, or **consent** on the part of the accused to possess it. A person cannot be guilty of possession of a weapon, for example, if he or she has no knowledge of having it on his or her person (someone dropped it into the person's backpack without the person knowing it, for example).

OFFENCES OF OMISSION

In some cases, the law requires a person to take a particular action in a particular circumstance, so it is an offence *not* to take the required action. These rules are sometimes called good Samaritan laws, and many of them have been created by the common law. For example, a parent is required to care for his or her child, and a doctor or teacher is required to report child abuse. In addition to creating offences based on these common law duties, statutes have imposed circumstance-specific statutory duties in response to dangerous behaviour. These include a driver's duty to give a breath sample when requested to do so by the police.

reasonable person
a hypothetical person on which a standard of behaviour is based for comparison with someone's actual behaviour

In determining whether a duty has been breached, the courts have traditionally compared the behaviour of the accused with the standard of behaviour of a **reasonable person** in the same circumstances, and have required that the omission be very closely connected to the harm that has resulted.

ACTION OFFENCES

Most of the offences in the *Criminal Code* are action offences: offences that require the accused to commit a certain act (striking, stealing, counterfeiting, and so on) in order to be convicted. An action offence may also include a requirement that the action of the accused caused a certain result (for example, the offence of assault causing bodily harm). This brings up the issue of causation.

Causation

Causation is an important element of proof in any offence that requires evidence of the consequences of an accused's action. Causation can be divided into two types: factual causation and legal causation.

Factual causation is established when it is shown that a consequence would not have resulted *but for* the actions of the accused. For example, a victim would not have died if the accused had not struck the victim with a tire iron.

Legal causation is a more complicated issue. The purpose of determining legal causation is to attribute fault as among more than one alleged cause. In determining legal causation, the court must measure the importance of one factual cause against all other factual causes of the same consequence. For example, if the victim was hit by a car, struck by lightning, and suffered from an incurable disease at the time the accused struck him or her, any of which could have led to the victim's death, the court has to determine which of the causes was the legal cause of the victim's death.

The *Criminal Code* provides guidance for resolving some common instances in which legal causation is at issue, but novel issues are resolved by referring to the common law concepts of foreseeability of consequences and culpable intervention by a third party.

Foreseeability, which will be discussed in chapter 10, is a test to determine whether a reasonable person could expect that a certain result may follow from his or her act. For example, it is foreseeable that someone may get shot if a person enters a bank with a gun.

Culpable intervention by a third party occurs when someone unexpectedly does some improper act that contributes to or causes the result or changes the chain of events or causation. For example, Uriah stabs Rhodida and Rhodida is taken to a hospital. Her injuries are not life-threatening, but at the hospital Doctor Patel makes a mistake and gives Rhodida the wrong medication. She dies. Whether Uriah will be charged with murder will depend on whether Doctor Patel's act altered the chain of causation. In a case like this, the question may be left for the trier of fact (the judge or jury) to determine whether the doctor's act caused Rhodida's death or whether it was simply incidental to the chain of events that foreseeably resulted from Uriah's actions.

Mens Rea

Imposing criminal sanctions in the Canadian legal system depends on a legal finding of moral guilt. To determine fault, the court examines evidence of the accused's state of mind at the time of committing the alleged offence. To be found guilty of a true criminal offence, the accused person must have

- made a choice to do something wrong,
- made the choice voluntarily or with free will, and
- known that the act was wrong.

If all of these elements are proven, then the accused is said to have the requisite *mens rea*, or "guilty mind." Most *Criminal Code* sections describe not only physical

causation
the element of an offence that involves whether an act or omission of one party resulted directly in the injury to the other party

factual causation
the situation where a certain result would not exist if a specific action or event had not occurred

legal causation
the situation where one or more actions could have caused a certain result and, for the purposes of a legal suit, the action that was most responsible for the result must be determined

foreseeability
a test to determine whether a reasonable person could expect that a certain result may follow from his or her act

culpable intervention
an unexpected action, often by a third party, that contributes to or causes a chain of events

acts but also the mindset of the accused at the time of committing those acts, using modifying words to define the criminal behaviour. Offences may depend not only on the action committed but also on how it is committed — for example, "wilfully," "recklessly," or "with intent to injure."

The modifiers chosen to define offences often bring public policy considerations into the criminal law, reflecting societal norms and expectations. Most *Criminal Code* offences require only proof of a **general intent** to commit a crime. However, offences such as break and enter with intent to commit an indictable offence (s. 348), wilfully obstructing a peace officer (s. 129), and first- or second-degree murder (s. 229) require proof of **specific intent** because of the language in the section of the Code.

INTENT

Intent is a key to *mens rea*. The law recognizes degrees of intent, which range from **direct intent** (the most serious in a criminal offence) to **negligence** (the least serious). There are many different degrees in between, and it is important to understand what degree of intent has to be proven to obtain a conviction for each specific *Criminal Code* offence. In general, offences that carry more serious penalties require a higher level of intent. One form of first-degree murder, for example, requires not only a specific intent to kill but also evidence of planning and deliberation on the part of the accused. Second-degree murder requires proof of the specific intent to kill. Manslaughter simply requires a general intent to injure the victim without any particular thought as to whether the victim will die as a result.

Intent is sometimes confused with **motive**. Motive is the "why" that explains the reason behind the accused's actions. The two concepts are related, but while proof of intent is necessary to establish *mens rea*, motive may be relevant only as evidence of intent (an element of proof of the crime) and as a factor to be considered for sentencing purposes. In fact, motive need only be proven if it is an *actus reus* element; for example, possession for the purpose of trafficking in an illegal substance is a more serious offence than simple possession.

LOWER LEVELS OF INTENT

At the lower end of the range of intent are issues of recklessness, wilful blindness, carelessness, and negligence. These lower levels of *mens rea* may be said to describe unjustifiable risk taking.

Recklessness describes a level of *mens rea* where the accused is aware of the potential harmful consequences of his or her action but takes an unjustifiable risk in the face of that knowledge, perhaps hoping that nothing bad will happen. The prosecution must prove that the accused appreciated the risk he or she was taking and that a reasonable person in similar circumstances would not have taken the risk given the potential consequences.

Wilful blindness is similar to recklessness except, instead of knowing of the risk, the accused needs to have refused to consider the possibility that the risk existed. Wilful blindness also applies where an accused suspected criminal consequences but did not confirm them and closed his or her mind to them. For example, a person who buys an expensive set of stereo speakers from a stranger in a bar for one-tenth their market value might be said to be wilfully blind to the fact that the

---

general intent
a level of *mens rea* where the accused need not have intended to commit the offence or cause certain results but must have intended to act in a way that resulted in the offence occurring

specific intent
a level of *mens rea* that requires the prosecution to prove that the accused meant to commit the offence or to cause the harm that resulted

direct intent
a level of intent (*mens rea*) where the accused has a clear intent to commit the offence or to cause certain results

negligence
the failure of a person to respect or carry out a duty of care owed to another

motive
the reason a person committed an offence

recklessness
a level of intent (*mens rea*) where the accused knows the potential consequences of his or her action and takes an unjustifiable risk despite that knowledge

wilful blindness
a circumstance in which the accused suspected the potential for criminal consequences but closed his or her mind to them

speakers are probably stolen. The purchaser is likely to be found guilty of possession of stolen property, contrary to s. 354 of the Code.

Carelessness is an even lower level of intent. An accused is careless when he or she fails to appreciate a risk that a reasonable person would have appreciated and avoided. The prosecution is not required to prove that the accused understood the risk he or she was taking.

Negligence is the failure to take the care that a reasonable person would use in the same circumstances. It does not involve any particular intent at all. Negligence as such has not traditionally been a part of the criminal law because of the absence of a *mens rea* element; however, some case law suggests that failing to take the precautions that a reasonable person would take in a similar situation may be the basis for criminal liability under some circumstances. Dangerous driving (s. 249), failing to provide the necessaries of life (s. 215), and careless use of a firearm (s. 86) are all *Criminal Code* offences where negligence can be the required *mens rea*.

Criminal negligence differs from ordinary or civil negligence in that it generally requires some level of *mens rea*, such as wanton and reckless disregard for the lives and safety of others. A motorist who engages in drag racing on a public road may be criminally negligent even if at the time there was no traffic and no apparent danger to others. Criminal negligence is established by proof of the accused's indifference to the consequences of this act.

ARGUMENTS AGAINST INTENT

It is possible for the accused to argue that he or she did not intend to commit an offence.

One argument against intent is a **factual mistake**. If a person accused of possessing a narcotic honestly believed that the substance was baking powder, the person cannot be said to have the intent to possess a narcotic. It would then be up to the prosecution to prove that either the accused was wilfully blind to the fact that the substance was in fact cocaine, or the accused's belief was unreasonable given the circumstances. If the prosecution fails to prove this, it can still obtain a conviction if it can convince the judge or jury that the accused's mistake was not material to the offence. For example, an accused's mistaken belief that his or her victim wished to be killed is not material to the offence of murder, since the law does not allow a person to consent to his or her own murder.

The issue of factual mistake was a recent hot topic in the law of sexual assault. Sexual assault requires proof that the sexual contact occurred without the consent of the victim. For a time, the common law allowed the accused to argue that he should be acquitted because he had an honest but mistaken belief that the victim had consented based on her failure to protest, her earlier behaviour, or even her choice of clothing. When the law was amended to eliminate this defence, defence lawyers argued that the level of intent was changed, creating an offence that attracted very serious penalties while requiring only a very low level of intent: negligence or recklessness. This area of law is still developing and involves both common law and statute law components.

Another argument against intent is that the actions of the accused were not consciously voluntary. For example, in *R v. Parks*,[12] the Supreme Court of Canada held that if a person can prove that a crime was committed while he or she was

carelessness
a level of intent (*mens rea*) where a person fails to appreciate a risk that a reasonable person would have foreseen

criminal negligence
actions that are defined as criminal under the *Criminal Code* even though they incorporate a level of *mens rea* falling below conscious intent— for example, indifference

factual mistake
an error made about the truth of a fact or the existence of a condition

sleeping or unconscious, he or she will be acquitted on the basis of not having the required intent to commit the crime.

No-Intent Offences

Almost all offences in the *Criminal Code* and other, similar statutes require proving some form of intent on the part of the accused. In general terms, society believes that a person should not be sent to prison or face serious punishment unless he or she is morally guilty — that is, he or she acted with intent in committing an offence.

However, some quasi-criminal offences (created mostly by provincial statutes or by regulations) require little or no mental element for a conviction. In general, these offences attract only fines or other punishments not involving imprisonment. The two types of these offences are absolute liability offences and strict liability offences.

ABSOLUTE LIABILITY OFFENCES

absolute liability offence
an offence that permits a conviction on proof of the physical elements of the offence (*actus reus*), with no proof of intention to commit the offence (*mens rea*) required

Absolute liability offences permit immediate conviction based on committing the physical aspect of the offence. For absolute liability offences, the prosecution has to prove only that the accused committed the prohibited act. The prosecution does not have to prove a guilty mind, fault, or negligence on the part of the accused. A person may be convicted of an absolute liability offence even if a reasonable person would have behaved in exactly the same way.

Once the *actus reus* of the offence is proven, the accused person's arguments and explanations have no effect. Examples of absolute liability offences can be found in the Ontario *Highway Traffic Act*. For example, the Act makes it an offence for a driver to drive his or her vehicle through a stop sign without stopping. If the prosecution proves that the driver did not stop at the stop sign, it does not matter if the driver did not know that the stop sign was there, if the driver was rushing to the hospital to deliver a baby, or even if the driver was trying to escape another vehicle that was chasing him or her. The driver failed to stop and so is guilty.

In *BC Motor Vehicle Reference re s. 94(2), Motor Vehicle Act*,[13] the Supreme Court of Canada decided that, on their face, absolute liability offences violate the principles of s. 7 of the *Charter of Rights and Freedoms* because they allow for the conviction of people without guilty minds. However, the court also held that an absolute liability offence would violate the Charter "only if and to the extent that it has the potential of depriving [the accused] of life, liberty and security of the person" as guaranteed by s. 7. Because failing to stop at a stop sign is punishable only by a fine and demerit points, the section of the *Highway Traffic Act* is not nullified by the Charter. For a detailed discussion of the Charter and the criminal law, see chapter 6.

STRICT LIABILITY OFFENCES

strict liability offence
an offence that depends for conviction only on proof of the physical element of the offence although there is no negligence on the part of the accused

For **strict liability offences**, the prosecution needs to prove only that the accused committed the *actus reus* of the offence; the court will assume, unless the accused can prove otherwise, that he or she was negligent in committing the act.

Strict liability offences differ from absolute liability offences in that an accused can provide explanations or defences to strict liability charges. If the accused can convince the judge that a reasonable person would have committed the *actus reus* of the offence under the circumstances, an acquittal will follow. In other words, the accused can prove that he or she was not negligent in doing what he or she did.

Examples of strict liability offences include polluting the environment and corporate violations of health, licensing, and safety requirements.

Attempts and Offences Involving Indirect Involvement

ATTEMPTS TO COMMIT CRIMES

Attempts to commit certain crimes are punishable. Section 24 of the *Criminal Code* states:

> 24. Everyone who, having an intent to commit an offence, does or omits to do anything for the purpose of carrying out his intention is guilty of an attempt to commit the offence whether or not it was possible under the circumstances to commit the offence.

The section also states that an attempt is an act that goes beyond "mere preparation" to commit the offence. The *actus reus* for an attempt does not depend on the proof of consequences. However, establishing intent alone (the *mens rea*) is not enough to convict without evidence of an act committed for the purpose of carrying out the intended objective. For example, Frank decides to deface a school with graffiti. If all he does is pick a date and time and buy spray paint, this is not enough to convict him of an attempt, since these acts amount only to mere preparation. However, if Frank is caught in the schoolyard with a spray can in his hand, but he has not yet defaced the building, he could be convicted of the offence of mischief.

Attempted crimes, often called **inchoate** (incomplete) **crimes**, are usually subject to less severe punishments than completed crimes. The three essential elements of an attempt are (1) intent, (2) some act or omission toward committing the offence, and (3) non-completion of the criminal act.

PARTIES TO AN OFFENCE

It is possible for a person to be charged, tried, and convicted of a serious criminal offence even if that person was not the main actor who actually committed the crime. Driving a getaway car, allowing a person who commits a crime to hide from police at your house, or helping someone plan a crime are all offences that are punishable by law if they are done willingly and knowingly.

The main **parties** that commit a crime are often called **principals** to the offence. Forms of secondary involvement in offences that are recognized in the *Criminal Code* include aiding, abetting, counselling, and being an accessory after the fact. People who engage in these activities will have their liability judged independently of the actions of the principals based on individual findings of *actus reus* and *mens rea*. If they are found guilty, secondary participants may be convicted of the same criminal offence as the principal offender and sentenced accordingly.

attempt
a criminal offence in which the offender took steps toward committing a crime but failed to complete it

inchoate crime
a crime that is incomplete or attempted

party
a person who has involvement in the commission of an offence, whether direct or indirect

principal
a person who is directly involved in committing an offence

Aiding and Abetting

aid
knowingly assist the commission of a crime

abet
intentionally encourage the commission of a crime

Aiding means knowingly assisting the commission of a crime in any way. The *actus reus* of aiding is material facilitation (helping) for a specified illegal purpose. **Abetting** means intentionally encouraging the principal to commit a crime.

Aiding and abetting, set out in s. 21(1) of the *Criminal Code*, are often charged together, and both offences require proof of direct or indirect intent. As a general rule, a person who is simply present and doesn't object to the crime being committed won't be convicted as an aider and abettor. If the person is under a duty to act and does nothing to stop the commission of a crime, he or she can be convicted of aiding or abetting by omission. For example, in *R v. Nixon*[14] a senior police officer who was in charge of a lockup was found to have aided and abetted an assault on a prisoner by failing to act under his statutory duty to protect a prisoner in his care.

Counselling

counsel
advise another person to be a party to an offence

Counselling is charged where a person advises, recommends, procures, solicits, or incites another person to be a party to an offence. There are two types of counselling offences. The first is counselling a crime that is never committed, contrary to s. 464 of the Code. This offence is subject to a lesser punishment, similar to an attempted but incomplete offence. The other type of counselling is a more serious offence and is set out in s. 22 of the Code. This offence involves being a party to an actual crime that is committed. The counsellor becomes a party to an offence and is subject to the same punishments faced by the principal actors.

Accessory After the Fact

accessory after the fact
a person who, knowing that another person has committed an offence, helps that person to commit a related offence (for example, converting stolen goods) or to escape prosecution

An **accessory after the fact** is, according to s. 23 of the *Criminal Code*, a person who, knowing that another person has committed an offence, "receives, comforts or assists" that person for the purpose of helping him or her to escape. There are two clear mental elements to this offence. First, the accused must know that the person he or she is assisting has been a party to an offence, and second, the accused must knowingly provide the assistance for the purpose of helping the party escape. A person who is an accessory after the fact is not considered a party to the offence, but he or she can be tried and sentenced under s. 463 of the Code as if guilty of attempting the offence.

KEY TERMS

abet

absolute liability offence

accessory after the fact

act

actus reus

aid

appeal

attempt

carelessness

causation

consent

conviction

counsel

criminal negligence

culpable intervention

direct intent

element

evidence

factual causation

factual mistake

foreseeability

general intent

hybrid offence

inchoate crime

included offence

indictable offence

intent

legal causation

mens rea

motive

negligence

offence

offence grid

omission

oral testimony

party

penalty part (of an offence)

physical evidence

possession

principal

procedural part (of an offence)

quasi-criminal

reasonable person

recklessness

sentence

specific intent

strict liability offence

substantive part (of an offence)

summary conviction offence

wilful blindness

NOTES

1. *Mental Health Act*, RSO 1990, c. M.7.

2. *Criminal Code*, RSC 1985, c. C-46, as amended.

3. *Highway Traffic Act*, RSO 1990, c. H.8.

4. *Controlled Drugs and Substances Act*, SC 1996, c. 19.

5. *Crimes Against Humanity and War Crimes Act*, SC 2000, c. 24.

6. *Compulsory Automobile Insurance Act*, RSO 1990, c. C.25.

7. *Canadian Charter of Rights and Freedoms*, part I of the *Constitution Act, 1982*, RSC 1985, app. II, no. 44.

8. *Canada Evidence Act*, RSC 1985, c. C-5.

9. *Youth Criminal Justice Act*, SC 2002, c. 1.

10. *R v. Marshall* (1986), 25 CCC (3d) 151 (NSCA).

11. *Highway Traffic Act*, RSO 1990, c. H.8.

12. *R v. Parks* (1992), 75 CCC (3d) 287 (SCC).

13. *BC Motor Vehicle Reference re s. 94(2), Motor Vehicle Act* (1985), 23 CCC (3d) 289 (SCC).

14. *R v. Nixon* (1990), 57 CCC (3d) 97; 6 WWR 253; 57 CR (3d) 349 (BCCA).

EXERCISES

Multiple Choice

1. Criminal offences that are listed in the *Criminal Code* are created by
    a. the federal government
    b. provincial governments
    c. municipal governments
    d. all of the above

2. Which of the following statutes is not generally included in an annotated edition of the *Criminal Code*?
    a. *Canada Evidence Act*
    b. *Highway Traffic Act*
    c. *Youth Criminal Justice Act*
    d. *Crimes Against Humanity and War Crimes Act*

3. The difference between negligence and criminal negligence is that criminal negligence has
    a. a *mens rea* component
    b. an *actus reus* component
    c. a due diligence component
    d. no defence available in court

4. What word describes the situation where a person is aware of the potentially harmful consequences of an act but acts anyway?

    a. mistake
    b. wilful blindness
    c. carelessness
    d. recklessness

5. What term describes provincial or municipal offences that are similar in nature to *Criminal Code* offences?
    a. no-intent offences
    b. quasi-criminal offences
    c. absolute liability offences
    d. strict liability offences
    e. included offences

True or False?

_____ 1. Quasi-criminal provincial offences can be found in the *Criminal Code*.

_____ 2. The *Highway Traffic Act* is an example of provincial legislation.

_____ 3. A person charged with any offence, whether criminal or quasi-criminal, must have intended to commit the offence in order to be convicted.

_____ 4. The common law, in the form of court decisions, must be consulted when interpreting *Criminal Code* provisions.

_____ 5. The *actus reus* is the physical component of a crime.

_____ 6. An accused may, in some cases, be convicted of a lesser, included offence if the prosecution fails to prove an aggravating element (for example, the use of a firearm).

_____ 7. Aiding means intentionally encouraging the commission of a criminal act.

_____ 8. A counsellor to an offence can actually be charged as a party to an offence under the *Criminal Code*.

Short Answer

1. Consider s. 245 of the Code: Administering Noxious Thing. Which terms or phrases in this offence will you need to research further to understand the offence properly?

2. Explain the main differences between criminal offences and quasi-criminal offences.

3. In what part of the *Criminal Code* would you expect to find the following offences?

   a. assault

   b. arson

   c. mischief

4. Write a scenario that demonstrates specific intent and one that demonstrates general intent.

5. Explain the differences among recklessness, carelessness, and negligence.

6. Describe the difference between aiding and abetting.

CHAPTER 6

Investigation of Crime, Police Powers, and the Canadian Charter of Rights and Freedoms

Chapter Objectives

After completing this chapter, you should be able to:

- Describe and explain the test for a reasonable search.
- Explain the process for obtaining a search warrant.
- Understand the requirements for arresting an individual.
- Identify the major individual rights protected by the *Canadian Charter of Rights and Freedoms*.
- Explain how the Charter affects crime investigations.
- Understand the test for excluding tainted evidence from trial.

Investigating Crime

Once a crime has been committed, it is up to the police to investigate it, collecting evidence to prove who committed the crime and how. The goal is to collect enough evidence to prove that a person is in fact guilty of the crime to the satisfaction of a judge or jury in court. To use the terminology from chapter 5, the police must find evidence to prove that the person is guilty of each element that makes up the equation of the offence.

While a person is being investigated under suspicion of committing the crime, he or she is referred to as a **suspect**. Once charges have been laid, the person becomes the **accused**.

Much of the investigation process is not governed by any law or statute; the police officer simply follows the guidelines for investigations produced by the police

suspect
a person the police are actively investigating with regard to an offence but who has not yet been charged

accused
a person against whom a criminal or quasi-criminal charge has been laid, but who has not yet been convicted

force. However, once the investigation begins to focus on a specific person, with the potential for infringing on his or her rights, the officer's actions are governed — and, in many ways, limited — by the rules set out in the *Criminal Code*[1] (specifically part XV), the *Canadian Charter of Rights and Freedoms*,[2] and the common law.

excluded
barred by a judge's order from being used as evidence at trial, often as a result of a breach of a Charter right in producing the evidence

Evidence that is discovered or obtained in a manner that is contrary to the Code, the Charter, or common law may be **excluded** from consideration in a trial. The decision to exclude evidence is made by the judge. In general, the defence will "move" (ask) to exclude the evidence; the judge will then send the jury, if any, out of the courtroom, listen to the arguments of both the prosecution and the defence, and decide whether the evidence can be considered or not.

Evidence that is excluded cannot be considered by the decision maker (the judge or the jury) in making a finding of guilt or innocence. If, in a trial by judge alone, the judge has heard the evidence in the course of the exclusion hearing, he or she must be careful to ignore the evidence when making the final decision. Even if the "tainted" evidence clearly suggests that a person committed a certain crime, the judge may rule that the prosecution is barred from using it at trial because it was obtained improperly.

As a result, it is very important that police officers understand what they can and cannot do when investigating a crime. This chapter discusses the rules governing the power of police to investigate crime and gather evidence against a suspect. The rules discussed here deal with the police powers of **search and seizure**, the proper procedure for arresting a suspect, and the various Charter rights that the officer must be aware of in conducting an investigation. Because the rights of individuals are considered of paramount importance in Canada, the Charter plays a role in all discussions of police investigative powers.

search and seizure
part of investigating offences, where the police inspect people or places and take into custody any physical evidence of crime that is found

Search and Seizure

Both statute law and common law give certain investigative powers to police officers. One of the most important investigative tools available to police is the ability to search private property and seize evidence, but this police power has limits. Section 8 of the Charter states, "Everyone has the right to be secure against unreasonable search or seizure." This section begs the question, "What is **reasonable**?" In the case *R v. Collins*,[3] the Supreme Court of Canada determined that a search will be reasonable if

reasonable
a subjective standard, used in the Charter or common law rules, of what is acceptable to society under the circumstances

- it is authorized by law,
- the law itself is reasonable, and
- the manner in which the search is carried out is reasonable.

AUTHORIZED BY LAW

authorized by law
conducted under the authority of a statute or with judicial authorization

A search is **authorized by law** if a statute exists that specifically allows the police to conduct the search in question or if the police officers obtain judicial authorization for the search before they conduct it. The *Criminal Code*, for example, authorizes the police to require a person to provide a breath sample on demand (s. 254) if the officer has reasonable grounds to believe that the person is operating a motor vehicle under the influence of alcohol (this is known as a "warrantless search"). This demand is considered a search under s. 8 of the Charter. Section 487 of the *Criminal Code* allows a justice of the peace or a provincial court (Ontario Court of Justice) judge, in appropriate circumstances, to issue a **search warrant** — a written authorization to conduct a search.

A warrant sets out the offence being investigated, the place that may be searched, the items that may be searched for, who may attend at the search, and when the search may be conducted. Failing to follow the terms of the warrant carefully may lead to the search being declared unlawful or without due authorization. For example, if the warrant allows officers to search a specific car and they search not only the car but also the garage in which it is found, they have overstepped the legal authority of the warrant. Any evidence they find in the garage may be tainted as having been obtained unreasonably.

The common law rule is that the warrant itself must be obtained legally and according to specific requirements; otherwise, the warrant is improper and the search is illegal. The usual procedure for obtaining a search warrant is for a police officer (the **informant**) to appear before a justice of the peace. The officer swears to the truth of an affidavit, which the Code calls an **information**, that sets out the grounds for believing that the items sought in a search warrant will result in discovering evidence of the commission of a crime. Sometimes, if the officer can't personally go to the courthouse, the justice of the peace issues a **telewarrant** under s. 487.1.

The issue of what constitutes reasonable and probable grounds for police action is a very important one. Law enforcement officers will encounter this issue in many facets of their work, not only with respect to search and seizure.

"Grounds" refers to the evidence on which an officer bases his or her desire to conduct the search. This evidence can come in many forms: verbal evidence from a third party (for example, a tip from an informer); eyewitness evidence (for example, observations that the officer has made in the course of surveillance of the outside of the building sought to be searched); or physical or documentary evidence (for example, a printed invitation to a film screening of what sounds, from the description, like child pornography).

"Reasonable" and "probable" are adjectives used to describe the quality and reliability of the evidence. Assessing the quality and reliability of an officer's grounds, and the degree to which they suggest that an offence has been or will be committed, is up to the justice of the peace.

In general, before issuing a warrant, the justice of the peace will look for specificity in the evidence, as well as credibility on the part of third-party sources. In *Hunter v. Southam Inc.*,[4] the Supreme Court of Canada held that, to be constitutional (consistent with a person's Charter rights), a search warrant must set out the reasonable grounds to believe that an offence has been committed and that the particular items to search for in a certain location will likely yield evidence of a crime. The description of the items must be detailed enough to allow the officers to identify the items and link them to the offence described in the search warrant; a search is not permitted to be what is commonly described as "a fishing expedition." There must also be a nexus (connection) between the location to be searched and the items being sought. The minimum requirements for issuing a search warrant are

search warrant
a written authorization to conduct a search

informant
for a document, the person, usually a police officer, who swears the facts in an application for a search warrant or on a charging document

information
a sworn affidavit that serves as an application for a search warrant

telewarrant
a search warrant that is issued by telephone or other telecommunication method, such as fax

- a description of the offence, including the name of the accused if known, the section of the Code that creates the offence being investigated, the identity of the victim, the date of the crime, the circumstances of the offence, and so on;
- a list of the items to be seized;
- the location to be searched; and
- the informant's reasonable grounds (reasons and evidence supporting those reasons) for believing that the evidence will be found in the specified location.

If the proper procedures are not followed to obtain the warrant, or if the warrant is issued without sufficient grounds, it is considered invalid and the search that it authorizes is considered unlawful. As a result, any evidence discovered through the search may be excluded from the trial of the accused.

Section 489 of the Code does allow for "plain-view" seizures of items that are not named in the search warrant if the items are found during a lawful search and are in plain view of the police officers. To seize these items, the officers must have reasonable and probable grounds to suspect that they may be evidence of an offence. For example, if police officers are searching a house for stolen jewellery and they look in the freezer and find, instead of jewellery, neatly bundled hundred-dollar bills, they may be justified in seizing the cash as evidence of the sale of stolen goods. However, the police would not likely be able to support the seizure of $36.71 in mixed bills and change from the pocket of a parka in the accused's hall closet.

THE LAW IS REASONABLE

For a search to be reasonable under s. 8 of the Charter, the law that authorizes the search must be reasonable. This requirement applies to two different kinds of law: the statute that authorizes the search or the search warrant, and the statute that specifies the way the warrant is obtained.

The courts have upheld s. 254 of the *Criminal Code*, which allows for warrantless demands for breath samples. Ordinarily, this kind of random search would not be allowed; however, an exception has been made to permit it on the basis of society's interest in reducing drunk driving and improving public safety on the roads. This balance between individual rights and social interests was discussed in chapter 4, where we examined how the courts analyze laws to determine whether they are consistent with the Charter.

The procedure for obtaining the warrant must be reasonable. For example, the information form provided to the justice of the peace to obtain the warrant must have room for, and be filled in with, a clear statement of the informant's reasonable and probable grounds. If the warrant is issued without these grounds filled in, or if the grounds are not reasonable but the justice of the peace accepts them anyway, the justice of the peace's action in issuing the warrant is unreasonable.

THE MANNER OF THE SEARCH IS REASONABLE

Even if the search is lawful and the law permitting the search is reasonable, the evidence obtained as a result of the search may be excluded from trial if the manner in which the police conducted the search was unreasonable. It is not reasonable, for example, for police who are looking for stolen vehicles in a garage to rip out the garage walls or dismantle the plumbing.

COMMON LAW POWERS TO SEARCH AND SEIZE

Even without a warrant or a specific statutory authorization, the common law provides that the police may, in certain narrow circumstances, conduct a search. The common law supports warrantless searches where the search is

- incidental to the arrest of a person,
- consented to by the person searched or a person in possession and occupation of the premises searched, or
- incidental to the general powers of the police (for example, during the Reduce Impaired Driving Everywhere [RIDE] program).

If a police officer has a legal right to arrest a person, that officer also has a common law right to search the person, for the safety of both the officer and the person. The common law recognizes that police officers must be able to assure themselves that the arrested person will not be in a position to harm them or to escape custody. A reasonable search for weapons or other dangerous items may be conducted at the time of the arrest — the officer does not have the right to conduct a full cavity search of the person, to take blood or DNA samples, or to search the person's house.

In conducting a search incidental to arrest, the police can take only those actions that are consistent with the purpose of the search — namely, ensuring personal safety. In general, this amounts to a pat-down of the suspect's body through clothing. In the recent Supreme Court of Canada case of *R v. Mann*,[5] a police officer conducting a pat-down felt a soft bulge in a suspect's sweatshirt pocket. Upon reaching into the pocket, the officer found illegal drugs. The drugs seized were later excluded from evidence because the court decided that reaching into the pocket for something soft (that is, something that did not appear to pose a threat to safety) amounted to an illegal search and seizure.

Consent to a search is another complicated matter. The police must take steps to ensure that the consent is informed and voluntary — that the person who consents understands what he or she is consenting to and is not feeling threatened by the officer making the request. The officer must also ensure that the person consenting to the search of a building actually has the legal right to give such consent. The person must be the owner or occupier of the place to be searched and not just a guest.

consent
the informed, voluntary approval by one party of the actions of another

Programs like RIDE or even routine roadside checks for seat belt use, licence and registration, or insurance are constantly being challenged under the Charter. Police are, in general, not allowed to simply conduct random checks of people's virtue. Absent a legally recognized exception, they must have reasonable grounds to suspect that an offence is being committed before beginning an investigation. The RIDE program has been allowed by courts because it fulfils a pressing social need (reducing drunk driving) but interferes in only a minimal way with the rights of the drivers who are stopped.

The related issue of "investigative detention," whereby the police randomly detain a person, even briefly, on a hunch (less than reasonable grounds) is discussed below, in the section on arbitrary detention.

Arrest

arrest
the act of taking a suspect into police custody

The issue of **arrest** is one of the most complex and important to a police officer. In all cases, officers should refer to the rules for arrest set out in the Code.

Arrest is the lawful restriction of liberty that consists of words of arrest and a physical demonstration of detention. In other words, a police officer arrests a person when the officer makes a statement like "You're under arrest" and then puts the person in the back seat of the police cruiser. Stopping an individual to ask for identification is not generally considered an arrest. However, if the person is given reason to form the impression that he or she is not free to go, the stop may amount to investigative detention, which has been a controversial issue in recent years.

Arrest is dealt with in part XVI (Compel Appearance of Accused) of the *Criminal Code*. Arrests are usually made for one of three reasons: to ensure that the person appears at trial for crimes he or she is accused of committing, to prevent a person from beginning to commit an offence, or to stop the person in the process of committing a crime. If a person is suspected of committing an offence that is not serious and there is no reason to believe that the person will not appear in court when required, the police officer need not arrest the person but may simply issue a document called an **appearance notice** to the person, which directs the accused to be at a certain court at a certain date and time.

appearance notice
a formal document, given to a person charged with a minor offence, that sets out the requirement to attend court for trial at a certain date and time

Arrests may be made either with an arrest warrant or without one. The process for obtaining an arrest warrant is described in ss. 504 to 514 of the Code. As with a search warrant, an arrest warrant is obtained by applying to a justice of the peace or a provincial court (Ontario Court of Justice) judge. An informant (usually a police officer) must appear before a justice of the peace and swear an information that identifies the person involved, alleges that the person has committed an indictable offence, and states that the person is or is believed to be located within the jurisdiction of the justice of the peace. The justice will review the adequacy and form of the information, and, if it is proper, the justice must then decide whether issuing a **summons** is enough or whether an arrest warrant is necessary.

summons
a document that may be delivered to a person accused of a crime requiring that person to be in court at a certain date and time to answer the charges

A summons is simply an order that the accused person appear in court at a certain date and time to answer the charge made against him or her. No arrest is involved.

If, however, the justice of the peace decides, on the basis of the offence alleged against the accused person or the evidence produced at the warrant hearing, that the public interest requires that the accused be arrested, then the justice may issue a warrant for the arrest of the accused.

According to s. 495(1) of the Code, with certain exceptions, a police officer may lawfully arrest a person without a warrant if that person has committed an indictable offence, or the officer has reasonable grounds to assume that the person is about to commit an indictable offence, or the person is found committing a criminal offence of any kind.

The Canadian Charter of Rights and Freedoms

The *Charter of Rights and Freedoms* (see appendix C and chapter 4) sets out those individual rights that Canadians believe are fundamental to a free and democratic society. In broad language, the Charter establishes rules that all levels of government must follow in their efforts to regulate the lives of citizens. These rules have been extensively challenged in the courts, and the common law surrounding each section of the Charter is already complex and well developed.

Among other things, the Charter protects the individual's right to freedom of expression and association; to be free from unreasonable search and seizure and from arbitrary detention; and to enjoy life, liberty, and security of the person.

The Charter applies equally to laws (both statute law and common law) and to the actions of the government and its representatives. In stating that the Charter applies to laws and government actions, we mean that a law that infringes on the rights and freedoms of individuals can be struck down unless that law represents a reasonable limit "prescribed by law as can be demonstrably justified in a free and democratic society" (s. 1). Government action that infringes a Charter right will attract "such remedy as the court considers appropriate and just under the circumstances" (s. 24(1)).

Any discussion of how the Charter applies to a section of the *Criminal Code* or an action of a police officer will first involve establishing that a right has been infringed (or breached), then determining whether the infringement is sufficient to attract a **remedy** and then what the remedy will be. For example, evidence collected as a result of breaching the right may be excluded from use at trial.

remedy
an award or order provided by the court to redress a legal wrong

THE CHARTER AND THE CRIMINAL CODE

The *Charter of Rights and Freedoms* and the *Criminal Code* often conflict. The Charter, which is part of the constitution of Canada and therefore paramount (above all other statutes), protects the legitimate interests of individuals to be protected from unreasonable actions of the state. The Code, a federal statute, protects the legitimate interests of society to be protected from crime and the people who commit crime.

Because the Charter is a constitutional document, it overrides the Code at every turn — no section of the Code that contravenes the Charter is lawful. If a section of the Code is found to be unlawful under the Charter (often called "unconstitutional"), that section may be struck down by a judge and declared to be of no force and effect. Unless the decision of the judge is later overturned, a law or part of a law that has been struck down cannot be enforced in any situation, not just in the case in which it was found to be unconstitutional. This process was discussed in chapter 4.

The actions of police officers are also subject to the Charter. As agents of the government, the police are required to behave at all times in a way that does not infringe on the Charter rights of individuals. This is particularly true when the police investigate crimes. As discussed above, if evidence of a crime is obtained in a manner that infringes the Charter rights of the accused, that evidence may be excluded from the trial of the accused under s. 24(2) of the Charter.

What follows is a brief discussion of the various sections of the Charter that apply to criminal investigations.

ARBITRARY DETENTION (SECTION 9)

Section 9 of the Charter protects an individual's right not to be arbitrarily detained. In addition, s. 10(a) guarantees the individual's right to be informed of the reason for the arrest or detention.

Detention by the police for the purposes of these sections involves restraining a person's liberty. Whether a person's liberty has been restrained is treated, by judges, as a question of fact, which means that it depends on the particular circumstances of each case. Judges have ruled, for example, that a police officer at the scene of a car accident has detained people simply by telling them to sit in the back seat of a police cruiser. In that instance, the police officer, in directing the people to enter the cruiser, assumed control over people's movements in a circumstance where they believed that they would face serious legal consequences if they did not obey.

The common law test for determining whether a detention is arbitrary involves considering the following factors:

- whether there is an articulable cause for the detention,
- the extent and duration of the detention, and
- the conduct of the police.

Articulable cause means a reason for detaining someone that arises out of information known to the police officer that indicates that detention is necessary or justified. For example, if a police officer receives a report that a crime is in progress at a certain store and, on approaching the store, sees two people running from it, that officer has articulable cause to stop and detain them, if only to get information on what the people may have seen in the store before leaving.

For a detention to be lawful, police must have some reason, beyond simple suspicion, to detain a person. In recent years, the issue of "investigative detention" has attracted attention. Investigative detention is a practice that has no express basis in law (no statutory provision allows it), and the term has come to describe the practice of detaining a person for the purpose of gathering information. Investigative detention generally amounts to detention without articulable cause, because the police do it not on the basis of information, but to obtain information.

In the case of *R v. Mann*, discussed above, Mr. Mann was stopped in the street by police who were cruising the area after reports of a break-in. The police knew the name of the break-in suspect, but even though Mr. Mann gave a different name (his own) when he was questioned, the police detained and searched him, discovering marijuana, which led to his arrest.

Although the *Mann* case turned not on the issue of investigative detention, but rather on the issue of search incidental to detention, the Supreme Court made some comments about investigative detention — namely, that it is not specifically provided for by law. However, the court opted not to take a hard-line approach against investigative detention. This suggests that police actions, in stopping people in suspicious circumstances, will be tolerated at least to a narrow degree by the court, but that clear violations of arrest and seizure rules will lead to Charter remedies. Investigative detention, like many other investigative issues, remains ripe for interpretation under the common law.

RIGHT TO COUNSEL (SECTION 10(b))

When people are detained or arrested by the police for any reason, s. 10(b) of the Charter protects their right to

1. instruct counsel (a lawyer) without delay, and
2. be informed of that right upon arrest or detention.

A person's right to retain counsel includes the right to do so in private and to be informed of the availability of legal aid and duty counsel services.

The police also have a duty to refrain from questioning people until they have either exercised or waived (given up) their right to counsel. This is subject to the requirement that people exercise their right to counsel (for instance, call a lawyer) within a reasonable time. A person is not able to put off being questioned indefinitely simply by refusing to call a lawyer.

To **waive** the right to counsel, the individual must make a clear statement that he or she understands the right to counsel and does not wish to exercise that right. Judges generally don't want to accept a waiver of the right to counsel unless it is made in clear, unambiguous terms. Some people hesitate to call a lawyer because they feel they cannot afford one. For this reason, good police practice means not only advising suspects of the existence of legal aid and duty counsel, but also providing relevant phone numbers so that the suspect knows how to access these services.

If the police fail to inform the person of the right to counsel or fail to allow the person to exercise the right (for example, by providing a private room and a phone) prior to questioning him or her, any answers that individual gives to police questions may be ruled **inadmissible** at trial as a result of this Charter breach.

DEPRIVATION OF LIFE, LIBERTY, AND SECURITY OF THE PERSON (SECTION 7)

Section 7 of the Charter states clearly that the government may not take away a person's life, liberty, or security of the person except in accordance with the principles of **fundamental justice**.

In some ways, s. 7 is a general statement that serves as the basis for the rights that follow in ss. 8 through 14 of the Charter. Each of those sections establishes a specific right that can be seen as an aspect of the right to life, liberty, and security of the person.

Fundamental justice is a broad concept that includes the right to remain silent when detained by the authorities. Police officers violate this right if their conduct effectively or unfairly deprives someone of the right to choose whether to speak to police. Police should not assume that people are guilty when they assert their right to silence.

RIGHT TO BE TRIED WITHIN A REASONABLE TIME (SECTION 11(b))

The right to be tried within a reasonable time is protected by s. 11(b) of the Charter. The inclusion of this right in our Charter led, in the years following proclamation of the Charter, to the dropping of hundreds of charges because of excessive delays between the time of arrest and the time of trial.

waive
give up a legal right

inadmissible
refers to evidence that was obtained in a manner that breached a Charter right and is disallowed by a trial judge so that the prosecution cannot use it as part of its case against the accused

fundamental justice
the basic tenet of the Canadian system of rights and freedoms that requires that all persons investigated for and accused of a crime receive procedural protections to ensure that they are treated fairly throughout the process

There are four factors to consider when determining whether a time delay is unreasonable:

1. *The length of the delay* If the delay is reasonable, then the determination ends here.

2. *The explanation for the delay* The delay in going to trial must be caused by the government, the courts, or the prosecution. If the delay has been caused, in whole or in part, by the accused person or his or her lawyers, it will likely not be found unreasonable.

3. *A waiver by the accused* A valid waiver of the right to a speedy trial must be understood, clear, unambiguous, and freely given by the accused.

4. *Resulting prejudice* A delay is more likely to be considered unreasonable if the accused's ability to answer the charges has suffered as a result of the delay, for example, when so much time has passed that the witnesses whom the accused had intended to call in his or her defence have died or moved away and cannot be located.

stay of proceedings
a decision by a judge to drop the charges against an accused; usually the result of improper actions on the part of the police or the prosecution

The remedy for a breach of this right is a **stay of proceedings**, meaning the charges are dropped and the accused person is free to go.

REMEDIES FOR INFRINGEMENT OF CHARTER RIGHTS (SECTION 24)

If the actions of the police are found to have infringed the Charter rights of a person accused of an offence, s. 24 of the Charter provides options to the judge for providing redress to the accused.

Section 24 is divided into two parts: s. 24(1) allows the judge to award "such remedy as the court considers appropriate and just under the circumstances"; s. 24(2) allows the judge to exclude from the trial any evidence that is found to have been obtained in a manner that infringed a Charter right if "it is established that, having regard to all the circumstances, the admission of [the tainted evidence] in the proceedings would bring the administration of justice into disrepute."

In criminal trials, the second part of the section is used most often. The person alleging the Charter breach and requesting that the evidence be excluded from the trial must establish for the judge that the requirements of s. 24(2) have been met.

Once it has been established that the police have infringed on the rights of the accused in obtaining evidence, the accused must establish that the evidence was obtained as a result of the Charter breach. For example, if the police conduct an illegal search of the home of the accused and find a blood-stained shirt, it seems clear that the evidence (the shirt) would not have been found had the police not conducted the illegal search. On the other hand, if the police conduct an illegal search of the home of the accused and, during the search, the accused enters with his or her lawyer and admits to having committed the crime, there does not appear to be a connection between the Charter breach and securing the evidence (the admission of guilt).

The final question to be asked under s. 24(2) (once the breach of the right and its connection to finding the evidence are established) is whether admitting the tainted evidence in the trial will result in an unfair trial. The common law test for excluding evidence under s. 24(2) has three elements:

1. assessing the effect of admitting or excluding the evidence on the fairness of the trial (including considering the type of evidence concerned),

2. assessing the seriousness of the Charter violation, and

3. assessing the effect that admitting or excluding the tainted evidence from the trial will have on the public's confidence in the justice system.

Each of these elements is subjective in nature. The judge must determine first whether admitting the evidence would be unfair to the accused. He or she should also consider whether excluding the evidence would be unfair to the prosecution and to society as a whole.

The judge must then consider the severity of the Charter breach. If it is a minor breach — a small defect in the form of the search warrant, for example — or if the police officer committed the breach unintentionally and in good faith, the evidence will not likely be excluded. A major breach, on the other hand, or a breach conducted knowingly and in a high-handed way by the police officer (for example, entrapment — where the accused is set up to commit a crime by the police), will generally lead to the exclusion of the evidence.

The final element is the most difficult. The judge must decide whether admitting the tainted evidence at trial could bring the administration of justice into disrepute (make it seem unfair). The standard for judging this is to consider what a reasonable person who is dispassionate and fully understands the facts of the case would think.

On the basis of applying this three-part test to the facts of a case, the judge will decide whether to admit the tainted evidence and allow the prosecution to use it in its case against the accused. The decision can have a major impact on the outcome of the trial.

Police officers who know and understand how the Charter affects police investigations can make sure they always act in a way that ensures that the evidence they discover will not be excluded from trial.

KEY TERMS

accused

appearance notice

arrest

authorized by law

consent

excluded

fundamental justice

inadmissible

informant

information

reasonable

remedy

search and seizure

search warrant

stay of proceedings

summons

suspect

telewarrant

waive

NOTES

1. *Criminal Code*, RSC 1985, c. C-46, as amended.
2. *Canadian Charter of Rights and Freedoms*, part I of the *Constitution Act, 1982*, RSC 1985, app. II, no. 44.
3. *R v. Collins*, [1987] 1 SCR 265.
4. *Hunter v. Southam Inc.*, [1984] 2 SCR 145.
5. *R v. Mann*, [2004] 3 SCR 59, 2004 SCC 52.

EXERCISES

Multiple Choice

1. Which of the following is not a requirement of a valid search warrant?
   a. the accused's criminal record
   b. a description of the offence
   c. the location to be searched
   d. the items to be seized
   e. when the search may be conducted

2. The *Charter of Rights and Freedoms* guarantees which of the following rights?
   a. the right of the accused to remain silent
   b. the right of the accused to be advised by a lawyer
   c. the right of all people to earn a living
   d. the right of all people to be free from unreasonable search and seizure
   e. a, b, and d

3. For a search to be reasonable,
   a. the law that authorizes the search must be reasonable
   b. the way the search is conducted must be reasonable
   c. the procedure for obtaining the search warrant must be followed exactly
   d. all of the above
   e. none of the above

4. Police may conduct a search without a warrant or legal authorization if
   a. the search is incidental to the arrest of a person
   b. the search is consented to by the person searched
   c. the search is consented to by the person in possession of the premises being searched
   d. a and b
   e. a, b, and c

5. The legal right of a police officer to search someone who has been arrested is based in

a. the common law

b. the *Charter of Rights and Freedoms*

c. the *Criminal Code*

d. a and c

e. none of the above

True or False?

T   1. Items that are not specifically named in a search warrant may be seized if they are in plain view and the officer has reasonable grounds to suspect that they are evidence of the commission of an offence.

F   2. The law does not permit police to arrest a suspect without a warrant.

F   3. Section 11(b) of the Charter guarantees an individual's right to counsel upon arrest or detention.

F   4. The Code and the Charter have equal importance and neither has authority over the other.

T   5. Failing to inform an arrested person of his or her rights is a breach of the Charter.

Short Answer

1. List three circumstances when police may conduct a search according to the common law.

a.

b.

c.

2. Describe the process by which a judge must decide to admit or exclude evidence that has been obtained in a manner that contravenes the Charter.

3. When is a search considered lawful?

CHAPTER 7

Criminal Pre-trial Issues

Chapter Objectives

After completing this chapter, you should be able to:

- Discuss the difference between s. 469 (most serious) and non–s. 469 offences with regard to bail hearings.
- Identify the issues relevant to the decision to grant or refuse pre-trial bail.
- Understand the reasons an accused may be found mentally unfit to stand trial.
- Describe the different pleas available to an accused and discuss how plea bargains may be arrived at.
- Explain the reasons behind Crown disclosure.

Introduction

Canada's justice system requires that any person charged with an offence (whether criminal, quasi-criminal, or other) should have the right to be tried for that offence in a court of law. The person charged with the offence has the right to require the Crown attorney (the prosecutor in a criminal case, who represents the state) to **prove beyond a reasonable doubt** that the accused has in fact committed the offence and that the accused is guilty of the *actus reus* and *mens rea* of the offence. Accused people are also entitled to have a lawyer represent them in the trial to help them defend against the charges.

However, the trial can't be held as soon as the accused is arrested and charged with the offence. It often takes several months, and sometimes several years, before the trial is held. There are many reasons for this delay: the accused and his or her lawyer must have time to prepare for the trial, the police must be allowed to complete their investigation of the offence, time must be found in the court's already busy schedule to conduct the trial, and so on. In fact, our court system is often so overburdened and the delays before trials so long that under the *Canadian Charter of Rights and Freedoms*,[1] protection of an accused's right to be tried within a

proof beyond a reasonable doubt
the level of proof that the prosecution must provide in a criminal trial to obtain a conviction

reasonable time of the laying of charges (s. 11(b)) is often invoked by accused people and their lawyers in an effort to have the charges thrown out of court. The right to a trial within a reasonable time was discussed in chapters 4 and 6.

The length of the pre-trial period raises an important question: what do we do with accused people between the time they are arrested and charged and the time they are actually tried? The pre-trial period also allows for other issues and procedural matters to be dealt with before the trial starts. This chapter will discuss some of the pre-trial issues.

Pre-trial Detention and Bail

As mentioned above, the period of time between the arrest of the accused and the trial is often several months or even a year or more. What is done with the accused during that time? Section 11(d) of the Charter states that the accused has the right "to be presumed innocent until proven guilty according to law in a fair and public hearing." If he or she is presumed innocent, we cannot simply leave the person in prison until the trial; the accused must, in most cases, be set free to await trial. Otherwise, we are presuming his or her guilt before a trial has taken place, given that imprisonment is one of our most serious forms of punishment for those found guilty of an offence.

On the other hand, there are public interest reasons to hold certain accused people in prison pending trial. They may have been charged with a particularly serious crime, they may be likely to commit further serious crimes if released, or they may be likely to flee rather than appear to attend their trial if they are released.

The *Criminal Code*[2] and the common law attempt to balance the interest of the public to be protected from the accused with the accused's right to be presumed innocent and to be protected from arbitrary detention. The Code and the common law do this by creating procedures by which a justice (either a judge or a justice of the peace) decides whether the accused should be released or kept in custody while awaiting the trial.

These procedures are divided into two categories, depending on the seriousness of the offence. For less serious offences (those *not* listed in s. 469 of the Code), the accused must be granted a bail hearing at which he or she must be granted an unconditional release unless the Crown can **show cause** as to why the accused should have conditions placed on his or her release or not be released at all. For serious crimes (those listed in s. 469 of the Code: treason, alarming her Majesty, intimidating Parliament, inciting to mutiny, sedition, piracy, piratical acts, or murder), the accused is held in prison pending trial unless he or she makes an application to be released.

The following is a brief discussion of these two procedures.

BAIL AND LESS SERIOUS OFFENCES

For less serious or **non–s. 469 offences**, s. 503 of the *Criminal Code* provides that the accused is entitled to be brought in front of a justice of the peace within 24 hours of the initial arrest and detention. This section describes the responsibilities of police officers to ensure that individuals arrested either with or without a warrant

show cause
another name for a bail hearing, where the prosecution is required to show cause as to why the accused should not be released before trial

non–s. 469 offence
a less serious *Criminal Code* offence for which, at a bail hearing, the onus is on the prosecution to show cause why the accused should not be released pending trial

be brought before a justice and dealt with according to the law. Failure to do this may be considered a violation of a person's right to be free from arbitrary detention (s. 9 of the Charter).

It may, however, not be practical for a bail hearing (which is described in s. 515 of the Code) to proceed right away. The accused's lawyers, for example, may need time to assemble the evidence and witnesses they need to persuade the justice to release the accused. Under s. 516 of the Code, the justice presiding over the **bail** (or **judicial interim release**) hearing may grant an adjournment (postponement), of no more than three days, at the request of either the defence or the prosecution. The justice may grant a longer adjournment, but only with the consent of the accused.

Onus at the Hearing

At the hearing, the **onus**, or burden of proof, is on the Crown to prove, on a balance of probabilities, that the accused either should not be released at all pending trial or should be released on certain **conditions**. If the Crown fails to meet this onus, the accused must be released on his or her own **recognizance** (promise to return for the trial). This is covered by s. 515 of the Code.

Section 515(6), however, describes certain situations where the onus to demonstrate why the accused should be released shifts to the accused, even though he or she is charged with a less serious (non–s. 469) offence. This is called a **reverse onus** because it reverses the general rule that, because of the presumption of innocence, the prosecution is required to prove the accused's guilt rather than the accused being required to prove his or her own innocence. The reverse onus situations are as follows:

1. The accused is charged with committing a non–s. 469 indictable offence while on bail for another indictable offence.
2. The accused is charged with committing a non–s. 469 indictable offence under s. 467.11, 467.12, or 467.13 (in connection with organized crime).
3. The accused is charged with an offence relating to terrorism, such as ss. 83.02 to 83.04, and 83.13 to 83.23.
4. The accused is charged with an offence under the *Security of Information Act*[3] (see s. 515(6) for the specific list of offences).
5. The accused is charged with a non–s. 469 indictable offence and does not ordinarily live in Canada (s. 515(6)(b)).
6. The accused is charged with committing an offence under ss. 145(2) to (5) while the accused was free after being released in respect of another offence under s. 679, 680, or 816 (s. 515(6)(c)).
7. The accused is charged with committing an offence punishable by life imprisonment under s. 5(3), 5(4), or 6(3) of the *Controlled Drugs and Substances Act*[4] or is charged with conspiring to commit such an offence (s. 515(6)(d)).

In these situations, the accused must show why he or she should not be detained.

bail
the release of a person accused of a crime before trial, with or without conditions

judicial interim release
bail

onus
burden of proof; the necessity for a certain party to prove a certain fact

condition
a requirement that limits the freedom of an accused who has been released on bail or on parole

recognizance
a promise

reverse onus
a situation where, instead of the prosecution being required to prove all aspects of an offence (which is the norm), the accused bears the burden of proving a fact or allegation

Grounds for Ordering Detention

At the end of the show cause hearing, the justice may order detention, release without conditions, or release with conditions. Detention may be ordered on any of three grounds:

1. the **primary ground** that detention is necessary to ensure that the accused appears at trial (s. 515(10)(a)),
2. the **secondary ground** that detention is necessary to protect the public (s. 515(10)(b)), or
3. the **tertiary ground** that detention is necessary for any other just cause that the justice determines maintains confidence in the administration of justice (s. 515(10)(c)).

The judge will consider the secondary ground only if detention is not justified according to the primary ground. The justice will consider the tertiary ground only if detention is not justified on either the primary or the secondary grounds.

Evidence at the Hearing

Section 518 sets out the evidence that may be presented at a show cause hearing. As in a trial, the prosecution can present evidence at the bail hearing that tends to prove that the accused committed the offence. The rules of evidence for bail hearings are, however, much more open than they are for a trial.

To prove that the accused should not be released, for example, the Crown may present evidence that the accused has a criminal record or that the accused is, at that time, charged with other offences. At the trial, the Crown generally can't present evidence of the accused's criminal record, since this evidence is considered too prejudicial to the accused.

Other forms of evidence that may not be admissible at trial may be presented at the show cause hearing. **Hearsay evidence** — where one person gives evidence as to what another person said rather than what that person did — is generally admissible at the bail hearing but not at trial. This often takes the form of "will say" evidence, where a police officer testifies at the bail hearing as to what various witnesses will say at trial. At the bail hearing, for example, a police officer may give evidence as simple as "Raj Singh will say at trial that he saw Bob Jones stab the victim." At trial, Mr. Singh will be required to appear and give this evidence himself so that the defence lawyers can cross-examine him and test his evidence.

Forms of Release

For less serious offences, our justice system assumes that the accused will be released on his or her own undertaking at the bail hearing. If the Crown has shown cause, however, the justice may order other bail conditions or order that the accused be detained in jail.

Bail with conditions means that the accused is released as long as he or she complies with certain requirements as set out by the justice. The conditions that may be imposed are set out in s. 515(2) of the *Criminal Code*. They include giving an **undertaking** (promise) and entering into a recognizance with or without **sureties** (money guarantees) and with or without a **deposit**. If, after bail has been

---

primary ground
a ground for ordering detention of an accused at a bail hearing for a non–s. 469 offence; based on the judge's belief that the accused is unlikely to appear at trial if released

secondary ground
a ground for ordering detention of an accused at a bail hearing for a non–s. 469 offence; based on the judge's belief that the accused poses a danger to the public

tertiary ground
a ground for ordering detention of an accused at a bail hearing for a non–s. 469 offence; based on the judge's belief that there is some justifiable reason necessary for the administration of justice

hearsay evidence
information that comes from a source that does not have direct knowledge of the truth of the information

undertaking
a promise or monetary payment made as security for a recognizance

sureties
monetary guarantees that a person will appear at court to answer the charges against him or her; this money is forfeited if the accused does not appear as required

deposit
partial payment of a surety

granted, the justice is satisfied that the accused has contravened or is about to contravene any summons or appearance notices or has committed an indictable offence, the justice can revoke or cancel bail and issue an arrest warrant, as described in s. 524 of the Code.

BAIL AND MORE SERIOUS OFFENCES

Whereas bail hearings may be held by judges or justices of the peace for less serious offences, bail hearings for **s. 469 offences** fall within the jurisdiction of a superior court judge (Superior Court of Justice, in Ontario). The rules governing release hearings for persons charged with s. 469 crimes are set out in s. 522 of the Code.

Onus at the Hearing

People who are accused of a s. 469 offence do not have an automatic right to a bail hearing. They must apply to the superior court judge to be granted such a hearing. Because they are accused of serious offences, once they have applied for a hearing they face the onus of proving to the judge, on a **balance of probabilities**, that they should be released. If they fail to do so, they must be detained until the trial. Proving something on a balance of probabilities means proving that it is more likely to be true than it is not to be true. This is a lower standard of proof than the "beyond a reasonable doubt" standard that must be achieved to support a conviction at trial.

Grounds for Ordering Release

The judge must have grounds for ordering that a person accused of a s. 469 offence be released. These grounds are, in general, the reverse of the grounds for detention listed above for bail hearings involving less serious offences. To be released, accused persons must prove that they will appear at the trial and that they are not a threat to the public.

Evidence at the Hearing

According to s. 522(5), the rules of evidence at the bail hearing for a s. 469 offence are similar to those for the bail hearing for a non–s. 469 offence.

Forms of Release

It is rare for a person accused of a s. 469 offence to be granted unconditional release pending trial. In most cases, if release is granted, it will be subject to some fairly serious conditions, including the posting of significant sureties (money guarantees).

BAIL REVIEW

An accused person or a prosecutor may request a review of a detention or release order (or a condition of them) before the trial starts. The review provisions are found in s. 520 (review by accused) and s. 521 (review by prosecutor). In Ontario, review applications must be brought before a judge of the Superior Court of Justice.

s. 469 offence
a *Criminal Code* offence of such seriousness that, at the bail hearing, the accused has to show cause why he or she should be released (a reverse of the usual onus in bail hearings)

proof on a balance of probabilities
the level (standard) of proof that someone accused of a s. 469 offence must provide at a bail hearing to be released pending trial

The accused may apply for a bail review either to allow him or her to be released from detention, or to remove conditions placed on his or her release. The prosecution may apply for bail review to convince the judge that the accused should in fact be detained or should face more onerous conditions upon release.

New evidence may be introduced at a bail review hearing, including evidence of the behaviour of the accused since the original bail hearing. The judge may decide simply to dismiss the review application and leave the bail order as is or modify the order, as long as the modifications still comply with the law of bail.

Post-trial bail — while awaiting the appeal of a conviction — will not be dealt with here.

Fitness To Stand Trial

The mental condition of the accused always plays a role in a criminal trial. As discussed in chapter 5, most offences include a mental element (the *mens rea*), without which the accused cannot be found guilty. So, the mental condition of the accused at the time the offence took place is a very important issue. If, because of some form of **mental disorder**, the accused was incapable of having the mental intent required for the offence, he or she cannot be found guilty of the offence.

mental disorder
a disease or condition of the mind under s. 16 of the *Criminal Code* that results in the accused lacking the mental ability to intend to commit a crime

The mental condition of the accused at the time of the trial is also important. For a trial to be fair, the accused must be mentally capable of understanding what is going on; of understanding the consequences he or she faces as a result of the trial; and of understanding, instructing, and receiving advice from his or her lawyer. If the accused is mentally incapable of these things, the trial cannot proceed.

The accused, the prosecutor, or the court may bring an application under s. 672.23(1) of the *Criminal Code* to determine the accused's **fitness to stand trial**. A person is deemed "unfit to stand trial," as defined under s. 2, if he or she is

fitness to stand trial
the accused's mental competence, at the time of trial, to understand the trial and what is at stake

unable on account of mental disorder to conduct a defence at any stage of the proceedings before a verdict is rendered or to instruct counsel to do so, and, in particular, unable on account of mental disorder to

(a) understand the nature or object of the proceedings,

(b) understand the possible consequences of the proceedings, or

(c) communicate with counsel.

A person who is found to be unfit to stand trial may be committed to a mental institution until either he or she is fit to stand trial or he or she is acquitted because the Crown cannot establish a *prima facie* case against the accused. Being unfit to stand trial does not save the accused from facing the charges, and perhaps being convicted of them — it simply delays the trial.

It is important to note that an accused's mental state can change over time. The person may be mentally capable of forming the intent required for an offence at the time of committing it but may not be mentally capable of standing trial several months later. On the other hand, the accused may not be mentally capable of forming the intent yet still be mentally capable of standing trial.

Disclosure

The police investigate the commission of offences. From their investigations, they determine who they believe committed a particular offence and provide evidence to the prosecution that tends to prove that the accused committed the offence. The prosecution uses this evidence at trial.

Accused people have no police force working for them to prove their innocence. In almost all cases, they do not have the resources to conduct an independent investigation of the offence to check the work of the police and to discover evidence the police may have missed that proves that someone else committed the crime.

Since our criminal justice system is based on the presumption of innocence, and since the common law (arising out of s. 7 of the Charter) has determined that accused people have a right to know the case that will be made against them and to make full answer and defence to that case, we have developed a system of **disclosure** that requires the police and the Crown prosecutors to provide to accused people and their lawyers all evidence in their possession related to the particular offence. This is often called Crown disclosure.

The accused's right to be able to make **full answer and defence** is at the core of our notion of fundamental justice, as set out in s. 7 of the Charter. Full answer and defence involves not only the opportunity for the accused to present his or her case at trial but also the accused's right to know what evidence the Crown has against him or her, to have an opportunity to contest and refute that evidence, and to know of any evidence that the police have found that may tend to prove that the accused did not, in fact, commit the offence or that another person did.

This introduces the issue of **culpability**. Culpability means guilt or responsibility. A culpable person is responsible for or guilty of an offence. Evidence is **inculpatory** if it tends to prove that the accused committed the offence; evidence is **exculpatory** if it tends to prove that the accused did not commit the offence.

So, the accused and his or her lawyers have the right to request that *all* relevant evidence be disclosed to them by the Crown before the trial begins so that they have the opportunity to prepare for the trial. All relevant evidence must be disclosed, whether the material is inculpatory or exculpatory, and regardless of whether the Crown intends to introduce the evidence at trial.

The initial disclosure should be provided before the accused is asked to choose a mode of trial (by judge or by judge and jury) or to plead (guilty or not guilty; see below). There is also a continuing obligation on the Crown to disclose new information and evidence, as it is uncovered or discovered, to the accused. These disclosure obligations are not reciprocal. This means that the defendant is not obliged to disclose his or her own evidence to the Crown. This apparent imbalance is intended to address the imbalance in power between the accused (an individual, often with no resources) and the Crown (a government agency, with an entire police force providing it with investigative resources).

The disclosure requirement extends through the Crown prosecutors to the investigating police officers themselves. The police have a statutory and common law duty to disclose to the Crown prosecutor all relevant information that has been discovered during an investigation, even if that evidence tends to prove the innocence of the person the police believe committed the offence. If the police fail to do this, the accused is entitled to a remedy. If evidence has been lost or destroyed either by the

disclosure
the requirement that the prosecution and police provide to the defence any and all evidence relevant to the charges against an accused

full answer and defence
a principle of fundamental justice whereby the accused person must be provided with the information and the means to have the opportunity to defend against the charges

culpability
guilt or responsibility

inculpatory
proving guilt; evidence that tends to show that a person committed an offence

exculpatory
proving innocence; evidence that tends to show that a person did not commit an offence

stay of proceedings
a decision by a judge to drop the charges against an accused; usually the result of improper actions on the part of the police or the prosecution

abuse of process
a course of action on the part of the police or the prosecution that misuses court process or ignores the spirit of that process and interferes with the accused's ability to make full answer and defence; threatens to bring the administration of justice into disrepute

adjournment
postponement of a trial

mistrial
a declaration by a judge that the trial of an accused cannot be allowed to continue due to unfairness to the accused, and that a new trial must be conducted

police or by the prosecution and this loss affects an accused person's ability to make full answer and defence, the charges may be stayed. A judicial **stay of proceedings** is a ruling that stops the prosecution altogether. To be granted a stay, the defence must establish that the accused's right to a fair trial has been denied or irreparably harmed, or that the non-disclosure was in bad faith (motivated by improper reasons) or constitutes an **abuse of process** — an improper action or series of actions on the part of the police that undermines the fairness of the criminal procedure.

REMEDIES FOR NON-DISCLOSURE

If the Crown does not make full disclosure to the defence, several remedies can be granted by the court. The court grants a remedy by making an order — a formal decision bearing the seal of the court.

- The court can grant an **adjournment** (postponement of the trial to a later date) to allow the defence to incorporate previously undisclosed evidence into their case.

- A **mistrial** can be declared. A mistrial ends the trial without imposing a conviction (or granting an acquittal) and it forces the Crown to begin its case again with a new jury, giving the accused more time to prepare.

- A judicial stay of proceedings can be ruled, meaning the accused is free to go, though it is possible that the Crown will lay the charge again.

- The judge may disregard the evidence that was not disclosed and withhold it from the jury in a jury trial, forcing the Crown to prove that the accused is guilty without having the benefit of the tainted evidence.

- The Crown may be ordered to pay the accused's legal costs incurred as a result of the Crown's failure to disclose the evidence.

Pleas and Plea Bargaining

plea
a statement of a legal position (guilty or not guilty); a legal argument or basis for a claim

The first step in the trial process is entering the accused's **plea** into the trial record. If the accused pleads guilty to the charges, there is no need for a trial, and the court proceeds directly to the step of sentencing. Sentencing is discussed in greater detail in chapter 9.

If the accused does not enter a plea, he or she is deemed to have pleaded not guilty. Once an individual has pleaded not guilty, the Crown must prove beyond a reasonable doubt at trial that the accused committed the offence.

PLEA BARGAINS

plea bargain
an agreement between the defence and the prosecution as to how the accused will plead and what punishment the prosecution will seek

A **plea bargain** is a negotiated agreement between the prosecution and the accused as to how to settle one or more charges against the accused. The purpose of a plea bargain is either to narrow the scope of the trial, so that it focuses only on the most serious charge(s) (which saves trial costs and the justice system's time), or to avoid a trial altogether. In general, in negotiating a plea bargain, the Crown is looking to gain a guaranteed conviction or to obtain a conviction to a lesser charge when the evidence does not support the original charge; and the accused is asking, in exchange, for leniency when it comes to sentencing. Because avoiding an unnecessary trial saves the public money, the court has a public policy interest in supporting plea bargaining. The judge is not obligated to accept the sentencing suggestions put forward by the parties as part of a plea bargain, but he or she is motivated to do so, based on public policy.

The bargain may include the accused agreeing to plead guilty to one charge and the prosecution agreeing to withdraw another. It may involve the accused and the prosecution agreeing to a guilty plea on a lesser but included offence (see s. 662) — for example, a plea of guilty to assault when the accused is charged with assault causing bodily harm.

Plea bargains struck between the Crown prosecutors and the lawyers for the defence are discussed before the judge only when an agreement is reached. If an accused offers to plead guilty to a lesser but included offence and the Crown prosecutor refuses to accept the offer, the Crown may not then attempt to use the accused's offer to plead guilty to the lesser offence as evidence to prove that the accused is guilty of the original offence.

Section 606(4) allows the court, with the consent of the prosecution, to accept a guilty plea for another offence arising out of the same circumstances without drafting a new information. The other offence is not necessarily included in the offence charged, but it must arise out of the same incident. For example, a person charged with attempted murder may plead guilty to assault. The facts supporting attempted murder (an attack on the victim) also support assault. This saves a great deal of time and resources, since the Crown does not have to go through the whole process of laying a new charge when a plea bargain is made.

Plea bargains are considered essential to an efficient justice system because they encourage guilty pleas and reduce the number of cases that actually go to trial.

PLEA OPTIONS

According to ss. 606 and 607 of the Code, the accused person has four plea options. He or she can

1. plead guilty,
2. plead not guilty,
3. plead not guilty as charged but guilty to a lesser, included offence or other offence, or
4. enter a special plea.

SPECIAL PLEAS

A **special plea**, described under s. 607 of the Code, is one that does not depend on the question of guilt or innocence. Instead, it invokes the common law principle of *res judicata*.

Res Judicata

If the accused has already been charged with and tried for an offence (has gone through a trial), he or she cannot be retried for the same crime arising out of the same circumstances. Often called "double jeopardy," this situation is prohibited by the principle of ***res judicata*** (Latin, meaning "the issue has already been

special plea
a statement, other than guilty or not guilty, made by an accused when he or she is required to enter a plea to the charges

res judicata
Latin for "already decided"; a special plea with which the accused argues that the charges against him or her have already been dealt with in a court of law

decided"). Where an accused believes that the prosecution is seeking to retry him or her for a crime that has already been addressed by the court system, the accused can enter a special plea of either autrefois acquit or autrefois convict. These pleas arise in very specific and rare situations and are governed by ss. 607 to 611 of the Code.

acquit
find an accused not guilty of an offence

autrefois acquit
French for "previously acquitted"; a special plea by which the accused alleges that he or she has already been charged, tried, and acquitted of the offence that is currently being charged

autrefois convict
French for "previously convicted"; a special plea by which the accused states that he or she has already been charged, tried, and convicted of the offence that is currently being charged

AUTREFOIS ACQUIT   If the accused has already been tried and **acquitted**, he or she cannot be retried for the same offence but may enter the special plea of **autrefois acquit** (French, meaning "previously acquitted") under s. 607(1)(a) of the Code. This plea is not generally available where the accused has been tried but the trial has ended in a stay of proceedings or other ending that does not result in an acquittal.

AUTREFOIS CONVICT   If the Crown tries to initiate the same charge after having obtained a conviction of the accused for the charge in the past, the accused can enter the special plea of **autrefois convict** (French, meaning "previously convicted") under s. 607(1)(b). If the Crown can distinguish between the charges (prove that the new charge arises out of different circumstances than did the first), the multiple convictions may survive.

Elections

election
choice

As discussed in chapter 5, the way a charge is to be tried — by way of summary conviction or by way of indictment — has an impact on the court in which the trial will be held and who the trier of fact will be. If the offence charged is a hybrid offence, the prosecution makes the first **election**: whether they wish to try the accused by way of summary conviction or indictment.

Trial by summary conviction involves no preliminary hearing. The trial is held in the provincial court (Ontario Court of Justice) before a judge alone. No jury is involved.

Trial by indictment gives the accused the right to a preliminary hearing (also called a preliminary inquiry; see below) unless the accused waives the right, either by

- electing to be tried by a provincial court judge (without a jury), or
- waiving the preliminary hearing while still electing to proceed in the superior court (in Ontario, the Superior Court of Justice).

In some cases, a preliminary hearing will also be dispensed with when the attorney general for the province takes the unusual step of preferring the indictment (forcing the matter to trial without holding a preliminary hearing). For more information on preferred indictments, see s. 574, which was amended in 2004.

Trial by indictment also gives the accused the right to elect the mode of trial: (1) in front of a provincial court judge alone, (2) in front of a judge of the superior court alone, or (3) in superior court with a judge and jury.

Once the accused has made his or her election, the accused has only limited rights to change his or her mind, or to re-elect. If the initial election was to proceed in the provincial court, the accused has until 14 days before the scheduled start date for the trial to re-elect to have the trial in the superior court (in front of a judge or a judge and jury).

If the initial election was to proceed in the superior court with a judge alone, the accused has until 15 days after the end of the preliminary hearing to re-elect either to proceed in the superior court by judge and jury or to proceed in the provincial court before a judge.

If the initial election was to proceed in the superior court with a judge and jury, the accused has until 15 days after the end of the preliminary hearing to re-elect either to proceed in the superior court by judge alone or to proceed in the provincial court before a judge.

If the accused wants to re-elect and change his or her mind at any other time, he or she must obtain the consent of the prosecution to the re-election.

The choice of mode of trial can be a very important tactical one. The provincial court route is often faster. The choice between a superior court judge alone and a judge and jury may depend on the complexity of the evidence, on the seriousness of the offence, or on many other factors. If the prosecution is proposing to introduce certain kinds of evidence that may have a tendency to make the accused "look bad," the accused and his or her lawyers may feel that a judge alone, who may be accustomed to considering such evidence, will be more likely to return a fair verdict than a jury would be. For example, a judge who is used to hearing the evidence of young children may be better able to focus on the content of the evidence rather than on his or her feelings of sympathy for the child witness. Or, where the prosecution will be introducing evidence of past behaviour (called "similar fact evidence"), which is admissible only to prove or disprove one aspect of the offence, an experienced judge may be better able to avoid coming to the conclusion that, for example, "once a violent drunk, always a violent drunk." The general belief is that members of the public on a jury are more likely to be improperly influenced against the accused upon hearing sensitive evidence and therefore less likely to accept technical defences in such cases than a judge might be.

Preliminary Inquiry

In the following discussion, keep in mind that preliminary inquiries are available only for indictable offences tried in the superior court and that an accused can waive his or her right to a preliminary inquiry.

Once a not-guilty plea has been entered for an indictable offence, a **preliminary inquiry**, or "prelim," will usually be conducted before the trial in accordance with part XVIII of the *Criminal Code*. The purpose of the prelim is to force the Crown to prove to a judge that the available evidence is sufficient to require the accused to stand trial for the offence charged. This inquiry is often called a **charge screening device**.

As provided in s. 548, before trials of certain offences, provincial court judges will hold a hearing to inquire into the charge and determine whether there is sufficient evidence to warrant placing the accused on trial (often called "committing" the accused to trial). On hearing the evidence, the judge will either order the accused to stand trial or discharge the accused.

preliminary inquiry
a judicial hearing where the prosecution must demonstrate that it has enough evidence to prove, if uncontested and accepted by the trier of fact, that the accused is guilty of the charges against him or her

charge screening device
a preliminary inquiry

The test at the preliminary inquiry is whether there is sufficient evidence that, if believed, could result in a conviction. The test must be met with respect to each offence (count) charged. Where an accused is charged with more than one offence, the judge may find that there is sufficient evidence to support a trial on some of the charges but not others. In this case, the judge will commit the accused to stand trial only on those supported charges. Where the evidence at the preliminary hearing warrants, the judge can also commit the accused to trial for new offences or counts that were not part of the original set of charges. If an accused is not committed on any of the charges, he or she is discharged. This means the accused is free to go.

KEY TERMS

abuse of process	non–s. 469 offence
acquit	onus
adjournment	plea
autrefois acquit	plea bargain
autrefois convict	preliminary inquiry
bail	primary ground
charge screening device	proof beyond a reasonable doubt
condition	proof on a balance of probabilities
culpability	recognizance
deposit	*res judicata*
disclosure	reverse onus
election	s. 469 offence
exculpatory	secondary ground
fitness to stand trial	show cause
full answer and defence	special plea
hearsay evidence	stay of proceedings
inculpatory	sureties
judicial interim release	tertiary ground
mental disorder	undertaking
mistrial	

NOTES

1. *Canadian Charter of Rights and Freedoms*, part I of the *Constitution Act, 1982*, RSC 1985, app. II, no. 44.

2. *Criminal Code*, RSC 1985, c. C-46, as amended.

3. *Security of Information Act*, RSC 1985, c. O-5.

4. *Controlled Drugs and Substances Act*, SC 1996, c. 19.

EXERCISES

Multiple Choice

1. Which of the following is not a recognized remedy for non-disclosure of relevant state evidence to the defence?

   a. a judicial stay of proceedings

   b. costs against the state

   c. an apology from the Crown or police

   d. a mistrial

2. Which of the following is considered a special plea?

   a. autrefois acquit

   b. *quid pro quo*

   c. not criminally responsible

   d. guilty with an explanation

3. People who are accused of committing a s. 469 offence

   a. have an automatic right to a bail hearing

   b. must apply to a superior court judge to be granted a bail hearing

   c. have no right to a bail hearing

   d. a and b

   e. none of the above

4. The mental condition of an accused at the time the offence took place

   a. always plays a role in a criminal trial

   b. never plays a role in a criminal trial

   c. is an important issue in a criminal trial

   d. affects the *mens rea* element

   e. a, c, and d

5. The principle of disclosure requires

   a. the Crown prosecutors to disclose to the defence all evidence in their possession

   b. the police to disclose to the prosecution all evidence in their possession

   c. the accused and his or her lawyers to disclose to the prosecution all evidence in their possession

   d. a and b

   e. a and c

True or False?

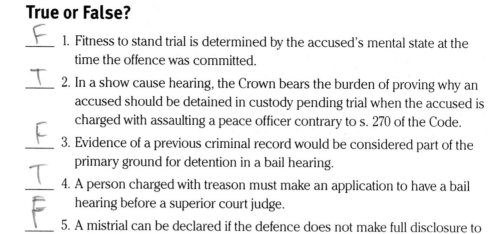

___F___ 1. Fitness to stand trial is determined by the accused's mental state at the time the offence was committed.

___T___ 2. In a show cause hearing, the Crown bears the burden of proving why an accused should be detained in custody pending trial when the accused is charged with assaulting a peace officer contrary to s. 270 of the Code.

___F___ 3. Evidence of a previous criminal record would be considered part of the primary ground for detention in a bail hearing.

___T___ 4. A person charged with treason must make an application to have a bail hearing before a superior court judge.

___F___ 5. A mistrial can be declared if the defence does not make full disclosure to the Crown.

Short Answer

1. Do you agree with the rules governing the onus of proof at show cause hearings? Why or why not?

2. What are sureties?

3. Why is it important for investigating officers to turn over to the Crown all material that is relevant to a crime?

CHAPTER 8

Criminal Trial Issues and Defences

Chapter Objectives

After completing this chapter, you should be able to:

- Describe the basic process of a criminal trial.
- Differentiate between an information and an indictment and explain the elements required for both.
- Explain the difference between a peremptory juror challenge and a challenge for cause.
- Understand the three standards of proof and explain the meaning of reverse onus.
- Identify the two types of defence and the major subcategories under each type.

Introduction to the Criminal Trial

Once a person has been accused of a crime, charges have been laid, and the pre-trial issues discussed in chapter 7 have been dealt with, the accused person is brought to trial.

PEOPLE INVOLVED IN THE TRIAL

In general terms, a criminal trial involves five different parties: the trier of fact, the trier of law, the prosecution, the defence, and the witnesses.

The **trier of fact** is either the judge (in a trial by judge alone) or the **jury** (in a trial by judge and jury). The trier of fact is the party that will make final decisions, based on the evidence, about what is true and what is not true. For example, the trier of fact will decide whether or not the accused was the person who pulled the trigger.

The **trier of law** is always the judge. It is the judge's job in every trial to interpret the law and apply it to the proven facts of the case. The judge, for example, decides the legal question whether a specific piece of evidence should be admitted

trier of fact
the person or people who must decide what facts have been proven at a criminal trial (either the judge or the jury)

jury
a group of 12 citizens who are chosen to act as the trier of fact in a criminal trial

trier of law
the judge who interprets the law and applies it to the facts as found by the trier of fact at a criminal trial

into the trial. If the trial is by judge alone, the judge will act as both trier of fact and of law. In trials by judge and jury, the judge will interpret the applicable law for the jury and, once all the evidence has been presented, will instruct the jury on how they must apply the law to the evidence presented at trial.

The **prosecution** is conducted by the Crown attorney (or attorneys) who have been nominated to present the evidence and arguments to prove that the accused is guilty of the offence.

The **defence** is conducted by the accused and his or her lawyers, whose job is to refute (counter and raise doubts about) the evidence presented by the prosecution and to produce evidence of their own that will cause the trier of fact to doubt that the accused is guilty of the offence.

The witnesses are people who appear at the trial to tell the court what they know about the offence or the accused. Witnesses may be brought to court by the prosecution or by the defence and are required to swear or affirm that their testimony will be true.

Both the prosecution and the defence may also introduce physical evidence at the trial such as a weapon, a photograph, or the results of DNA tests. This physical evidence plays a role, along with the verbal evidence of the witnesses, in convincing the trier of fact of the guilt or innocence of the accused.

THE TRIAL PROCESS

The trial process is a formal one. Trials can be as short as a few hours or as long as several months. The following is a brief overview of the stages in a normal jury trial after the charges have been laid, the bail hearing has been held, the plea has been entered, and the committal and/or elections, if applicable, have been made. Each stage will be discussed in greater detail below, with the exception of sentencing, which is covered in chapter 9.

The typical stages of a trial are as follows:

- The jury is selected.
- Any pre-trial motions are heard.
- The charges are read and the plea is entered into the trial record.
- The prosecution makes its opening statement.
- The defence makes its opening statement.
- The prosecution presents its evidence.
- The defence presents its evidence.
- The judge instructs the jury on how to apply the law.
- The jury deliberates and delivers its verdict.
- The judge listens to submissions from both sides and renders a sentence.

First, the jury is selected. This will be dealt with in greater depth later in this chapter. Once a jury has been selected, the trial itself may begin.

The second step is hearing any pre-trial motions. Pre-trial motions are brief hearings on a specific issue that needs to be addressed before the trial itself can proceed. For example, if the defence feels that certain pieces of evidence have been obtained in a way that contravened the rights of the accused under the *Canadian*

---

prosecution
the Crown attorney or attorneys who are given the task of proving an accused guilty of an offence

defence
the lawyers representing the person accused of an offence in a criminal trial

Charter of Rights and Freedoms,[1] the defence may bring a motion to exclude that evidence from trial. Motions are brought before the judge alone, since they concern questions of law. If the judge rules that the evidence should not be admitted into the trial under s. 24(2) of the Charter, the jury will never know that the evidence existed.

The first two steps — selecting the jury and hearing pre-trial motions — may take place in reverse order if, in the opinion of the parties and the judge, the motions will take several days or weeks. This is done to avoid bringing the jurors to the courthouse and disrupting their lives and then making them wait through several days of motions that they cannot attend.

Once the pre-trial motions are completed, the trial begins with the reading of the charges against the accused. The accused's plea is entered, and the two sides (the prosecution and the defence) are given the opportunity to make opening statements to the jury about what they intend to prove at the trial.

The prosecution is then required to present its evidence against the accused. Any witnesses presented by the prosecution may be cross-examined by the defence to test the trustworthiness of their evidence. As discussed in chapter 5, the prosecution must be very careful to present evidence to prove each element of the offence with which the accused is charged. Failure to do so will result in a failure of the prosecution and the acquittal of the accused.

After the prosecution finishes presenting its case to the jury, the defence usually presents evidence of its own. Once again, any witnesses called to testify by the defence may be cross-examined by the prosecutors. The defence may simply try to present evidence that undermines the evidence presented by the prosecution, or it may attempt to prove certain recognized defences that, if accepted by the jury, may lead to the acquittal of the accused. Defences will be explained in more detail later in this chapter.

Once all the evidence has been presented, the judge reviews the evidence for the jury, providing them with **instructions** on how to apply the law to the facts as they may find them. For example, the judge may say to the jury, "If you find as a fact that the accused intended to cause the death of the victim when she struck him with the baseball bat, then you must find the accused guilty of murder. If, on the other hand, you find that the accused had no such intention, you must find her guilty of manslaughter."

The jury is then asked to consider all the evidence, along with the instructions given to it by the judge, before rendering a **verdict**. The jury members are escorted to a private room to discuss the evidence and to reach a consensus with respect to a verdict. The jury then re-enters the courtroom and returns its verdict: guilty of the offence charged, guilty of a lesser but included offence, or not guilty.

Once the jury's verdict has been delivered, the trial is over. Chapter 9 will discuss sentencing and appeals.

INFORMATIONS AND INDICTMENTS

Two types of **charging documents** are used in criminal law. The charging document is what brings the criminal charges against the accused and begins the process toward trial. It contains individual charges or offences (known as **counts**) that the accused is alleged to have committed.

instructions
directions given to the jury by the judge at the end of a trial advising it on how to apply the law to the facts of the case

verdict
the decision as to the guilt or innocence of the accused

charging document
a written document, either an information or an indictment, that sets out the charges against a person accused of an offence

count
a single charge on a charging document

information
a form of charging document used for less serious offences

indictment
a form of charging document used for serious (indictable) offences

The first type is an **information**, and it is a document, usually sworn by a police officer, that contains a criminal charge against an accused. It is used only for offences tried in provincial court (Ontario Court of Justice) or youth court. The other kind of charging document is an **indictment**. An indictment is usually signed by the prosecutor and is used for offences tried in superior court (in Ontario, the Superior Court of Justice).

The Information

An informant, who is typically a police officer, swears to a justice of the peace that he or she has knowledge or reasonable and probable grounds to believe that the accused committed the offence in question. The information must contain a list of each court appearance and the purpose for it, the names of all court officials present, all elections made by both the prosecution and the accused, any detention orders, the outcome of a preliminary inquiry if one has been held, and any adjournments.

The *Criminal Code*[2] requires that a document called a Form 2 be prepared by the informant. Police departments have copies of this form for common offences so that the officers have to fill in only the accused person's name and the place and date of the alleged crime. Note that some offences — for example, public nudity (s. 174) and distributing hate propaganda (s. 319) — require the consent of the attorney general before an information can be sworn. This is an exception to the general rule that a police officer alone can bring a sworn information before a justice.

The Indictment

The indictment is the charging document that is used when the case progresses to superior court. The document used for the indictment is a Form 4 regardless of whether the accused has elected trial by judge and jury or by judge alone. The indictment sets out the history of the case in the same way the information does.

The meaning of the word "indictment" is tricky in criminal law because it has more than one definition. "Proceeding by way of indictment" refers to the choice that a Crown attorney makes when an offence is hybrid and can be pursued by way of a summary conviction or by indictment. The use of the word "indictment" in this context is different from the charging document that is referred to as an indictment.

Challenging the Charging Document

Informations and indictments must follow these five principles:

- Each count must relate to a single transaction (s. 581(1)).
- Each count must charge an offence known to law (s. 581(1)).
- Each count must charge only one offence (duplicity rule — see below).
- Each count must identify the act or omission alleged to be an offence (s. 581(3)).
- Each count must identify the transaction (s. 581(3)).

The information or indictment may be challenged by the defence if there are any deficiencies. Common types of deficiencies are discussed below.

INSUFFICIENCY Under ss. 581 and 583 of the *Criminal Code*, the charging document may be challenged for **insufficiency** if any crucial information that is necessary to give the accused adequate notice of the crime for which he or she is being charged is missing. In *R v. Cote*,[3] the Supreme Court of Canada held that the "golden rule" with respect to sufficiency is that the accused should be reasonably informed of the transaction alleged against him so that he or she can make full answer and defence of it at trial.

DUPLICITY The common law rule against **duplicity** prohibits the listing of two separate charges or offences in a single count on the charging document. Basically, it does not allow the informant to charge the accused with one offence and a second offence as an alternative for the same actions. For example, a single count cannot state that, on or about the 12th of June 2005, the accused committed assault causing bodily harm or murder. If such a count was allowed, the defence would not know which offence the prosecution would proceed with, and this would reduce its ability to defend the accused of the charges. If the charging document is unclear about what charges the accused will face at trial, it is improper.

IMPROPER JOINDER In many cases, it is easier and more efficient to bring an accused to trial at the same time for all offences he or she is accused of having committed, even if they do not arise out of the same incidents or circumstances. This is called **joinder** of charges.

Joinder of charges, however, can result in prejudice to the accused in that a jury may be more inclined to believe that a person charged with assault causing bodily harm is also guilty of shoplifting. If a person is charged and tried with a whole series of offences, all arising out of different incidents, the jury may also be more inclined to believe that the accused is guilty of at least some of the charges.

Therefore, to avoid unfairness to the accused, there are clear rules about which offences may be joined and which offences may not be joined. Sections 589 and 590 of the *Criminal Code* set out when joinder is inappropriate. Most important, a charge of murder cannot be joined with any other offence unless the other offence arises out of the same situation as the charge of murder or the accused consents to the joinder.

SAVING DEVICES OR REMEDIES Two saving devices are available to the court to remedy the above deficiencies: (1) the judge may order that the prosecution give the defence **particulars** of the unclear counts, or (2) the judge can amend the charging document to rectify the deficiency.

According to s. 587 of the *Criminal Code*, the judge can order the prosecution to give the accused more information and details of the accusation so that he or she can make full answer and defence and facilitate the administration of justice. This is a common remedy for insufficiency.

The court also has wide discretion to amend an indictment or information, as set out in ss. 601 and 795 of the *Criminal Code*. This is a common remedy for duplicity.

If an information or indictment is so deficient that it cannot be remedied, the judge may **quash** (overthrow or void) the charging document. The prosecution

insufficiency
a flaw in a charging document that causes it to fail to contain the required information to sustain the charge

duplicity
a flaw in a charging document where a single count contains two or more alternative offences so that the accused does not know against which offence to defend

joinder
where two or more charges or two or more accused persons are tried together in the same trial

particulars
details of a count

quash
overthrow or void

may still be able to appeal the order to quash the charging document, or if time permits, the prosecution may simply lay the charges again in proper form.

Juries

A jury in a criminal case typically includes 12 people. Jurors must decide unanimously on a conviction or an acquittal. The jury is involved only in determining guilt — it is not involved in sentencing. The one exception is that the jury may make recommendations about parole eligibility in second-degree murder cases. Rules relating to juries are found in ss. 626 to 644 of the *Criminal Code*.

If the accused elects to proceed to trial before a judge and jury, selecting the jury can become a long and contentious process. The jury is, after all, the trier of fact and as such has the ability to decide the fate of the accused.

Jury selection begins when prospective jurors are asked to appear at the local courthouse. One at a time, each person steps forward and the defence and the prosecution are asked whether they want to challenge the juror or are content with the juror. If the defence and the prosecution are satisfied with the juror, he or she is sworn and seated in the jury box. Both sides are entitled to a certain number of challenges of the jury pool.

PEREMPTORY CHALLENGES

peremptory challenge
the right of either party to a criminal jury trial to reject a prospective juror without giving a reason

Each side is allowed to exclude a certain number of potential jurors with no explanation. These are called **peremptory challenges**.

Where the accused is charged with an offence that is punishable by five or more years of imprisonment, each side has 12 peremptory challenges (except for cases that involve first-degree murder or treason, where both the prosecution and the defence are entitled to 20 challenges). Where the offence is punishable by five or less years of imprisonment, each side has only 4 peremptory challenges.

CHALLENGES FOR CAUSE

challenge for cause
the right of either party in a criminal jury trial to require that prospective jurors be questioned about certain aspects of the offence or the accused that may result in bias on the part of the jurors

Before jury selection begins, both the prosecution and the defence have the opportunity under s. 629 of the *Criminal Code* to request of the judge that every member of the jury panel (the group of citizens from which the jury is selected) be challenged or questioned regarding his or her feelings on certain subjects related to the accused or the offence. The goal is to screen out people who might allow their personal feelings to affect their impartiality. An Asian accused, for example, should not be tried by jurors who have expressed prejudices against Asians; a homosexual accused should not be tried by jurors who are homophobic.

If the judge agrees that a proposed concern is legitimate, a question is formulated to deal with the concern and asked of each prospective juror. This question is called a **challenge for cause**. If a potential juror's response indicates a lack of impartiality, that person will not be permitted to join the jury.

Proof of Facts

The Canadian criminal legal system has adopted the **presumption of innocence** as the basis for its procedure and its rules of evidence. The presumption of innocence means that a person who has been accused of a crime will be considered innocent until proven guilty by the trier of fact in a court of law. The presumption of innocence is a principle of fundamental justice (discussed in chapter 6) and is guaranteed by s. 11(d) of the *Canadian Charter of Rights and Freedoms*.

At trial, the prosecution must prove that the accused committed the offence. This proof is created through the use of evidence, which can take the form of either the oral testimony of witnesses or physical items.

The **burden of proof**, or onus, refers to the party that is required to provide the proof of a given fact or theory. In most cases, the prosecution has the burden of proof: it bears the burden of proving the elements of the offence and, therefore, the guilt of the accused. Situations that require the accused to prove a particular fact are called reverse onus situations.

The **standard of proof** is the level or degree of proof that the party must produce to be successful. In other words, the standard of proof refers to how convincing the proof must be. In general terms, there are three standards or levels of proof, each more difficult or strict than the last:

1. the **evidentiary standard**, meaning that the party must simply provide some evidence of the truth of the fact;
2. the **civil standard** (also known as the "balance of probabilities"), meaning that the party must prove that it is more likely than not that the fact is true; and
3. the **criminal standard** (also known as "proof beyond a reasonable doubt"), meaning that the party must prove the guilt of the accused to such a high degree that no reasonable person would have a real doubt as to its truth.

THE PROSECUTION'S BURDEN OF PROOF — PROOF BEYOND A REASONABLE DOUBT

The prosecution bears the burden of proving an accused person's guilt at trial to the criminal standard of proof: proof beyond a reasonable doubt. The fact that the prosecution's burden of proof must meet the highest standard results from the fact that, if found guilty of the offence, the accused faces the most serious punishment our justice system allows: imprisonment.

The key word in the criminal standard of proof is "reasonable." The prosecution does not have to eliminate *all* doubt to obtain a conviction — it simply has to provide proof beyond a reasonable doubt that is based on the evidence or the lack of evidence against the accused.

The trier of fact must be convinced beyond a reasonable doubt, on all the evidence, that the accused is guilty of the offence in order for a conviction to result. Note, however, that the prosecution does not have to prove each piece of evidence beyond a reasonable doubt. It is enough for the sum of the evidence to convince the trier of fact that the accused is guilty of the offence beyond a reasonable doubt.

presumption of innocence
the basis of criminal legal procedure and rules of evidence — that an accused person is considered innocent until proven guilty

burden of proof
the requirement that a certain party prove a particular fact at trial

standard of proof
the level to which a party must convince the trier of fact of a given allegation

evidentiary standard
a basic level of proof; an alleged fact meets the evidentiary standard when there is at least some evidence that the allegation might be true

civil standard
the level of proof that a party must achieve in a civil trial to be successful — proof on a balance of probabilities

criminal standard
the level of proof that the prosecution must provide in a criminal trial to obtain a conviction — proof beyond a reasonable doubt

THE DEFENCE'S BURDEN OF PROOF

The burden of proof in criminal trials falls on the prosecution. The defence is not required to present any evidence, and there is no obligation on the accused to prove his or her innocence or even to raise a doubt.

In some cases, however, the defence may choose to present evidence, if only in an attempt to create a reasonable doubt about the evidence presented by the prosecution. It is sufficient for the defence to meet the very low evidentiary standard of proof: to produce some evidence of facts alleged in its attempt to combat the prosecution's case. The defence does not have to prove its position beyond a reasonable doubt or even on a balance of probabilities; it only needs to cast doubt on the case presented by the prosecution.

Defences

defences
the arguments that the defence uses to contradict the prosecution's evidence against the accused

passive defence
a defence by which the accused and his or her lawyers simply assert (through cross-examination or in closing arguments by counsel) that the prosecution has failed to prove the accused's guilt beyond a reasonable doubt

positive (or affirmative) defence
a trial defence where the accused and his or her lawyers actively attempt to refute the evidence of the prosecution and perhaps introduce evidence of their own to clear the accused

directed verdict
an early verdict of acquittal based on the prosecution's failure to meet its standard of proof

The accused and his or her lawyers have many options when it comes to attempting to obtain an acquittal at trial. These options are called **defences**. In most cases, the accused will simply try to create a reasonable doubt as to the prosecution's case. This may be referred to as a **passive defence**, since it goes no further than refuting the allegations against the accused.

However, a number of other defences involve the accused and his or her lawyers attempting to prove that circumstances existed that negate the guilt of the accused, in most cases by proving that the accused did not have the required intent (*mens rea*) to commit the offence. These can be referred to as **positive (or affirmative) defences**.

PASSIVE DEFENCES

The simplest way to defend an accused against criminal charges is to assert that the prosecution has failed to establish proof beyond a reasonable doubt of an essential element of the offence — usually either the *mens rea* (mental element) or the *actus reus* (physical element). In such a case, the accused does not call any witnesses (though Crown witnesses may be cross-examined), nor does he or she testify or present an affirmative defence. Indeed, at the end of the presentation of the prosecution's case, the accused asks the judge (by bringing a motion) to rule that the prosecution has failed to provide sufficient evidence that, if accepted completely by the trier of fact, proves the accused's guilt. The judge may, at that point, rule that the prosecution has failed to meet its standard of proof and acquit the accused without requiring any evidence from the defence, even if a jury is involved in the trial. This is called a **directed verdict**.

In most cases, therefore, the defence lawyers will cross-examine the witnesses presented by the prosecution in an effort to create doubt in the mind of the trier of fact. They may try to prompt an eyewitness to the offence to admit that he is not absolutely certain it was the accused he saw committing the offence because, for example, he was not wearing his glasses at the time; they may attempt to prove that a witness has a motive for wanting the accused to be convicted of the crime even if he or she is innocent; they may even attempt to prove that the witness herself is unreliable as a result of her mental condition, abuse of alcohol or drugs, or history of lying in other circumstances.

In these situations, the defence is not attempting to prove anything new, but simply trying to undermine the credibility of the prosecution's evidence to create a reasonable doubt.

POSITIVE, AFFIRMATIVE, OR "TRUE" DEFENCES

True defences are those that involve the defence lawyers attempting to prove a new fact or facts that tend to negate the existence of one or more of the elements of the offence or tend to attack the charges themselves. These defences may be subdivided into three categories: justification, excuse, and entrapment.

Defences in criminal law are extremely complex and can't be dealt with adequately in the context of this chapter. What follows is simply a brief discussion of the basics of each defence.

Justification

Defences of **justification** are rare, but when proven, they negate the objective wrongfulness of the act and exempt the accused from the application of the *Criminal Code*. An example of using a justification defence is the medical use of marijuana. Although the statute states that using marijuana is an offence, the common law has developed to allow people suffering from painful medical conditions the right to use marijuana for therapeutic purposes. The use of the drug is not for a purpose that is wrong and that, in the opinion of judges who create the common law, should be punishable as a criminal offence. The accused may be justified, as a result of the medical condition, to use marijuana.

justification
a rare defence that negates the objective wrongfulness of an act and exempts the accused from the application of the *Criminal Code*

SELF-DEFENCE **Self-defence** can be a defence against assault if the force used was no more than was necessary to protect against the assault. The judge will consider the accused's subjective perceptions of the situation and the reasonableness of those perceptions. The rules governing self-defence are set out in s. 34(1) of the *Criminal Code*, which reads as follows:

self-defence
a defence that can be used against assault if the force used was no more than was necessary to protect against the assault

> 34(1) Every one who is unlawfully assaulted without having provoked the assault is justified in repelling force by force if the force he uses is not intended to cause death or grievous bodily harm and is no more than necessary to enable him to defend himself.

For an accused to claim a s. 34(1) defence: (1) the attack must have been unprovoked, (2) no intent can have been present to cause death or grievous bodily harm, and (3) the force cannot have been excessive. Provocation, for the purposes of s. 34, is defined in s. 36 of the Code and includes blows, words, and gestures. There are special provisions governing self-defence causing death or grievous bodily harm. These rules are stated in s. 34(2) of the Code:

> 34(2) Every one who is unlawfully assaulted and who causes death or grievous bodily harm in repelling the assault is justified if
>> (a) he causes it under reasonable apprehension of death or grievous bodily harm from the violence with which the assault was originally made or with which the assailant pursues his purposes; and

(b) he believes, on reasonable grounds, that he cannot otherwise preserve himself from death or grievous bodily harm.

In short, self-defence causing death or grievous bodily harm may be justified if
the accused reasonably thought that he or she was going to be killed or seriously
hurt and reasonably believed that there was no other way to prevent his or her own
death or serious physical harm.

DEFENCE OF PROPERTY   Sections 38 to 42 of the *Criminal Code* cover defences
of real and personal property. Section 38(1) permits people in "peaceable possession of personal property to prevent a trespasser from taking it if he does not strike
or cause bodily harm to the trespasser." If the trespasser persists in taking the property, he or she is deemed by s. 38(2) to have committed an "assault without justification." When this occurs, the defender of the property is entitled to use a reasonable amount of force, subject to the rules of self-defence, to prevent the offence. For
example, if Jim tries to steal Kim's purse, Kim is entitled to defend her purse by
grasping Jim's wrist and wrenching it away from her purse. The fact that Jim was
trying to steal Kim's property justifies Kim's assault on Jim. Kim is not entitled to
beat Jim unconscious with a baseball bat, however. It is important to remember
that the Code sets out slightly different rules for defence of personal property and
defence of a home.

Excuse

excuse
a defence that concedes
that the accused's actions
were wrong but claims
that external or internal
forces influenced the
accused

Defences of **excuse** concede that an accused's actions were wrong but claim that
external or internal forces influenced the accused so that the mental element required to establish the offence was not present. These defences usually depend on
physical involuntariness (drunkenness) or mental impairment (mental defect, disease, or infancy).

NECESSITY   Necessity is a type of a defence of excuse. It asserts that the accused
had no real opportunity to avoid breaking the law. The defence of necessity depends on proving three elements: (1) an urgent peril, (2) no reasonable legal alternative to the criminal action taken, and (3) a reasonable proportionality between
the peril avoided and the crime committed. Simply stated, the accused could avoid
some imminent disaster, calamity, or serious harm only by breaking the law.

For example, imagine that Karen was snowmobiling and fell through the ice in
a remote area of Algonquin Park. To avoid freezing to death, she broke into a
nearby cottage to warm and dry herself. It appears obvious that Karen committed
both the *actus reus* and *mens rea* of the indictable offence of breaking and entering
under s. 348 of the *Criminal Code*. The circumstances — the fact that she would
likely have died if she had not committed the offence — would probably provide her
with the excuse of necessity and lead to an acquittal.

Once the accused has raised some evidence of the defence of necessity, the
onus falls on the prosecution to prove that necessity did not exist.

duress
a defence that allows the
accused to be acquitted if
he or she committed the
offence under threat of
immediate death or
bodily harm

DURESS   The defence of **duress** is closely related to necessity since it involves
committing an offence to avoid some threatened harm. Duress itself is any unlawful

threat or coercion used by one person to induce another person to act or yield in a different way than he or she would if operating under his or her own free will. The defence of duress is very complicated, partly because it is both a *Criminal Code* defence and (with different requirements) a common law defence.

Section 17 of the Code states that an accused may be acquitted if he or she committed the offence under threat of immediate death or bodily harm by a person who is present at the time of the offence. The person who commits the offence must hold an actual subjective belief that the threat will be carried out in order to use the defence of duress.

MENTAL DISORDER   The defence of mental disorder is dealt with under s. 16 of the Code. If the accused suffers from some form of mental disorder, he or she is not considered capable of the *mens rea* of most offences.

An accused who uses the defence of mental disorder must give evidence of a disease or disorder that rendered him or her incapable of either appreciating the nature and quality of the impugned act or understanding the moral wrongfulness of the act. A successful defence of not guilty by reason of mental disorder (also called "not criminally responsible") may result in detention for treatment if the accused is found to be a danger to society. The person is typically committed to a hospital for an indefinite term until doctors prove that he or she has been cured and is no longer dangerous.

People may be found to be suffering from a mental disorder if they meet one of two tests. The mental disorder must have made them incapable (1) of appreciating the nature and quality of the act or omission or (2) of knowing that the act or omission is morally wrong. In general, the case law has determined that the term "disease of the mind" includes any abnormal condition, disorder, or illness that impairs the functioning of the human mind. However, mental disorder excludes self-induced states caused by alcohol or drugs, as well as temporary mental states such as hysteria or concussion.

The word "appreciates" in s. 16 has been defined to mean that the accused had an understanding beyond mere knowledge of the physical quality of the act.

AUTOMATISM   **Automatism** is similar to the defence of mental disorder because both defences flow from the idea that the accused cannot be held criminally responsible because of a mental deficiency. Automatism is involuntary or unconscious behaviour. In *R v. Rabey*,[4] the court expanded on the definition by writing that automatism is an "unconscious, involuntary behaviour, the state of a person who, though capable of action, is not conscious of what he is doing. It means an unconscious, involuntary act, where the mind does not go with what is being done."

An accused may be acquitted if he or she can prove a defence of non-insane automatism, a condition leading to involuntary action that negates the *mens rea* of the offence charged. In alleging automatism, there is an onus on the defence to provide at least some evidence of the accused's suffering from this unusual condition. With respect to non-insane automatism, *R v. Parks*[5] is an interesting case. In *Parks*, the Supreme Court unanimously upheld the trial court's ruling that the accused's sleepwalking (also called somnambulism) was not a "disease of the mind" and only the defence of non-insane automatism should be put to the jury.

automatism
involuntary or unconscious behaviour

PROVOCATION   Provocation is a defence that is available only to persons charged with murder. A successful provocation defence does not lead to the acquittal of the accused, however; it just serves to reduce the offence from murder to manslaughter on the basis that a provoked person does not form the required intent to murder someone.

To be successful, the defence must provide evidence that the killing was done in the heat of passion and as a result of a sudden act, attack, or insult. Provocation is codified in s. 232 of the *Criminal Code*:

> 232(1) Culpable homicide that otherwise would be murder may be reduced to manslaughter if the person who committed it did so in the heat of passion caused by sudden provocation.
>
> (2) A wrongful act or an insult that is of such a nature as to be sufficient to deprive an ordinary person of the power of self-control is provocation for the purposes of this section if the accused acted on it on the sudden and before there was time for his passion to cool.
>
> (3) For the purposes of this section, the questions
>
>> (a) whether a particular wrongful act or insult amounted to provocation, and
>>
>> (b) whether the accused was deprived of the power of self-control by the provocation that he alleges he received,
>
> are questions of fact, but no one shall be deemed to have given provocation to another by doing anything that he had a legal right to do, or by doing anything that the accused incited him to do in order to provide the accused with an excuse for causing death or bodily harm to any human being.

The wording of s. 232 shows that there are both objective and subjective elements to the defence of provocation. The objective component is whether the wrongful act or insult was serious enough to take away an ordinary person's self-control. The subjective component of the test is whether the accused acted on the provocation and did so before his or her passion cooled.

Four restrictions on the defence of provocation are detailed in s. 232 and the case law:

- Generally, the provoking act must come from the victim and not from a third party.

- The act or insult and the reaction must both be sudden.

- Provocation does not exist when the accused has incited the other person to react.

- Provocation does not exist where the victim was doing anything he or she had a legal right to do.

INTOXICATION   Intoxication or drunkenness in its extreme form may be used as a defence if it interfered with the ability of the accused to form the required level of intent to commit the offence. There must have been an extremely high level of intoxication for this defence to be accepted. Basically, the accused must have been in such a state that he or she was unaware of the specific criminal act committed.

The common law has held that intoxication is appropriate only as a defence to specific intent offences — offences where the accused must have had a particular intention in mind when committing the *actus reus* (for example, breaking and entering with the intent to commit an indictable offence, as discussed above). The intoxication defence cannot be used for general intent offences such as assault, sexual assault, assault causing bodily harm, manslaughter, and mischief, where the mental element of the offence is simply the intention to commit the *actus reus*. The *mens rea* for assault is simply the intent to strike someone, an intent that can be formed even by an extremely intoxicated person.

INFANCY Under Canadian law (s. 13 of the *Criminal Code*), a child under the age of 12 cannot be convicted of a criminal offence. An 11-year-old child who commits any criminal offence in Canada, including murder, cannot be held criminally accountable. The rationale for this law is that a person under the age of 12 does not have the maturity to be accountable for the *mens rea* element of the act.

Young people aged 12 to 17 who commit criminal offences are tried and sentenced according to the *Youth Criminal Justice Act*.[6] If the crime a youth over age 14 commits is particularly serious, the prosecution may seek to have the youth sentenced as an adult. This is permissible under s. 62 of the *Youth Criminal Justice Act*.

MISTAKE OF FACT Although **mistake of fact** can be interpreted as a defence to a criminal charge, it really amounts to the Crown failing to prove the *mens rea* element of the offence. Mistake of fact can be defined in the following way: the accused did not willingly or knowingly commit the act because he or she believed certain facts to be true. For example, Claire was at a party and took a coat that she believed to be hers from the coat rack. As it turned out, the coat belonged to Maria. Claire had an honest belief that the coat was hers. If Claire is charged with stealing the coat, her defence could be mistake of fact.

mistake of fact
a defence to a criminal charge that involves the Crown failing to prove the *mens rea* of the offence

Entrapment

Although included here, **entrapment** is not truly a defence. A successful entrapment argument involves a finding of guilt followed by a decision by the judge to stay the proceedings as a result of the actions of the police.

Entrapment involves a situation where the police lure, draw, or entice a person into committing a crime that he or she may not have committed otherwise. As a society, we do not consider it proper for the police to cause otherwise innocent people to commit offences, and then to arrest and charge them for those offences.

If entrapment is raised by the defence in a case tried before a judge and jury, the jury will first determine whether the accused is guilty or not guilty of the offence. If the accused is found guilty, the judge will then consider the entrapment issue. The accused must prove entrapment on a balance of probabilities. If a court finds that police officers entrapped the accused, the most common remedy is a stay of proceedings, which effectively ends the trial.

entrapment
a situation where the police lure, draw, or entice a person into committing a crime

KEY TERMS

automatism	insufficiency
burden of proof	joinder
challenge for cause	jury
charging document	justification
civil standard	mistake of fact
count	particulars
criminal standard	passive defence
defence	peremptory challenge
defences	positive (or affirmative) defence
directed verdict	presumption of innocence
duplicity	prosecution
duress	quash
entrapment	self-defence
evidentiary standard	standard of proof
excuse	trier of fact
indictment	trier of law
information	verdict
instructions	

NOTES

1. *Canadian Charter of Rights and Freedoms*, part I of the *Constitution Act, 1982*, RSC 1985, app. II, no. 44.
2. *Criminal Code*, RSC 1985, c. C-46, as amended.
3. *R v. Cote* (1977), 33 CCC (2d) 353 (SCC).
4. *R v. Rabey* (1977), 79 DLR (3d) 414 (Ont. CA), aff'd. [1980] 2 SCR 513.
5. *R v. Parks* (1992), 75 CCC (3d) 287 (SCC).
6. *Youth Criminal Justice Act*, SC 2002, c. 1, as amended.

EXERCISES

Multiple Choice

1. To convict an accused of a crime, the judge or jury must be convinced that
   a. it is more likely that the accused is guilty than not guilty
   b. beyond any doubt the accused is guilty
   c. beyond a reasonable doubt the accused is guilty
   d. the police collected all the relevant evidence

2. For an accused to claim self-defence under s. 34(1) of the *Criminal Code,* which of the following conditions must be present?

   a. the attack must have been unprovoked

   b. there was no intent to cause death or grievous bodily harm

   c. the force was not excessive

   d. all of the above

3. The trier of law in a trial is

   a. the prosecution

   b. the judge

   c. the jury

   d. the judge and the jury

   e. the defence

4. During jury selection, the defence and the prosecution

   a. are allowed to exclude a certain number of potential jurors with no explanation

   b. are allowed to challenge each juror

   c. may be granted the opportunity to question each juror for cause

   d. none of the above

   e. a and c

5. Which party bears the burden of proving the elements of the offence and the guilt of the accused?

   a. the defence

   b. the judge

   c. the jury

   d. the prosecution

   e. all of the above

True or False?

T 1. The Crown bears the burden of proving that an accused person committed a crime.

F 2. Proof beyond a reasonable doubt means the judge or jury cannot convict an accused person if they have any doubt in their minds that the accused committed the crime.

T 3. Balance of probabilities means that the trier of fact is more than 50 percent certain of the truth of a fact.

T 4. Necessity is an example of the type of defence known as an excuse.

F 5. The principle of fundamental justice is guaranteed by the *Criminal Code.*

Short Answer

1. Explain the concept of reverse onus, and cite an example from the *Criminal Code* that has not already been provided.

2. Why must a crime be proven beyond a reasonable doubt?

3. Explain the two types of duress defences, and provide an example of each.

CHAPTER 9

Criminal Offence Sentencing and Appeals

Chapter Objectives

After completing this chapter, you should be able to:

- Describe at least three objectives of sentencing.
- Explain the different kinds of sentences available to a judge.
- Identify aggravating and mitigating factors that may affect the sentence imposed for an offence.
- Understand the grounds available to each party for appealing a trial court decision.
- Describe the structure of courts for appeal purposes.
- Identify the powers of the appeal courts to change the decision of a trial court.

After the Verdict

The criminal trial ends with the announcement of the verdict: guilty or not guilty. Once the verdict has been announced, the jury is no longer needed and is dismissed by the judge. At that point, certain post-trial issues must be dealt with. The two most important of these are sentencing and appeals.

If the verdict is not guilty, the accused is free to go. In certain circumstances, however, the prosecution (in this case, the attorney general and his or her representatives in the Crown attorney's office) can **appeal** the decision of the court.

If the verdict is guilty, the next step is sentencing the accused — deciding what punishment he or she will face. The accused also has certain rights of appeal from a guilty verdict.

appeal
the review or challenge of a legal decision in a court of higher jurisdiction

Sentencing

sentence
the punishment imposed
on a person convicted of
an offence

The issue of **sentencing** is dealt with in great detail in part XXIII of the *Criminal Code*.[1] What follows is only an introduction to some of the concepts.

When an accused is convicted of an offence either after a trial or after a guilty plea, the court must impose a sentence. The range of sentences for each offence is described in the *Criminal Code*, often in the section that creates the offence itself.

RATIONALES FOR PUNISHMENT

The purpose and principles of sentencing are contained in s. 718 of the Code:

> 718. The fundamental purpose of sentencing is to contribute, along with crime prevention initiatives, to respect for the law and the maintenance of a just, peaceful and safe society by imposing just sanctions that have one or more of the following objectives:
>> (a) to denounce unlawful conduct;
>> (b) to deter the offender and other persons from committing offences;
>> (c) to separate offenders from society, where necessary;
>> (d) to assist in rehabilitating offenders;
>> (e) to provide reparations for harm done to victims or to the community;
> and
>> (f) to promote a sense of responsibility in offenders, and acknowledgment of the harm done to victims and to the community.

In general, once a guilty verdict is entered, the judge has the power to decide what sentence to impose, subject to the minimum or maximum sentence (if any) set out in the Code for the offence, the principles of sentencing listed above, and the case law precedents for sentences previously imposed for similar offences and similar offenders.

For example, the offence of assault under s. 266 of the Code carries with it, if tried as an indictable offence, a maximum sentence of five years in prison. This means that a judge may not sentence a person convicted of assault to eight years in prison. As well, if every other judge who has dealt with an assault conviction in the past has imposed a sentence of between one and three years, the judge in the present case must impose a similar sentence unless he or she is convinced this case is much more serious.

Section 718.1 sets out the fundamental principle of sentencing: "A sentence must be proportionate to the gravity of the offence and the degree of responsibility of the offender." The scope of sentences available under the *Criminal Code* is relatively narrow. Canadian law does not allow capital punishment (the death penalty) or corporal punishment (whipping, beating, or otherwise inflicting physical punishment), in part because of the prohibition against cruel and unusual treatment or punishment in s. 12 of the *Canadian Charter of Rights and Freedoms*.[2]

aggravating factor
in a sentencing context, a
circumstance of the
offence or the offender
that supports a more
serious punishment

AGGRAVATING AND MITIGATING FACTORS

Under s. 718.2 of the Code, the court can take into account any aggravating or mitigating factors when imposing a sentence. One or more **aggravating factors** (factors that make the crime more serious) may result in a harsher sentence than the norm; one or more **mitigating factors** (factors that make the crime less serious) may result in a lighter sentence than the norm.

Some examples of aggravating factors that may increase the sentence include the following: the crime was motivated by hatred of an identifiable group (hate crime), the crime was domestic (committed against a family member), the offender breached a position of trust with respect to the victim, or the offence was committed for the benefit of a criminal organization.

Mitigating factors that may lessen the sentence include the following: the accused was provoked by the victim, the accused is a first-time offender, and/or the accused has shown evidence of remorse or rehabilitation. Unfair or improper (though not necessarily illegal) conduct by law enforcement officials or prosecutors may also lead to a reduced sentence. An example is the Crown deliberately delaying the trial.

TYPES OF SENTENCES

The most common sentences imposed include **imprisonment** in a custodial facility (ss. 743 to 746), imprisonment to be served conditionally in the community (s. 742), a **fine** (ss. 734 to 737), a **suspended sentence** (s. 731(1)(a)), and **probation** (ss. 731 to 733.1). Imprisonment in a state-run custodial facility — a jail — is considered the most serious of the sentences, since it deprives the offender of his or her freedom.

Conditional imprisonment is served in the community. It is a form of house arrest. This type of sentence cannot be used for dangerous offenders or offenders who are likely to escape, but it is an alternative to jail.

Fines are often imposed for statutory or quasi-criminal offences, such as minor traffic or environmental offences. The ability of the offender to pay the fine must be considered before a fine is imposed.

A judge can impose a suspended sentence for offences that do not carry a minimum sentence. A suspended sentence means that the offender is released back into society subject to certain conditions set out in a **probation order**. If the offender breaches the conditions of the probation order before it expires (three years after it is issued), he or she faces being sentenced on the original offence and forced to serve the sentence. Several possible conditions can be included in a probation order, such as a prohibition against carrying firearms, an order not to approach or associate with certain people, or an order to stay away from certain places.

Offenders sentenced to probation must comply with the conditions contained in a probation order. Probation may be ordered on its own or along with a fine or a term of imprisonment, but not both. Thus, a person convicted of assault could be sentenced to one year in prison and two years of probation, subject to the conditions in the probation order. He or she may, instead, be sentenced to a fine of $1,000 plus two years of probation, subject to the conditions in the probation order.

In some cases, a person convicted of a less serious offence may be **discharged** either on an absolute or on a conditional basis. An absolute discharge (s. 730) has no conditions attached to it and takes effect right away. An accused who receives an absolute discharge has a criminal conviction against him, but is not required to serve time or pay a fine. A conditional discharge (s. 730) includes a probation order with conditions that can be in effect for up to three years.

mitigating factor
in sentencing for crimes, a fact or condition relating to either the offence or the offender that decreases the punishment (e.g., an early guilty plea or remorse)

imprisonment
incarceration in a prison, the most serious punishment allowable in Canada for persons convicted of offences

fine
a form of punishment, requiring the payment of money, generally used for quasi-criminal or minor criminal offences

suspended sentence
a form of punishment that involves delaying the imposition of the punishment indefinitely if the accused person complies with certain conditions, failing which the punishment is enforced

probation
a type of sentence that does not involve imprisonment but allows the accused to remain free, subject to conditions

probation order
the list of conditions that apply to a convicted person released on parole

discharge
the release of an accused after a finding of guilt, with or without conditions

Offenders who are sentenced to a prison term can usually apply for supervised release or parole before they have served the entire sentence.

PRE-SENTENCE REPORT

In deciding the type and harshness of the sentence to be imposed, the judge may hear submissions from both the prosecution and the defence. These take place at a sentencing hearing, without the jury present.

The judge may order a **pre-sentence report** under s. 721(1) of the Code. If ordered, the report is prepared by a probation officer before sentencing and filed with the court. The report usually contains information on the background and character of the offender, separate from the offence. The report gives the judge insight into the offender so that the sentence can be effective both in punishing the offender for the offence and in helping his or her rehabilitation.

pre-sentence report
a document prepared by a probation officer at the request of a judge that provides background on the offender for use in deciding on a sentence for the offender

Appeals

The verdict of the judge or jury in a criminal trial is not necessarily the final word. Both the prosecution and the defence have certain rights to appeal verdicts and sentences.

Appeals of decisions about indictable offences are dealt with in part XXI of the *Criminal Code*. Summary conviction offences are dealt with as a whole in part XXVII of the Code. What follows is a very brief introduction to the complex issue of appeals.

GROUNDS: THE BASIS FOR AN APPEAL

The basis for any appeal must be a party's allegation that some sort of **error** was made at trial by either the trier of fact or the trier of law. The alleged error itself is called the **ground for appeal**. If there is no ground for appeal, no appeal can be made. In most cases, parties who appeal a trial court decision will list several grounds for appeal in their appeal documents.

Grounds for appeal fall into three categories: questions of law, questions of fact, and questions of mixed law and fact. In most cases, the right to appeal is available to either the defence or the prosecution on a question of law; questions of fact or of mixed law and fact can be appealed only by the defence with **leave to appeal** (permission) of the court to which the appeal is to be brought.

When making an appeal on the ground of a **question of law**, the person appealing — the **appellant** — must show that the judge in the trial court misinterpreted or misapplied a legal rule and that the error had a material impact on the verdict. For example, the offence of first-degree murder involves a very specific *mens rea*: the accused must not only have intended to kill the victim, but the killing must also have been planned and deliberate. If, instead, the judge instructs the jury that it can convict the accused of first-degree murder if the jury believes that the accused attacked his or her victim without concern for whether the victim would die, the judge has made an error in law. That error could potentially have led the jury to wrongly convict the accused of first-degree murder even if the required planning and deliberation were not present.

error
a mistake made by the judge (or, less commonly, the jury) that might lead to an appeal

ground for appeal
a reason — generally an error made by the trier of law or of fact — for a party to be allowed to ask a higher court to reconsider the decision of a lower court

leave to appeal
permission to file an appeal

question of law
a ground for appeal that is available to either the defence or the prosecution that is based on the misinterpretation or misapplication of a legal rule at trial

appellant
the party that decides to appeal a court's decision to a higher court

When making an appeal on a **question of fact**, the appellant must show that the trier of fact made an error in deciding, on the basis of the evidence presented at trial, that a certain fact was true or false. The error must be glaring — it cannot simply be a difference of opinion. In general, the decision of the trier of fact must be completely unsupported by the evidence for the appeal court to intervene. For example, if all witnesses to the offence stated clearly that a tiny woman committed the offence and the jury still convicts the accused, a large man, of the offence, it could be argued that the jury has made a finding of fact that is not supported by the evidence.

An appeal on a **question of mixed law and fact** is based on an error that combines elements of the two. This type of appeal tends to arise in cases where the legal rule that was applied is one that turns very closely on particular facts. A case involving sexual assault is a good example. There can be no sexual assault where the contact complained of was consented to by the (adult) victim. From a practical standpoint, participants do not explicitly negotiate every stage in a sexual encounter. This means that where consent is contested, the circumstances must be closely examined on their specific facts. Any errors in this process of examining the evidence may later result in an appeal on a question of mixed law and fact.

APPEAL COURTS

The decision of a provincial court (Ontario Court of Justice) judge in a summary conviction matter must be appealed to the superior court (in Ontario, the Superior Court of Justice). The decision of a provincial court judge in an indictable matter is appealed to the provincial court of appeal (Court of Appeal for Ontario). The decision of a superior court judge or judge and jury must be appealed to the provincial court of appeal. In some cases, the decision of the provincial court of appeal may be appealed to the Supreme Court of Canada.

RIGHTS OF APPEAL OF DEFENCE AND PROSECUTION

The defence can appeal a decision of the trial court by right (without leave) on a question of law or, with leave from the court to be appealed to, on a question of fact or a question of mixed law and fact. If leave is granted, the defence can also appeal a sentence.

The prosecution can appeal only on a question of law.

PROCEDURE FOR APPEALS

The appeal is launched when the appellant files (in the appropriate court office) a notice of appeal or, when leave is required, a notice of the application for leave to appeal, which will set out the grounds on which the appeal is based. The notice must be served on the representative of the other party — the **respondent**.

Once an appeal has been launched and, if necessary, leave for the appeal has been granted, the appellant and the respondent must each prepare a detailed document called a **factum** that sets out the position of the party on the grounds for appeal. The factum cites the law (cases, statutes, and regulations), refers to evidence given at the trial and to the trial transcripts, and makes arguments to support the position of the party filing the factum. Once prepared, the factum must be served on the other party and filed with the court of appeal.

question of fact
a ground for appeal that is available only to the defence that is based on the validity of a piece of evidence presented at trial

question of mixed law and fact
a ground for appeal that is available only to the defence that is based on an error that combines elements of a question of law and a question of fact

respondent
the party that defends the original trial court decision when it is appealed by another party

factum
a document used in an appeal that sets out the grounds for the appeal, the facts of the case, and the legal arguments as to why the appeal should succeed or fail

Although the court of appeal has the right to hear oral testimony from any witness who appeared at trial (s. 683), in general the court simply reads the factums of the parties and hears oral argument from the lawyers for the two sides. The judges on the court of appeal are entitled to question the lawyers about legal points or interpretations or to clarify the parties' positions.

At the end of the hearing, the judges of the court of appeal have the power to take any of the actions described in the next section.

POWERS OF THE COURT OF APPEAL

Once the appeal hearing is over, the judges of the court of appeal have wide powers to revisit (or leave alone) the trial court decision.

On an appeal by the defence (s. 686), the court of appeal for the province can direct an acquittal, direct a new trial, dismiss the appeal, or uphold the conviction and alter the sentence. On an appeal by the prosecution (s. 686), the court of appeal can set aside the acquittal and direct a new trial, dismiss the appeal, alter the sentence, or substitute the acquittal with a conviction (if the trial was held with a judge alone). If the trial was held with a judge and jury, the court of appeal cannot substitute a conviction for an acquittal but must order a new trial.

SUMMARY CONVICTION APPEALS

For summary convictions, appeals of provincial court decisions go to superior court. Leave is not required. Further appeals are addressed, only on questions of law and only with leave, by the court of appeal. Further appeals may be launched to the highest court in Canada, the Supreme Court of Canada. The Supreme Court considers only appeals based on questions of law. Leave is always needed to bring an appeal to the Supreme Court of Canada unless one of the judges in the court of appeal dissented on a matter of law or the conviction or acquittal was set aside at the court of appeal level.

KEY TERMS

aggravating factor	mitigating factor
appeal	pre-sentence report
appellant	probation
discharge	probation order
error	question of fact
factum	question of law
fine	question of mixed law and fact
ground for appeal	respondent
imprisonment	sentence
leave to appeal	suspended sentence

NOTES

1. *Criminal Code*, RSC 1985, c. C-46, as amended.

2. *Canadian Charter of Rights and Freedoms*, part I of the *Constitution Act, 1982*, RSC 1985, app. II, no. 44.

EXERCISES

Multiple Choice

1. Which of the following is not a rationale for punishment?

    a. deterrence

    b. mitigation

    c. rehabilitation

    d. protection of society

    e. none of the above

2. Which of the following is not an aggravating factor?

    a. the consumption of alcohol

    b. the defacing of a synagogue

    c. a mob hit

    d. a teacher sexually assaulting a student

    e. none of the above

3. The jury is dismissed from the trial after

    a. the sentencing

    b. the verdict is announced

    c. the Crown presents its case

    d. post-trial issues are dealt with

    e. all of the above

4. Sentences are

    a. decided by the judge based on precedent

    b. decided by the jury based on the relevant *Criminal Code* section

    c. decided by the judge and the jury together

    d. decided by the judge based on the relevant *Criminal Code* section

    e. a and d

5. Which of the following is not a mitigating factor?

    a. the victim taunted the accused

    b. the accused has never committed an offence before

    c. the accused committed the offence on behalf of someone else

    d. the accused seems sorry to have committed the offence

    e. the accused is trying to kick a drug habit

True or False?

_F_ 1. The court has no discretion in imposing sentences, which are strictly prescribed by the *Criminal Code.*

_T_ 2. The fact that a crime was motivated by hatred of an identifiable group is an example of an aggravating factor.

_F_ 3. An absolute discharge has conditions attached to it.

_T_ 4. Improper or unfair conduct by the police or the Crown may be a factor in reducing a sentence.

_T_ 5. A judge can consider an offender's background and character when deciding on a sentence.

Short Answer

1. Briefly outline the rationales for punishing convicted persons. Which rationale do you think is the most compelling? Why?

2. Give an example of a ground for appeal on a question of law.

3. Explain why the prosecution can appeal only on questions of law.

PART IV

Introduction to Civil Law Disciplines

CHAPTER 10

Contracts and Torts: The Founding Principles of Civil Law

Chapter Objectives

After completing this chapter, you should be able to:

- Compare and contrast the way in which legal rights arise under contract law and tort law.
- Describe the basic principles of the relationship between two contract parties.
- Describe the nature of the remedies commonly awarded in a contract dispute.
- List some of the circumstances in which a contract will not be enforced by a court.
- Describe the basic principles of the relationship between a tortfeasor and the victim of a tort.
- Describe the nature of the remedies commonly awarded in a lawsuit based in tort.

Contracts and Torts: The Distinctions

This chapter introduces contracts and **torts**, the two legal disciplines from which nearly all other civil law principles flow. These two disciplines are hundreds of years old, and it would be impossible to introduce even their most basic principles properly in these few pages. A more realistic goal, adopted here, is to compare and contrast these disciplines in an effort to illustrate how the presence or absence of a contract between two parties influences the way in which legal rights arise and are enforced by the courts in the event of a dispute.

tort
literally, a "wrong"; in law, an injury — whether physical, emotional, economic, or otherwise — suffered by a person for which another person may be held liable

CONTRACTS

Contract law is a very broad legal discipline that encompasses a great number of situations, including commercial transactions, tenancies, family arrangements, employment relationships, personal service arrangements, and many other transactions. All situations that fall within contract law, however, have at their heart one common feature: an agreement (or alleged agreement) between two or more parties. The relationship between the parties is governed by the contract or agreement.

For example, you decide to buy a car. You negotiate the terms of purchase with the dealer, including the make, colour, year, price, and options. The contract will also state when you can pick up the car and when you have to provide payment. Your agreement with the dealer is described in the terms of your contract.

A contract can be oral or in writing. A written contract offers the parties the advantage of proof of the terms, whereas there are potential difficulties in proving an oral contract.

Because of the great differences between the kinds of relationships dealt with by contract, many subdivisions of contract law — such as landlord and tenant law, family law, and employment law — have evolved into specialized disciplines. These subdivisions have their own complexities and are often shaped and supplemented by specialized statutes (such as provincial landlord and tenant acts, family law acts, or employment standards acts), many of which represent the codification of branches of common law.

Nevertheless, a large body of general contract law remains a part of the common law and continues to evolve according to common law principles. This large and ancient body of law continues to govern all contractual relationships that don't fall neatly into a subdiscipline, or that are not adequately addressed by existing statutes. If, for example, a landlord and a tenant enter into a relationship that incorporates rights or responsibilities that extend outside the scope of the applicable landlord and tenant legislation (without violating that legislation) and a dispute arises over those new terms, the court will rely on the common law of contract to resolve the dispute.

In general, all issues that arise under contract law are decided by referring to the underlying agreement between the parties, although in some cases terms that are not explicitly incorporated into that agreement are read into it (added) by the courts. Because of this practice of looking to the agreement to settle the dispute, parties' legal rights in a contract dispute are said to flow from the contract itself.

TORTS

"Tort" is a French word that simply means a "wrong." The law of torts deals with wrongs, or injuries (physical, economic, or otherwise), inflicted by one party on another, usually outside the context of a contract. The result of the infliction of the wrong is that the injured party sues the wrongdoer (tortfeasor) for the injury suffered. Thus, although the parties may have known each other prior to the occurrence of the wrong, they are not in this particular relationship by choice. Examples of situations that may result in a tort claim are a car accident and a slip-and-fall accident on a slippery sidewalk.

Tort law is less extensively subdivided and codified than contract law. There are certain distinct branches of tort: intentional torts (such as assault), negligence, and nuisance/trespass. Certain types of tort have become the subject of statutes, such as environmental protection laws, which create offences that may be prosecuted by the government in a criminal or quasi-criminal manner. These statutes are designed to protect the common good by stopping parties from committing torts that will cause damage on a significant scale. As a result, a corporation that pollutes the water source for a community, causing health problems and deaths, can be prosecuted under the environmental protection statute and can also be sued by the individual victims under tort law.

A large number of *Criminal Code*[1] offences (typically, those offences that have an identifiable victim) describe actions that would also qualify as torts under the common law. In theory, most victims of criminal offences have the common law right to sue the perpetrator of a crime in civil court under the law of torts, regardless of whether the offence is prosecuted in the criminal system. In practice, most victims choose not to do this, because the remedies available in a tort dispute (most commonly money damages, discussed later in this chapter) are difficult to enforce against a criminal accused, who may be impecunious (broke) or incarcerated. But parallel criminal and civil tort cases do occur (the Todd Bertuzzi and O.J. Simpson cases are well-known examples), and, partly because of a difference in the criminal and civil standards of proof (criminal standards are discussed in chapter 8), the finding of culpability/liability in the two cases can differ.

In a tort case, in contrast with contract law, no underlying agreement is in place that establishes the rights between the parties. A **tortfeasor** (literally, "wrongdoer") and his or her victim are, in theory, "strangers" brought together by misfortune (although in reality many torts occur as a result of interactions between acquaintances or friends). The absence of an agreed-upon set of rights and responsibilities between the parties places tort liability outside the control of the parties involved: tort rights flow not from the parties' own plans but from the law itself.

tortfeasor
literally, "wrongdoer"; a person who commits a tort

Basic Principles of Contract Law

Strictly speaking, the law of contracts provides a **remedy** in the event of a **breach** (but will only rarely enforce the specific terms of an agreement) once certain required criteria are proven to exist. A party has breached the contract once there is a failure to do what was promised. The availability of a remedy for breach of a contract depends on the enforceability of that contract; in other words, a court will not provide a remedy unless the contract was created according to the rules of contract law.

remedy
an award or order provided by the court to compensate a victim for the commission of a legal wrong, such as a tort or a breach of contract

breach
the failure of one party to perform a contract or contractual obligation

FORMATION OF THE CONTRACT: INTENTION TO BE LEGALLY BOUND

Contracting parties must have the intention to be legally bound by the terms of the contract.

Offer

An **offer** exists at the point in negotiations where the terms of the contract have been set and one party, the offeree, must accept or reject the terms set forth by the offeror. There are four ways in which an offer can come to an end without being accepted:

offer
the proposal of a contract or a set of contract terms; an offer is not a contract until it is accepted

revocation
the withdrawal of an offer
by its maker

consideration
the benefit(s) flowing to
each party under a
contract

rejection
the refusal of an offer

counteroffer
a new offer that replaces
an original offer, often
with revised terms

lapse
the expiry of an offer that
has not been accepted by
a stipulated acceptance
time or on the occurrence
of stipulated conditions

- *Revocation* As long as the offer has not been accepted, an offeror may revoke (withdraw) or alter the offer at any time. An offeror has no duty to hold an offer open (in the absence of a contractual agreement to do so) because there has not yet been any **consideration** in return for the original offer. The revocation is effective only when it has been communicated to the offeree. This communication need not be direct.

- *Rejection* Once an offer is rejected, it is no longer valid or open for future acceptance.

- *Counteroffer* A counteroffer rejects the original offer by substituting a new or revised offer.

- *Lapse* An offer may lapse (expire) at a stipulated time or on the occurrence of a stipulated event. Alternatively, a lapse date may be implied after a reasonable period of time has passed without the offer being accepted.

Acceptance

In general, a contract is not complete until acceptance is communicated to the offeror. The contract is completed at the time the offeror hears or implicitly knows of the offeree's acceptance. Once a contract is "complete," it is legally binding on the parties — it can be enforced using the courts.

Consideration

Each party to a binding contract must receive a benefit under the contract. The benefit flowing to each party is known as consideration. An entirely one-sided promise is generally not enforceable because it implies no mutuality and therefore no consideration. Moral obligations, or present compensation for past performance, do not qualify as adequate consideration, and courts are not generally entitled or required to consider issues of fairness when determining the adequacy of consideration.

Capacity To Contract

A contract entered into by an individual who is found to be lacking the required **legal capacity** to enter into binding contracts may be unenforceable. Subject to certain exceptions, a party may lack the capacity to contract as a result of mental incapacity, drunkenness, or minimum age requirements.

legal capacity
the ability to enter into an
enforceable contract,
based on the absence of
factors (for example,
cognitive impairment)
that might impair capacity

Certainty of Terms

Contract terms must be precise and clear to enable the courts to understand the agreement and to ensure that the contract represents the contracting parties' intention. Previous dealings between the same parties can be consulted by the court to help interpret new contracts. Also, where terms are unclear or missing, they may be interpreted or filled in by the court by referring to an industry standard or norm. For example, Ontario's *Sale of Goods Act*[2] states that, in a contract for the sale of goods, if no agreement is reached as to price but there is an enforceable agreement to sell, the purchaser is held to a reasonable price.

CONTRACT TERMS

Written Terms

The interpretation of a contract is subject to established legal rules of construction. However, the courts will consider the fact that the meaning of a term may vary depending on local custom or the practices of a specific trade. The **parol evidence rule** provides that, in general, the meaning of the contract is determined without reference to external sources of evidence, such as other documents or oral testimony. This rule is applied less rigidly to standard form contracts, and more rigidly in circumstances involving parties that have individually negotiated the specific terms of their contract.

parol evidence rule
the rule that the meaning of a contract must be determined without reference to external sources of evidence, such as other documents or oral testimony

Implied Terms

The court will generally not imply "missing" terms into a contract; however, in the interests of business efficiency, a necessary term may be "read in." Factors such as past business dealings between the parties may be considered in determining the appropriateness of reading in a particular term.

Terms may also be read in by applying a statute. For example, the *Sale of Goods Act* provides that certain implied terms as to the description, merchantability, and fitness for purpose of goods sold be read into contracts that fall under the application of that legislation.

Exclusion Clauses

An **exclusion clause** is a contractual device that limits the contractual or statutory liability of a party in the event of a breach of the contract. It is a contract term like any other, negotiated between the parties. The standard rules of construction apply to these clauses no differently from any other term of a contract, but misrepresentation of the purpose of the exclusion clause, or serious unfairness (unconscionability) in its operation, may render the clause inoperative.

exclusion clause
a part of a contract that limits the contractual or statutory liability of a party in the event of a breach of the contract

representation
a statement or claim made during contract negotiations that, though not necessarily a term of the contract, may be relied on by a party in deciding whether to enter into the contract

CONTRACTUAL DEFECTS

Misrepresentation

Representations are statements or claims made by contract parties in the course of negotiations. Although they may **induce** a party to make the contract, they are not necessarily incorporated into the document as a contractual term or obligation. As a result, **misrepresentations** do not automatically give rise to an award of **damages** under *contract* law because there has been no contractual breach. There may, however, be *tort* liability for negligent or wilful misrepresentation.

To constitute a **contractual defect** (that is, a factor that affects the enforceability of the contract), a misrepresentation must

- be based on a fact that is asserted to be true,
- have been false when it was acted on, and
- have induced the other party to make the contract.

A representation made on the basis of opinion, and not on fact, may be treated in the same way as a factual misrepresentation if it is provided by a person with

induce
persuade or bring about

misrepresentation
a representation based, either innocently, negligently, or intentionally, on incorrect information

damages
losses suffered as a result of the breach of a contract or the commission of a tort, or compensation awarded for contract or tort losses

contractual defect
a legal problem with a contract that can either invalidate a contract or give rise to damages without invalidating the entire contract

special expertise or knowledge of the subject matter. There are three types of misrepresentation:

- *Fraudulent misrepresentation* A statement that is made that is known to be false or is made recklessly, without any regard to its truth, is a fraudulent misrepresentation. Misrepresentations of this type give rise to the tort of deceit. Remedies that may be awarded to the innocent party may include an award of damages under tort law and/or the right to **rescind** (to not carry out one's side of) the contract.

- *Negligent misrepresentation* A statement of fact, or a statement of opinion made by a person with special knowledge or expertise, that is untrue or inaccurate and that has been **reasonably relied on** to the detriment of another is a negligent misrepresentation, provided that the person making the statement or the party with special knowledge rendering the opinion did not take reasonable care under the circumstances to ascertain the truth of the claim. The innocent party will be found to have "relied on the misrepresentation to his or her detriment" if he or she has taken action, because of the misrepresentation, that has caused a loss of some sort. Remedies that may be awarded to the innocent party may include damages and the right to rescind the contract.

- *Innocent misrepresentation* A statement of fact that is not true but was made by one who believes it to be true is an innocent misrepresentation. Although this may give rise to a right of the other party to rescind the contract, no damages will be awarded unless the representation can be shown to be a term of either a **collateral contract** (one that is related to but separate from another contract) or an implied term of the main contract.

Mistake

There are three types of mistake under contract law: common or mutual mistake, unilateral mistake, and a situation called *non est factum*. With the exception of common mistakes, once proven, a mistake may render a contract unenforceable.

- *Common or mutual mistake* Such a mistake exists where both parties have made the same error (are mistaken about a fundamental aspect of the contract). If the party requesting the right to rescind the contract on grounds of mistake was at fault in causing the mistake (even if it was accidental), this remedy is not available to him or her.

- *Unilateral mistake* Such a mistake exists where one party, with the full knowledge of the other, is mistaken. This mistake arises both in situations of fraudulent misrepresentation (described above) and in situations involving one party's acceptance of an offer that the offeror knows is a result of a mistake. Obviously, in such cases, only the innocent party is entitled to rescind the contract.

- ***Non est factum*** This is a Latin phrase loosely translatable as "I didn't sign that." Modern law has changed the meaning of the phrase to something closer to "I didn't *intend* to sign that" or "This is not my deed or doing." A party may **plead** (base his or her case on) *non est factum* in a situation where he or she has signed the wrong contract or has signed a contract

rescind
to opt, generally with good legal reason, not to carry out one's side of a contract, as if the contract had never been made in the first place

reasonable reliance
reasonable actions by one party, generally based on representations or actions by the other party, that may result in losses that a court will compensate

collateral contract
a contract that is related to or depends on, but is separate from, another contract

non est factum
Latin for "I didn't sign/make [this contract]"; a legal doctrine that can be pleaded, based on a narrow set of circumstances, in an attempt to render a contract unenforceable

plead
argue or claim

under a complete misunderstanding about its nature. This is an exception to the general rule that, once signed, a document is binding. For a party to successfully plead *non est factum*, the mistaken document must be different in quality or nature, not merely content, from the intended document. Also, the party claiming *non est factum* must not have been careless in signing the document.

Illegality

The general rule is that illegal contracts are unenforceable. There are two types of illegality:

- *Common law illegality* The common law concerns itself primarily with contracts that are contrary to public policy. For obvious reasons, the court will not enforce a contract to kill someone or to share the proceeds of a robbery. Other examples include contracts to defraud the revenue service, contracts to corrupt public officials, contracts that attempt to deny the jurisdiction of the courts, contracts to commit a tort, or contracts that the court concludes are of an immoral nature.

- *Statutory illegality* This type of illegality arises where a breach of a statute is inherent in the fulfillment of a contractual obligation — one party has promised to do something that is contrary to legislation (such as to divide land in contravention of Ontario's *Planning Act*[3]). In concluding that a contract is void because of statutory illegality, it is often necessary to consider the purpose of the relevant statute.

Problems with Formalities

Formal requirements are attached to certain categories of contracts. The absence of these formal requirements, or **formalities**, renders the contract void. The general rule is that an oral contract is enforceable, but this rule is altered by statute in some cases — for example, in the case of contracts falling under the Ontario *Statute of Frauds*,[4] the *Sale of Goods Act*, and the *Consumer Protection Act*,[5] which all require that certain contracts be in writing. An agreement to sell real estate must be in writing and under seal in order to be enforceable.

formalities
procedural or formal requirements, such as writing, a seal, or a signature (typically prescribed by statute), that are necessary to make certain kinds of contracts enforceable

Duress

A contract is void for reasons of duress if, in signing the contract, a contracting party was influenced by threats of bodily harm against himself or herself or his or her family.

Undue Influence

A presumption of undue influence may exist in circumstances that involve relationships of a special personal or professional nature: the voluntariness of the contract may be put in question when one of the parties is perceived to be in a position of power over the other. Once raised, the presumption of undue influence must be successfully rebutted (proven incorrect) before the contract is considered valid.

For example, if an elderly woman enters into a contract to sell her house to her lawyer for $50, she, or her heirs, could challenge the contract on the basis of undue influence exerted by the lawyer on the woman. The simple fact that the lawyer is in a position of trust, is feared and respected by the woman, and has some measure of control over her actions is enough to make undue influence an issue. The lawyer is then required to prove to the court that he did not exert undue influence on the woman in convincing her to sign the contract, or the contract will not be enforceable.

Unconscionability

unconscionability
serious unfairness in a contract; unfairness that no reasonable person would accept and no honest person would propose

A judge may set aside a contract for gross unfairness by applying the doctrine of **unconscionability**. An unconscionable contract is one in which there is gross or extreme one-sidedness, such that an honest and fair person would not propose it because it is so unfair to the other person. A two-part test must be satisfied to be successful in a claim of unconscionability. It must first be established that a substantial inequality of bargaining power existed between the parties and that the exertion of power by the influential party created the unfair result. Once the inequality of bargaining power is established, the onus shifts to the party in the position of power to establish that, although the power existed, it was not exercised. Because a valid contract need not involve equal consideration (equal benefits on both sides), a "bad" bargain is not in itself sufficient cause for applying this doctrine.

PERFORMANCE AND BREACH

Frustration

frustration
a legal doctrine that releases the parties to a contract from their responsibilities under the contract when something (a circumstance or an object, for example) necessary to the performance of the contract no longer exists

A contract may be determined by a court to be **frustrated** in circumstances where false assumptions about future events have substantially altered the contract conditions. In the event that performing the terms of the contract is impossible or increasingly difficult, the doctrine of frustration allows the court to terminate or alter the contract's terms in an attempt to preserve the original "flavour" of the bargain. The doctrine does not apply in circumstances where a reasonable person could have contemplated the future event and no provision was added to the contract to plan for it. The *Frustrated Contracts Act*[6] states that where a contract becomes frustrated, moneys paid are recoverable and sums owing are not enforceable, thus placing parties in their precontractual positions.

Remedies

The party who sues or brings the lawsuit is called the plaintiff; the party who has to defend the lawsuit is called the defendant. Often, when there has been a breach of contract, the innocent party (the party who did not breach the contract) will sue the "breaching party."

A remedy is the order a judge makes to compensate the innocent party for the breach of contract. Contractual remedies offered by the courts are designed either to put the innocent party back into the position he or she would have been in had he or she not entered the contract, or to put the innocent party into the position he or she would have been in had the contract been fulfilled. There are a few situations where the court will order the parties to complete the contract (specific performance), usually only if a monetary payment (damages) will not address the breach of contract appropriately.

Damages may be calculated on any one of the following three bases:

- **Restitution** The plaintiff may seek reimbursement or return of the benefits conferred on the defaulting defendant. Restitution is most appropriate where the plaintiff, relying on the defendant's promise, has transferred something of value to the defendant. In an attempt to guard against unjustly enriching one party at the expense of another, restitution puts the parties back into their precontractual positions. For example, Joanne agrees to buy Ali's car. Joanne pays Ali a deposit of $500. Ali changes his mind and decides not to sell her the car. Joanne sues Ali. The court orders Ali to return Joanne's deposit of $500, thus putting Joanne in the same position as before they entered into the agreement.

- **Reliance** The plaintiff may seek an award of damages that includes expenses incurred from relying on the contract. Protecting the reliance interest is most often a concern where the plaintiff's position has changed and restitution is not an option. An attempt is made to undo the harm that reliance on the defendant's promise has caused by putting the plaintiff in a position that is *similar* to the precontractual position.

- **Expectation** The plaintiff may seek to recover the value of the benefits he or she expected to receive upon fulfillment of the contract. This kind of remedy attempts to place the plaintiff in a position similar to what was expected had the contract been performed. Compensation according to expectation is the most common contract law remedy.

A court order may also grant an order for **specific performance**, which requires the parties to complete the obligations of the contract. Specific performance is available only where the payment of money damages is inadequate. The sale of real estate is often considered an appropriate situation in which to request specific performance. This is based on the theory that all land is unique and that its loss cannot be compensated with an award of monetary damages.

QUANTIFICATION OF DAMAGES   The burden of establishing with evidence the extent of damages suffered is on the plaintiff as the party requesting the award of damages. Receipts, bank statements, and income tax documents and statements are examples of the kind of evidence that the plaintiff must provide the court in order to support the claim for damages. In situations where damages are impossible to quantify accurately, an estimate based on evidence is sufficient.

MITIGATION OF DAMAGES   A plaintiff cannot recover damages that he or she could have avoided. **Mitigation** refers to the avoiding or reducing of the plaintiff's losses, and the plaintiff has a responsibility or **duty to mitigate**. Courts will often reduce an award of damages by the amount that could have been reasonably mitigated. The plaintiff must do that which is expected of a reasonable person to minimize his or her losses resulting from a breach of contract.

For example, if a dentist breaches a contract of employment by firing a dental assistant for no sufficient cause, the dentist is in general liable to pay the employee for her lost income over the life of the contract. The dental assistant is not allowed, however, to just sit at home and collect the money from her former employer; she has an obligation to look for and obtain another suitable job so that her losses (for

restitution
the return of benefits to put contracting parties back into their precontractual position

reliance
dependence on a promise or contract, including the expenditure of money in dependence on the contract

expectation
anticipation of benefits from a contract being fulfilled

specific performance
a court order requiring a party in default to fully perform his or her obligations under a contract

mitigation
minimizing a party's damages from breach of contract or from the commission of a tort

duty to mitigate
a party's responsibility to minimize his or her damages from breach of contract or from the commission of a tort

which the dentist is liable) are reduced. If she does not do so, a judge could reduce the amount of damages awarded to her as a result of her failure to mitigate her damages.

remoteness
the degree to which the consequences of a contract breach or the commission of a tort results, directly or indirectly, from the breach or the tort

REMOTENESS The **remoteness** test provides that only those losses that flow naturally from the contractual breach are recoverable. Only those damages that can be reasonably foreseen at the time of forming the contract will pass the remoteness test and are therefore recoverable.

For example, if the dental assistant discussed above has been improperly fired by the only dentist in town, she may be able to recover from the dentist her costs of moving to another town to take another job (and, thus, mitigate her damages) because, at the time the contract was entered into, it was reasonably foreseeable that the dental assistant would be forced to move to another town to find work if she were fired. On the other hand, if the dental assistant drives her brand new car into a tree because she is so angry at the dentist that she is not paying attention to her driving, she will not likely be able to force the dentist to pay for the car repairs. It is not reasonable to expect the parties to an employment contract to foresee that improperly firing an employee could lead to a smashed car.

Basic Principles of Tort Law

Tort law applies to a wide range of legal disputes involving injuries to people or property, usually outside the context of contract. Because of the breadth of the doctrine, tort law is divided into subcategories, the most important of which are negligence and intentional torts. The defendant in a tort suit is the tortfeasor, and the remedy sought by a tort victim is almost always monetary damages.

All torts require proof of fault as a basis for imposing liability, although fault is measured differently for different classes of tort. The most important distinction between negligence and intentional tort is the presence or absence of intent. Where there is intent, the general principles of intentional tort will apply, but where there is only recklessness, carelessness, or negligence, the principles of negligence will govern. Finally, other torts, such as nuisance, cannot readily be classed in either category.

negligence
a tort law concept based on the failure of a person to respect or carry out a duty of care owed to another

duty of care
a legal duty owed by one person to another based on a relationship or on the doctrine of foreseeability

standard of care
the standard by which discharge of a duty of care is measured, which depends on the relationship between the parties and the circumstances under which the duty arises

NEGLIGENCE

The traditional law of **negligence** operates independently of both contract and property rights and is based on those rights flowing from relationships between people. The **duty of care** is the central principle of negligence law, without which no liability can flow, no matter how awful the conduct of the alleged tortfeasor.

As its name implies, negligence does *not* depend on intentional wrongful action or recklessness for the imposition of liability. Instead, negligence judges the execution of every duty of care by reference to a corresponding **standard of care**, and imposes tort liability wherever a tortfeasor's behaviour falls below the standard and the damages suffered by the victim are not considered to be too remote.

Duty of Care

One person's duty of care to another person is the foundation on which fault is established in a negligence action. In the absence of a duty of care, there is no liability in negligence because the law is unwilling to place obligations on people without reason or reciprocity.

The successful proof of a duty of care depends on **foreseeability** — that is, the plaintiff must prove, first, that the defendant acted despite a foreseeable risk of injury and, second, that the plaintiff was within the scope of foreseeable victims of that injury. If the defendant, in committing the tort, could foresee that a particular person or class of persons might be injured by his or her actions, then the tortfeasor is said to have had a duty of care to that person or class of persons.

Duties of care often accompany relationships — neighbour to neighbour, host to guest, parent to child — but they can also arise between strangers, as between two drivers on a highway. Foresight need not be actual. A tortfeasor who is thoughtless as to the potential victims of his or her actions will usually be held accountable on the basis that foresight was reasonable in the context. For example, a homeowner owes a duty of care to people using the sidewalk in front of his or her house to make sure that it is as reasonably free and clear of snow and ice as circumstances permit.

foreseeability
a test to determine whether a reasonable person could expect that a certain result may follow from his or her act; typically, an objective precondition to imposing a duty of care or to imposing liability for a particular class of damages

Standard of Care

Once a duty of care has been attributed to the alleged tortfeasor, the court must determine whether that duty has been met. To do that, the behaviour of the tortfeasor is compared with a legal standard of care appropriate to the circumstances. The standard used corresponds with the nature of the duty of care, with some duties, such as those between a parent and child, attracting a higher standard of care than others (such as duties owed to strangers). The basic tort standard of care, applied in the absence of special factors, is that of a reasonable and prudent person in the same circumstances.

Causation

Many mishaps involve the convergence of unfortunate circumstances. Multiple tortfeasors acting independently may contribute to one set of injuries, and the victim may even be partially at fault. It is up to the court to allocate fault (and liability) among the different negligent parties according to the rules of causation.

To impose tort liability for an injury, the court must accept the plaintiff's argument that the actions of the defendant were the "cause in fact" of that injury or, in circumstances of multiple causation, that they were a significant and substantial factor in the occurrence of the injury. To establish cause in fact, the plaintiff must prove to the court that the actions of the defendant were a major contributing factor, if not the only contributing factor, to the occurrence of the event that caused the plaintiff's injuries. Where the actions of more than one defendant contribute to the chain of events leading to the plaintiff's injuries, the court must review each individual action in isolation to determine which ones constituted significant and substantial factors. This last inquiry turns on whether there is a substantial connection between the action and the injury. The plaintiff may be found to have contributed to his or her own injury. One of the most familiar examples of this is that of the

contributory negligence
the role that a plaintiff or victim may play in negligently contributing to the cause of or aggravation of his or her own injury

car accident victim whose injuries are aggravated by failure to wear a seat belt. In such a case, the plaintiff is said to have been **contributorily negligent**.

Once it has been determined that the defendants made significant and substantial contribution to the harm, the court must allocate liability among them. If the individual causes are found to be divisible, each defendant will be responsible for part of the damages. If the causes are indivisible, the defendants will be found jointly and severally liable for the harm. In joint and several liability, each defendant and all defendants are accountable for all of the harm, and the plaintiff may pursue any or all of them for payment. For example, car A stops properly for a red light. Car B, following behind, does not stop in time and rear-ends car A. Car C rear-ends car B. The driver of car A is injured and sues the drivers of car B and car C for damages. The judge finds both drivers/defendants responsible (jointly liable) for driver A's injuries. As between the defendants, the judge allocates 60 percent liability to driver B (severally liable) and 40 percent to driver C (severally liable).

In some cases, the multiple causes of an injury do not all occur at the same time. A minor injury may predispose a victim to a future, much more serious, injury, or a later injury may compound an earlier one. In such cases, the court must reconcile the rule that defendants take their victims as they find them (discussed later) with the principle that defendants should be held responsible only for foreseeable damage substantially connected to their own actions. To do this, the court usually tries to determine which part of the injuries proven at trial would have occurred without the defendant's own negligence, and will not hold the defendant liable for that part unless a rule, such as the "thin skull rule" (discussed later), dictates otherwise.

Remoteness

One tortious action may trigger a long chain of different kinds of damage. Not every kind of damage in the chain will be a consequence that the tortfeasor might have foreseen, and the severity of damage may also exceed all normal expectations. Common law has limited the scope of tortfeasors' liability in such cases, imposing instead responsibility for a defined scope of damage by reference to foreseeability and remoteness. As in contract law, tort law will not provide compensation for injuries that were not reasonably foreseeable at the time of the improper action.

The foreseeability test in this context is different from the objective measure used in the context of the duty of care. Actual foresight is usually necessary, although a tortfeasor is responsible for all *possible* foreseeable consequences of his or her actions. It is not necessary that a consequence be probable or even likely. Where the variety or the extent of damage far exceeds the defendant's actual foresight, he or she will usually argue that the damage was "too remote" to be foreseeable. As in contract law, the victim cannot claim damages from the defendant for losses that no reasonable person could have foreseen at the time of the action that led to the lawsuit (either the breach of contract or the negligent act).

Before liability will be imposed, it must usually be shown that a reasonable person could have foreseen each type of harm proven to have resulted from the wrongful act. For example, a defendant who runs over a poodle may be responsible for the dog's veterinarian bills and even for the tranquilizers required to calm down the distraught owner. However, the defendant will not likely be held responsible for the breakdown of the owner's marriage that arguably occurs as a result of the owner's spouse blaming the owner for allowing the dog to be killed. Foreseeability of the *extent* of harm, however, is not always necessary. A defendant who is capable of foreseeing one degree of injury will often be held responsible for more serious damage.

Indirect damage or damage aggravated by an intervening act or risk raises issues of causation, discussed above, and a defendant is entitled to argue that he or she is liable for only limited damages or for none at all because of a break in the chain of causation between the wrongful act and the injury. However, not all secondary causes are intervening acts. In some cases, aggravating circumstances may themselves be the subject of foresight (or even of control) by the defendant.

In some personal injury cases, the courts have chosen to modify the normal rules of remoteness. A rule sometimes called the "thin skull doctrine" applies in circumstances where the tort plaintiff suffers from an unusual physical or mental vulnerability that may not be easily detectable but that predisposes him or her to unusually serious injury. A tortfeasor, in injuring such a plaintiff, "takes the victim as he finds him" and may be liable for damage beyond the damage that would be foreseen by a reasonable and prudent person.

Negligence and Contract Remedies in Business Relations

Because the violation of the terms of an explicit contract is generally easier to prove than the violation of an unwritten duty of care, the choice of contract remedies over tort liability is an important motivation for contractual relations. Nevertheless, it is a mistake to view the spheres of tort and contract as completely independent. Business relations, as with social relations, can create duties of care, and a layer of negligence responsibility underlies many contracts. Even virtual strangers, bound only by the simplest terms of bargain and sale, may owe a duty of care to each other. The law of product liability is a good example. Product liability is the name given to a hybrid area of the law that depends on both negligence and contract concepts that allow parties to recover damages incurred through losses or injuries from defective or dangerous consumer goods.

For example, the manufacturer of a sports drink can be found to owe a duty of care to the person who buys it, the customer. A problem with the sports drink that causes the customer to be violently ill gives rise to both a breach of contract (the manufacturer did not provide the customer with the sports drink that was intended to be purchased) and a tort (the manufacturer caused the customer to become ill).

OCCUPIERS' LIABILITY

Occupiers — people who have control over property with or without other ownership rights — have long been attributed a duty of care with respect to others invited or even trespassing onto the property. In Ontario, this responsibility has been codified in a statute called, naturally enough, the *Occupiers' Liability Act*.[7] (Other provinces have similar statutes.) The degree of control required to form the basis of occupiers' liability does not have to be permanent or exclusive — there may be multiple occupiers on one parcel of property, and an occupier's tenure need last only as long as the incident that attracted the tort suit.

Ontario's *Occupiers' Liability Act* has eliminated the different standards of care owed at common law. Previously, an occupier owed a lesser standard of care to a trespasser than to an invited guest. Now, an occupier of premises has an obligation to take reasonable care that people coming onto the premises are reasonably safe while there. The occupier is held to a standard of what is reasonable under the circumstances.

Although the Act makes it clear that the occupier cannot create a danger for trespassers, the Act also states that a trespasser is deemed (assumed) to have willingly agreed to any and all risks involved in being on the premises.

Consider the situation of someone who snowmobiles across a farm field without permission of the farmer. The Act prohibits the farmer from creating any dangers for the snowmobiler (which the farmer might be tempted to do, to discourage snowmobiling) even though the snowmobiler is deemed to have willingly assumed all risks involved in taking his snowmobile across the farmer's field without permission.

Another application of the duty of care under the *Occupiers' Liability Act* is related to "host liability" — the concept that a host should be responsible for the injuries that a drunken guest suffers while at the host's premises. Injured people (plaintiffs) have argued, with varying degrees of success, that the Act imposes a duty on the host of the party to make sure that guests do not injure themselves or others as a result of being intoxicated while at the party.

INTENTIONAL TORTS

Intentional torts are different from negligence in that they are committed by a tortfeasor who intends to cause harm, loss, or damage to someone or something. A tort is intentional as long as the tortfeasor foresaw the occurrence of the relevant consequences as substantially certain. An intentional tort is different from the tort of negligence; in negligence, the tortfeasor does not demonstrate the duty of care in doing something that is otherwise permissible.

Trespass to the Person

assault
under the common law, a threat of injury

Assault is an intentional tort that involves a *threat* of contact by a tortfeasor who has the means to carry out the threat. Note the difference here between the tort of assault, which involves only the threat, and the criminal offence of assault, which includes both the threat and the carrying out of unwanted contact with another person. Intentional acts that involve actual direct or indirect physical contact and an intent to threaten, harm, or offend constitute **battery**. Because assault and battery are often present together, there is some blurring of the boundaries between the two; however, each is a separate tort, and assault (threat) by itself can attract liability, although quantifying the damages for an assault alone may be difficult.

battery
under the common law, a usually negligent or intentional act of physical contact

Intentional torts also include intentionally inflicting mental suffering and false imprisonment (including even momentary detention by any person, not just by the police). In general, almost any violation of personal integrity can qualify as an intentional tort if the necessary combination of intent and action is found to be present and the tortfeasor cannot prove a defence.

Trespass to Property or Goods

trespass
the wrongful entry onto or damage to the property of another

Because the law accords rights to property owners, establishing a duty of care is unnecessary in **trespass** cases: any intentional entry upon or injury to real property (land) or personal property (possessions) constitutes the tort of trespass.

Because property owners have a right to exclusive possession of their property, any invasion of the boundaries of private property is tortious, regardless of whether any damage is done. Trespass to real property is probably the most familiar form, but trespass to personal property (often described as theft or conversion) is also actionable in tort and can attract damages that would be unavailable in a criminal action for theft.

Intentional Business Torts

The common law also recognizes a number of discrete "business" torts, some with a historical definition. These include deceit (or fraud), conspiracy, interference with contractual relations (including inducing breach of contract), and interference with business relations (a tort that doesn't depend on contract interference). Each of these torts depends for proof on an intent-plus-action analysis, which is done by referring to a historical "formula" of legal requirements. For example, Jetsgo, the discount airline that declared bankruptcy on the eve of March break in 2005, sued WestJet, another airline, alleging that WestJet interfered with customer relations.

Defences

The most important defences to intentional torts are (1) the consent of the victim and (2) the self-defence of the tortfeasor. Other defences include legal licence or authority and necessity. A defendant seeking to avoid tort liability bears the burden of proof in alleging a defence — that is, he or she must put before the court sufficient evidence to establish, on a balance of probabilities, the validity of the defence.

NUISANCE

The doctrine of **nuisance** (in contrast to trespass, discussed above) deals with interference with another person's use and enjoyment of his or her property. To constitute nuisance, an invasion of property need not be intentional or even negligent. As long as the possibility of an impact on the plaintiff's use is foreseeable to the defendant before the action is taken, that action can constitute nuisance. Nuisance need not and often does not involve an entry by the defendant onto the plaintiff's land. It may instead be the result of the defendant's ostensibly legitimate use of his or her own private property, which may have harmful effects on the plaintiff's use. For example, loud noises, bad odours, or shade from a new shed cast over a neighbour's cabbage patch may be considered nuisances that attract tort liability. Even a neighbour's noisy air conditioner may give rise to a lawsuit.

In assessing damages, the courts can award a remedy for almost any kind of interference, temporary or permanent, with an owner's "use and enjoyment" of the property in question. Any interference beyond that which would not be tolerated by the "ordinary occupier" in the position of the plaintiff will be compensated with damages.

nuisance
a tort law concept generally used to describe something that interferes with another person's use and enjoyment of his or her property

STRICT LIABILITY AND THE RULE IN RYLANDS v. FLETCHER

Because there is no deterrent value in punishing people for their non-negligent (or non-trespassing) actions, the law of tort requires an element of **fault**, usually described as negligence, before liability will be imposed. However, some circumstances cry out for an exception to this rule, especially where damage from

fault
responsibility for an action

non-negligent actions is serious and prevention may have been possible. Exceptions to the rules of tort law are found most often in legislation. For example, environmental statutes hold present occupiers liable for expensive environmental damage caused by their predecessors.

The common law offers at least one example of such an exception. The *Rylands v. Fletcher*[8] doctrine allows for the imposition of **strict liability** (non-negligent liability) in certain cases that involve the escape of water, chemicals, or other dangerous forces from one property onto another. In these cases, the damage to the victim's property does not have to be negligent or intentional — the fact of the damage is sufficient ground for liability in all cases except for those involving an "act of God." The principle behind imposing strict liability is that there is a social benefit in requiring those who make risky or dangerous use of their own land to account for even the non-negligent consequences of that use, because they are presumably the parties most able to control the danger.

strict liability
in the civil law context, liability that depends only on proof of the consequences of an action, even though there is no negligence on the part of the tortfeasor

KEY TERMS

assault	negligence
battery	*non est factum*
breach	nuisance
collateral contract	offer
consideration	parol evidence rule
contractual defect	plead
contributory negligence	reasonable reliance
counteroffer	rejection
damages	reliance
duty of care	remedy
duty to mitigate	remoteness
exclusion clause	representation
expectation	rescind
fault	restitution
foreseeability	revocation
formalities	specific performance
frustration	standard of care
induce	strict liability
lapse	tort
legal capacity	tortfeasor
misrepresentation	trespass
mitigation	unconscionability

NOTES

1. *Criminal Code*, RSC 1985, c. C-46, as amended.
2. *Sale of Goods Act*, RSO 1990, c. S.1, as amended.
3. *Planning Act*, RSO 1990, c. P.13.
4. *Statute of Frauds*, RSO 1990, c. S.19.
5. *Consumer Protection Act*, RSO 1990, c. C.31, as amended.
6. *Frustrated Contracts Act*, RSO 1990, c. F.34.
7. *Occupiers' Liability Act*, RSO 1990, c. O.2.
8. *Rylands v. Fletcher* (1868), LR 3 HL 330.

EXERCISES

Multiple Choice

1. Which incident(s) can form the basis of both a criminal charge and a tort lawsuit?
   a. a person enters a stranger's house by force and removes valuables
   b. a person enters a stranger's house by force and removes nothing
   c. a person threatens to slash his girlfriend's face with a knife, but doesn't
   d. a and c
   e. all of the above

2. A contract in which one person agrees to transfer a brand new car to another person for $5 is unenforceable
   a. on the basis of insufficient consideration
   b. if it's not in writing
   c. because of the doctrine of *non est factum*
   d. if one of the parties lacks legal capacity to contract
   e. for any or all of the above

3. Could a landowner be liable for a chemical spill that occurred on his or her land (contaminating nearby waterways) before he or she even purchased the land?
   a. no, never
   b. only if he or she knew about it at the time of purchase
   c. only if the possibility of a previous spill was foreseeable at the time of purchase
   d. only if he or she signed a contract guaranteeing that his or her use of the land would be contamination-free
   e. possibly, based on the doctrine of strict liability

4. A has his 10-year-old car repainted and tells B the car is 5 years old. B buys the car on the basis of its being only 5 years old. This is a case of

   a. negligent misrepresentation

   b. fraudulent misrepresentation

   c. innocent misrepresentation

   d. mutual mistake

   e. unilateral mistake

5. A has his 10-year-old car repainted. B buys the car believing it is only 5 years old, but doesn't tell A this. This is a case of

   a. mutual mistake

   b. innocent misrepresentation

   c. unilateral mistake

   d. common mistake

   e. negligent misrepresentation

True or False?

_____ 1. Some aspects/areas of contract and tort law have been codified by statute.

_____ 2. The victim of an assault and battery can sue his or her attacker under tort law, whether or not criminal charges have been laid.

_____ 3. A "not guilty" finding in criminal court means that the victim of the crime will automatically be unable to recover civil damages for the same incident.

_____ 4. A person can be found liable under tort law for the consequences of ostensibly legal activities carried out on his or her own property.

_____ 5. A sales contract is unenforceable if it contains no term setting a price for the goods sold.

_____ 6. A person can be held liable in tort for untrue statements he or she made in the process of negotiating a contract.

_____ 7. A parent cannot enter into an enforceable contract with his or her own child.

_____ 8. A contract designed to allow the enforcement of the bribe of a police officer may be struck down by a court even if the contract conforms with all applicable rules of contract formation.

Short Answer

1. A mother sues a condom manufacturer for the costs of raising her daughter, conceived and born as a result of breakage of a condom during normal sexual intercourse. Based on your knowledge of tort and contract law, do you think her lawsuit will succeed? Should she sue under contract law or under tort law? From an ethical standpoint, do you feel she should succeed or not, and why?

2. Eddie "The Baby" Hertz finds out that his rival Big Dool has a contract out on his head. Fortunately for Eddie, Nubs and Dirt Boy (the goons hired to carry out the deed) have refused to proceed because, based on their knowledge of a recent failed business venture, they don't think Big Dool is good for the money.

    a. Can Big Dool sue for specific performance of the contract? Why or why not?

    b. Can he sue for damages? If so, how might they be calculated?

c. If you believe that this sort of contract is never enforceable in court, why would parties like Big Dool and the goons enter into a contract in the first place?

3. Two teenage boys are roughhousing in a department store, making loud comments about the other shoppers, and generally being a nuisance. A security guard decides to "teach them a lesson" by detaining them, accusing them of shoplifting, and threatening to call the police. Can the boys — or their parents — sue the guard or the store on the basis of a tort? If so, what tort(s)?

CHAPTER 11

Property, Family Property, and Tenancies: The "Rights To" Disciplines

Chapter Objectives

After completing this chapter, you should be able to:

- Describe the function and status of property rights in Canada.
- Understand the basic principles of property law.
- Describe the basic rights of property owners and the legal mechanisms by which these rights are enforced.
- Explain the impact of familial relationships on property rights.
- List ways in which the criminal law protects property.
- Describe the basic rights and responsibilities of both parties to a landlord–tenant agreement.

The Concept and Function of Property Rights

Perhaps one of the strongest human instincts is to protect property. Because acquiring basic goods (such as food) and territory (such as a place to build a shelter) is essential to survival, human beings have always been motivated to work to acquire these things and to protect them from those who might take them away. Acquiring the necessities of life requires effort, and consequently community support for a system of rules to protect property has always existed in human societies.

There is enormous diversity in the way in which societies define and administer property rights. Some societies see property as being individual, with items of property belonging to a single owner (even if others are allowed to use the property); others see property as being familial (owned by a family unit); and still others, though less commonly today, see property as belonging to a wider group, even to the community or society as a whole. In many modern societies, all three modes of ownership coexist, depending on the kind of property.

Societies also differ widely in their rules about how property ownership is to be transferred or how property is to be protected. For example, in societies where property and property rights are very highly valued, extremely severe penalties (including, for example, physical mutilation) may follow the theft of property of comparatively modest commercial worth. More commonly, however, the goals of property administration are to preserve the peaceful use and enjoyment of the fruits of one's labour, and to allocate those "fruits" among members of the society in an orderly way. Establishing clear rules about who controls what property is simply a way to minimize interpersonal disputes.

The Status of Property Rights in Canada

In Canada, property is protected both under the common law and by statute, and the determination and administration of property rights is dealt with in a wide range of statutes. As a result, we can reasonably conclude that property is a relatively important concept in Canadian society. Nevertheless, Canadian lawmakers and the citizens who elect them have so far declined to take a step that has been taken in some other common law countries — protecting (or *entrenching*) individual property rights in the constitution, under the *Canadian Charter of Rights and Freedoms*.[1] Because the Charter, as part of the constitution, is the highest law of the land, and because it does protect many other types of individual rights, such as the right to "life, liberty, and security of the person" (see s. 7), our legal system, when considered as a whole, seems to place a lesser value on property rights than on the right to personal security. Because of this hierarchy of values, there are considerable limits on what a person can do to protect his or her property from attack by another person, and the penalties imposed by Canadian law for interfering with property rights are usually less severe than those imposed for physical assaults and other crimes against the person.

Basic Principles of Canadian Property Law

WHAT IS PROPERTY?

As a concept, property is subjective — that is, its content and application are subject to the changing values and circumstances of society. There continue to be new disputes about what kinds of things can be the subject of property rights. While tangible resources such as land and objects have been the subject of property protection for centuries, more recent years have seen the granting of property and quasi-property status to **intangibles**.

intangibles
things or concepts that may be the subject of a property right without having a physical form

Individuals or corporations may acquire property rights in, among other things, artwork, music, literary works, trademarks, and genetically engineered plants or animals. These forms of property are governed by copyright, trademark, or patent law and are called **intellectual property**. The technology in your cell phone is protected by laws governing intellectual property. Intellectual property can be extremely valuable. The Waterloo company, Research in Motion Limited (RIM), is involved in a multi-million dollar patent dispute with an American company over ownership of a patent for the Blackberry, a wireless personal digital assistant.

Property status can also be accorded to intangible business assets such as "goodwill," a concept that describes a company's ability to retain customers through the benefit of its reputation.

Finally, the concept of personal property has in some cases been extended to apply to the human body and personality. While tort law deals with resolving disputes that involve physical and emotional injury, property concepts have sometimes been used to protect physical integrity and body parts and substances. For example, some courts have allowed a donor to assert a proprietary interest in semen samples. Some jurisdictions have extended property or quasi-property status to privacy and to "personality" in some circumstances, allowing remedies for the violation of interests in these. For example, in Ontario, the *Freedom of Information and Protection of Privacy Act*[2] regulates access to personal information gathered by public institutions. The outer limits of the property concept continue to be tested as information and innovation become the most valuable commodities of our time, demonstrating that law is responsive to changes in society.

REAL PROPERTY AND PERSONAL PROPERTY

Canadian law recognizes a distinction between **real property** (generally land) and **personal property** (generally anything other than land). These two broad categories of property are governed by the same basic principles, but these are applied differently for each category, notably with respect to transferring and registering rights.

FEATURES OF THE PROPERTY CONCEPT

A "Bundle" of Rights

Property may be defined as rules between people in relation to things, and it is useful to understand the property concept as a "bundle" of rights and obligations designed to protect some of the *interests* of property holders. A full complement of rights includes

- the right to possession and use of the property,
- the right to exclude others from possession, and
- the right to transfer some of these rights to others.

Not all property holders are entitled to all rights with respect to all of their property. For example, each joint owner of co-owned property lacks rights of exclusion with respect to the others, making proprietorship a matter of degree. Nor are rights absolute. Property owners are obliged to use their property in accordance with common law and statutory rules. The more complete the bundle of rights held by one person, the more completely that person's interests will be respected. The flexibility of a property concept based on multiple rights allows for sharing the benefit of property within a society.

intellectual property
intangible property, including copyrights, trademarks, and patents

real property
land and affixed dwellings; real estate

personal property
property without a land or real estate component — physical possessions (chattels)

Ownership and Title, Possession and Control

One of the most important potential "splits" of the bundle of property rights is that between ownership of property (title) and physical control over property (possession).

Title is a legal concept that guarantees a traditional set of rights, including possessory rights, in property. Title is usually passed through formal means: inheritance, gift, or purchase. It is typically established by **instruments** (documents with legal effect) such as deeds or transfers. Title can include and determine possessory rights.

Possession is a physical fact, and, in the right circumstances, may also be a legal conclusion. A person who can establish physical control over property may acquire rights because of that possession. Possession is normally acquired by action — taking or moving in — combined with the intention to take control. Possession itself is important evidence of title, and in some cases, possession may afford a stronger interest than title. Many legal battles are the result of conflicts over the separation of ownership and possessory rights. For example, a landlord, as owner of the apartment building, may disagree with the way in which a tenant, as the lawful possessor of an apartment, exercises possession.

REAL PROPERTY (LAND-OWNING) CONCEPTS

Tenure

The tenurial system — in which all lands are owned by the monarchy — as it existed in England was imported into Canadian common law through colonization, when all Canadian lands became the property of the British Crown. Our constitution transferred this ownership to the Canadian government. As a result, no Canadian land is ownerless — the Crown is the ultimate owner. This state of affairs has led to problems with respect to the rights of aboriginal peoples, who have been forced to establish their pre-existing property rights through negotiation with the government. While most ancient tenurial concepts are irrelevant to modern society, the concept of **escheat** still permits the government to reclaim ownership of property when a person dies intestate (without a will and with no legal heirs). Ownership of the land also reverts (goes back) to the government when a corporation ceases to exist while still holding title to the land.

The Physical Scope of Property Rights

In general, a landholder is entitled not only to the surface of the land, but also to the air directly above the land, to the earth below, and to the support provided by the subsurface. The landholder may grant some of these rights to another, such as rights to mineral deposits in the subsurface, or, where property includes the bank of a lake or river, rights of access to and use of the water. Legislation may limit the right of landholders to use water flowing through or under their land, and the law of trespass or nuisance can be used to protect landholders against damage to their own lands from their neighbours' use of water. Finally, the law allocates rights on expanding and reducing land boundaries through the processes of erosion and accretion that occur naturally.

---

title
ownership based on rights acquired or conferred through legal transactions or instruments

instrument
a formal legal document

possession
rights acquired or conferred through physical occupancy or control

escheat
a reversion of property to the Crown when there is no will or heir to inherit it or when a corporation that is the legal owner of property is dissolved

Landholding and Capacity

Both individuals and corporations are entitled to hold Canadian land, but restrictions apply in some cases. Provincial legislation often restricts the rights of minors to dispose of their land with full autonomy and grants disposition rights to the courts or to parents or guardians. Persons ruled mentally incompetent also face restrictions on their rights as owners. Non-citizens may hold Canadian land, but provincial legislatures can restrict ownership rights of non-residents. A corporation's right to hold and dispose of land depends on permission found in the statute or instrument granting corporate status.

Estates in Land

The legal concept of an **estate** describes the extent of an owner's interest in a parcel of land. In a tenurial system like ours, landholders do not own the land itself (since the government is the ultimate owner) but rather an interest in the land. The ownership of an estate in land entitles the holder to possession of the physical land. Our property law is based on the rule that possession must never lapse — all land must always be possessed by someone — and a person in actual possession may exclude others from access to the land.

estate
an interest in land

The following are the three most common kinds of estates in land that a person can hold:

- *Fee simple* A fee simple is the greatest possible estate, with the potential of continuing forever. Ownership of land in fee simple means that the owner has the unfettered right to use and dispose of the land as he or she wishes. Most land in Canada is owned in fee simple, with the owner having absolute right to the property subject only to the underlying right of the government (see the discussion of escheat above).

- *Life estate* The holder of a life estate in land has the right to exclusive possession of the land "for life," after which time the land passes to somebody else. Who that somebody else will be is something over which the life estate holder generally has no control, and he or she cannot sell the land during his or her lifetime. A typical situation that results in a life estate is a gift, by will, of land to a spouse for life and then, on the spouse's death, to a child in fee simple.

- *Leasehold estate* A leasehold estate generally confers rights of possession only to a tenant for a limited time. The landlord and tenant relationship in Canada is now primarily governed by contract and statutory rules, but it has its roots in property law. Most Canadian leaseholds are of short duration, but it is possible for a leasehold estate to last several lifetimes.

Transferring Real Property

Most land is transferred either by deed or transfer document (paper or electronic) or by succession (inheritance). In both cases, the *Statute of Frauds*[3] requires that land transfers be in writing. The written instruments describing transfers are later used to trace title to land, such that an unbroken "chain of title" between the current owner and the Crown constitutes evidence of title. This tracing process depends on the registration of instruments at county registries. Many parts of Canada still rely on this deed registration system. In the remaining jurisdictions, it has been replaced (or is being replaced) by the Torrens or land titles registration system. This system provides certified evidence of the *state* of title, rather than the actual instruments, so that title may be guaranteed to a new owner without the necessity of researching the validity of title. Additionally, the availability of title insurance has reduced the scope of title searches.

Government Expropriation of Private Land

expropriation
the reclaiming of private
land by the government

In addition to the voluntary transfer of title to land (by gift, sale, inheritance), landholders may lose title when property is **expropriated** or taken over by the government under applicable legislation. Landholders subject to government expropriation can dispute the applicable legislation, the specific mandate of the government body in question, or the amount of compensation offered, but the basic right to expropriate is one of the oldest characteristics of the tenurial system. For example, a government may expropriate land from its owners to build a highway.

Multiple Owners

Individual parcels of land can have multiple owners, and the structure of the co-ownership may be determined by the owners themselves or may be imposed by another, such as in the case of an inherited interest. Co-owners of land can be joint tenants or tenants in common, depending on the nature of their rights ("tenants" in this context means owners; the term has nothing to do with leasing or renting).

- *Joint tenants* own a piece of property together. They have identical rights with respect to (1) possession, (2) the type of estate owned, (3) title to the property, and (4) duration of ownership. They obtain title to the property by way of the same instrument, at the same time, and they must transfer title at the same time. Each owner has the right to enjoy the full physical extent of the property, and no tenant can exclude another from any part. Joint tenants enjoy the right of survivorship. When any one of them dies, that person's interest passes entirely to the remaining joint tenants — it cannot be bequeathed to someone else by will. However, it is possible for a joint tenant to sever (cut) the joint tenancy by conveying his or her interest to another person. The joint tenants then become tenants-in-common.

- *Tenants-in-common*, by contrast, can have divergent interests with respect to a single piece of property. They may obtain their interests in the property at different times, under different instruments. They each own a specific share of the property (for example, one tenant may own 10 percent, another 30 percent, and another 60 percent) and may sell, give as a gift, mortgage, or will their share of the land independently of the other tenants.

Rights in the Land of Others

A person can acquire rights in the land of another in several ways. These rights, usually limited and well defined, can arise by contract or by other means (such as use), and they form an exception to the law of trespass.

- **Licences**, as personal agreements, are not property interests but may give rights to use land. Licences are not "attached" to land and generally are valid only between the original parties. They need not be the subject of a contract but may arise through behaviour demonstrating an expectation on the part of one party that is encouraged by another.

- **Easements** are special property interests tied to land. They depend on the existence of both a dominant tenement (the parcel of land that benefits from the easement) and a servient tenement (the parcel of land that bears the easement burden). Dominant and servient tenements must be owned separately, but since the easement is tied to the properties, it binds all successive owners. Common easements in residential areas include power line rights-of-way and mutual driveways. In rural areas they may include access paths to "landlocked" property. Usually, telephone companies and cable companies are able to service individual parcels of land because of easements that not only give these companies access to the land but also allow them to dig, if necessary, to complete the work.

licence
permission to use another's land for a specific purpose; does not give any other rights

easement
a limited property interest (often a right of access) that "attaches" to and is passed on with the land; it can either be a benefit or a burden

Adverse Possession and "Squatting"

Because of the importance in law of possession as an indicator of property rights, it is possible, under special circumstances, for a person in possession (having physical control) of land to exclude the title holder from possession. This occurs through the doctrine of **adverse possession**. The most notorious adverse possessors are **squatters**, who move onto apparently vacant land and eventually defeat the property rights of the paper title holder. More common is the adverse possession of much smaller parcels, as in the case of a neighbour who erects a fence beyond the boundaries of his or her own property and through long use acquires rights in the enclosed strip. The modern doctrine of adverse possession is based on the failure of the title holder to exercise his or her right to exclude trespassers for a period exceeding a provincial statutory limitation. The title holder loses this right if the adverse possessor can show that he or she took possession with intent to exclude the owner, such that the owner is in fact dispossessed of the land. The true owner cannot be excluded by adverse possession under land titles until the land has been in land titles for more than 10 years.

adverse possession
a legal doctrine by which rights in land are acquired or are sought to be acquired through possession unaccompanied by title

squatter
a person who occupies or controls property to which he or she does not have formal legal title

PERSONAL PROPERTY LAW

The law relating to personal property is less formal than that relating to land. In general, personal property can be transferred without the need for a written instrument, and it is not necessary to prove ownership through a traceable chain of title. However, systems exist to register and trace the ownership of certain types of property such as cars and firearms. The police need to be able to determine the owner of a car involved in an accident. You, as the potential purchaser of a used car, need to be certain that the seller is indeed the lawful owner of the car. In the case of personal property, possession is generally easy to prove, and in the absence of evidence to the contrary (such as evidence of theft, or bailment, discussed below) the person who has possession of property is presumed to be the owner.

One situation that is an exception to the general "havers keepers" rule of property law is **bailment**, a situation in which one person holds the property of another. In bailment situations, there is generally a responsibility on the part of the holder to protect the property of the owner. Avoiding this presumed responsibility is the reason behind most of the "exclusion of liability" clauses and notices used by parking lots, shipping companies, airlines, and other services that are in the business of temporarily holding the property of others.

How the Criminal Law Protects Property

Because it is impractical to deal with all violations of property rights — especially rights to personal property — through civil lawsuits, the criminal law incorporates a number of property-related offences. The most obvious example is theft, also known as conversion. The theft provisions in the *Criminal Code*[4] protect not only tangible property, but also intangibles. See, for example, s. 326, which deals with the theft of telecommunication service.

Although damage to real property (land) is often the subject of civil suits, victims of such damage can also have recourse to the criminal law, which criminalizes activities such as arson or the destruction of documents of title.

Finally, the criminal law protects property in less direct ways as well by making it an offence, among other things, to forge a signature or to possess break-in tools.

Family Property: Balancing Merit and Need

As was mentioned above, although property law has its roots in the common law, in a number of situations the common law rules have been altered by statute. One of these situations is in the context of family relationships.

Marriage and family relations have long been the subject of legislation in the Commonwealth and in Canada. Common law countries have historically viewed women as different from men when it comes to property. For many years, the common law prohibited married women from owning property in their own right, and presumed that women's needs would be met through the financial support of their spouses. Although there are no longer any legal restrictions on women's property rights in Canada, our family law still concerns itself with the issue of spousal interdependence.

There are good reasons for this focus. Many families, often in an effort to care for dependent children and to carry out household chores, arrange their affairs so that, at certain times throughout the course of a marriage, one partner bears a disproportionate share of the burden of income earning, while the other pursues non-earning work. The pattern, of course, is no longer as closely tied to gender as it used to be — although women are still more likely to carry the burden of child care, there are many instances in which a family has a stay-at-home dad. There are also childless families in which one spouse supports both partners for a period of time while the other spouse pursues an education. Although arrangements like these may prove very practical while a marriage lasts, they can lead to inequalities in property ownership that can operate unfairly if a marriage breaks down.

EQUALIZATION UNDER PROVINCIAL STATUTES

To reduce the impact of these inequalities, all Canadian provinces have legislation designed to "equalize" family property on marriage breakdown. Ontario's equalization provisions are found in the *Family Law Act* (FLA).[5] Under the FLA, a spouse does not acquire an ownership interest in property owned by the other spouse, but does have a right to an **equalization payment** if the parties separate. The equalization payment equals one-half the difference between the **net family property** of one spouse and that of the other. Net family property is the value of all property owned on a chosen "valuation date" (often the date of separation, but it depends on the circumstances) after deducting

- debts and liabilities, and
- the value of property owned on the date of marriage.

Certain property is excluded from the calculation of property owned on the valuation date, including gifts and inheritances from third parties after the date of marriage. The **matrimonial home**, however, is never excluded, and the matrimonial home is not deducted from the owner's net family property even if it was owned before the marriage.

THE MATRIMONIAL HOME

A matrimonial home is defined by the FLA as property that the spouses ordinarily occupied as their family residence at the time of separation. The matrimonial home is given special treatment in the equalization of net family properties, and the FLA also provides for special rights of possession (occupancy rights) and rights against alienation (rights prohibiting sale) of the matrimonial home. Both spouses have an equal right of possession of a matrimonial home. No spouse may sell or mortgage a matrimonial home without the consent of the other spouse or without a court order. Depending on the needs of the parties, one party may be granted the right to live in the matrimonial home (often after compensation is paid to the other party for giving up his or her own right), or the home may be sold and the proceeds equalized.

EQUALIZATION OF PROPERTY UNDER TRUST LAW

While it is easiest and most common for couples to rely on equalization rules under provincial legislation to settle family property disputes, not all separating couples are covered by this legislation. Each family law statute contains a definition of "spouse" that depends on certain conditions (typically the sex of the parties, the duration of cohabitation, and the presence of children). Ontario's *Family Law Act* defines "spouse" as either of two people who have married each other or have entered in good faith into a marriage that may be voidable. The definition no longer refers to heterosexual spouses, as a result of a number of court decisions over the past couple of years in which the common law definition of marriage (which referred to heterosexual couples) was struck down as being unconstitutional.

Where a couple's relationship falls outside the bounds of family legislation, a party seeking redress of property-related inequities may assert a claim for property that is legally owned by the other party on the basis of **trust** law. A party who

equalization payment
a payment ordered from one spouse to another, under family property legislation, that is designed to equalize property holdings on separation

net family property
a statutorily defined value of the property owned by one spouse that may be subject to equalization under family property legislation

matrimonial home
a dwelling that meets criteria making it subject to special treatment under family property law

trust
a complex legal doctrine based on the rights of a person in the property of another

succeeds in bringing such a claim will be granted relief in the form of an order (by the court) that the other party holds an interest in the disputed property "in trust" for the claiming party. The effect of such an order is to prevent the title owner from disposing of or using the property without compensating or taking into account the interest of the other party.

DOMESTIC CONTRACTS

Parties may contract out of family law rules by means of a "domestic contract." Part IV of the FLA provides that domestic contracts and agreements to amend domestic contracts must be in writing, signed by the parties, and witnessed. There are three kinds of domestic contracts:

marriage contract
a contract entered into before or during marriage that addresses the rights and obligations of the parties during the marriage or upon separation

cohabitation agreement
a contract entered into before or during cohabitation (the parties are not married) that addresses the rights and obligations of the parties during cohabitation or upon separation

separation agreement
a contract entered into by married persons or cohabitants after separation that addresses the rights and obligations of the parties after separation

- **Marriage contracts** may be made by people who are married or who intend to marry. These contracts may address the rights and obligations of each party during the marriage or on separation, including ownership or division of property, support obligations, and the right to direct the education of children, but not the right to custody of or access to children. Any provision in a marriage contract that purports to limit a spouse's right to possession of the matrimonial home is unenforceable.

- **Cohabitation agreements** may be made by people who are cohabiting or who intend to cohabit. Cohabitation agreements may address the rights and obligations of each party during cohabitation or on termination of the relationship, including ownership or division of property, support obligations, and the right to direct the education of children, but not the right to custody of or access to children. If the parties to a cohabitation agreement marry, their cohabitation agreement is deemed to be a marriage contract.

- **Separation agreements** may be made by married persons or cohabitants who have separated. A separation agreement may include provisions as to each party's rights and obligations, including ownership or division of property, support obligations, the right to direct the education of children, and the right to child custody and access.

Tenancies: Occupancy Rights and the Property of Others

Another key area in which the common law of property has been altered by statute is in the context of residential tenancies. Although most people today view landlord–tenant relationships as being essentially a matter of contract, tenancy relationships have property law roots in the concept of the leasehold estate. Because of the importance that the law accords to the concept of possession, the rights of a tenant, although they may be largely administered by contract, are strengthened by the fact of possession of real property. Another factor contributing to the comparatively strong legal rights of residential tenants is the existence of a public policy motive to promote people's security when it comes to a need as basic as shelter.

All Canadian provinces have passed legislation that imposes certain limits on the terms that landlords and tenants can include in the contracts that they make with each other. The balance between the rights of landlords and tenants has been a "live" political issue in modern times, and landlord–tenant legislation has a history of frequent amendment. Ontario's current landlord–tenant statute is the *Tenant Protection Act, 1997*.[6] A detailed review of that legislation (and the legislation in place in other provinces) is beyond the scope of this book. However, since law enforcement officers are often called upon to intervene in landlord and tenant disputes, it is useful to have a general knowledge of the kinds of rights typically contained in this kind of legislation. A very general discussion of typical provisions follows here. Note, however, that provincial legislation varies; to be certain whether a particular rule applies in a jurisdiction, the legislation itself should be consulted.

A RIGHT TO PEACEFUL AND EXCLUSIVE ENJOYMENT

Most landlord–tenant legislation guarantees tenants the right to occupy and "enjoy" (use) the rented premises free from unexpected intrusions by the landlord. In general, a landlord cannot enter the rented premises without being invited (for example, to fix something), or without providing a legislated period of notice to the tenant (usually at least 24 hours). These basic rules may be suspended or altered in cases of emergency, or in cases where the tenant is moving out soon and is required to provide access for the purpose of showing the premises to new or prospective tenants. But, in general, a landlord has no right to perform unannounced "inspections" or to enter rented premises when the tenant is not at home.

KEEPING UP THE PROPERTY

Most landlord–tenant statutes have provisions governing maintenance of the property and the landlord's duty to keep the premises in good repair. Typically, the premises must meet a certain level of livability before they are determined to be "legal" for the purpose of tenancy, and these standards must be kept up for the duration of the tenancy. Tenants, of course, are responsible for day-to-day maintenance such as cleaning, and may be held liable to the landlord for unusual damage to the property (normal "wear and tear" will not give rise to liability).

A RIGHT TO NOTICE OF TERMINATION OF THE TENANCY

Because of the public policy interest in security when it comes to shelter, many provisions of landlord–tenant legislation deal with the issue of termination of the tenancy and the parties' rights to notice of termination. Legislation on this issue varies widely, but all jurisdictions provide for a minimum period of notice on both the landlord's and the tenant's part. Even in the absence of a stated lease term (many tenants rent month to month and not on the basis of a longer lease), it is generally impossible or illegal to exclude a tenant from leased premises without at least a month's notice, even if the tenant is not paying the rent or is otherwise in breach of the tenancy agreement. As a result, a tenant who comes home to find that the locks on the door have been changed and he or she cannot get in is almost always entitled to be let back in (unless the eviction process under the Act has been finalized).

distrain
keep and resell the personal property of another; traditionally, a landlord's remedy that allowed the taking of a tenant's property as compensation for a default (typically non-payment of rent or property damage), now either banned or strictly constrained in all Canadian jurisdictions

Tenants are also required to provide notice of termination, although they often enjoy shorter notice requirements (though rarely less than a month). If tenants leave before the expiry of a term lease (such as a 12-month lease), they may be liable for payment of rent for the months they were supposed to stay, although they may be allowed to sublet the premises to a new tenant, and the landlord has a duty to minimize his or her losses by replacing the tenants as soon as possible. Finally, in some very limited instances, a landlord may have a right to **distrain** (keep and resell) the personal property of an absconding tenant who owes money for non-payment of rent or for damage to the property, but this remedy is usually (in Ontario, always) enforceable only when it is directed by a court order.

KEY TERMS

adverse possession	licence
bailment	marriage contract
cohabitation agreement	matrimonial home
distrain	net family property
easement	personal property
equalization payment	possession
escheat	real property
estate	separation agreement
expropriation	squatter
instrument	title
intangibles	trust
intellectual property	

NOTES

1. *Canadian Charter of Rights and Freedoms*, part I of the *Constitution Act, 1982*, RSC 1985, app. II, no. 44.

2. *Freedom of Information and Protection of Privacy Act*, RSO 1990, c. F.31.

3. *Statute of Frauds*, RSO 1990, c. S.19.

4. *Criminal Code*, RSC 1985, c. C-46, as amended.

5. *Family Law Act*, RSO 1990, c. F.3.

6. *Tenant Protection Act, 1997*, SO 1997, c. 24.

EXERCISES

Multiple Choice

1. The *Criminal Code* protects property interests by imposing liability for the following offences:

    a. fraudulent concealment

    b. mischief

    c. unauthorized use of a computer

    d. destroying documents of title

    e. all of the above

2. Canadian law has recognized property or property-like interests in

    a. family pets

    b. Internet domain names

    c. one's spouse's medical school degree

    d. frozen spermatozoa

    e. all of the above

3. Which of the following is not covered under intellectual property law?

    a. a patent for an invention

    b. the copyright for a painting

    c. a trademark for a new laundry detergent

    d. a person's collection of books

    e. the copyright for a book

4. Property rights can apply to

    a. land and buildings

    b. personal possessions

    c. intangible possessions

    d. the human body and personality

    e. all of the above

5. Legal possession of property can result from

    a. legal title

    b. inheritance

    c. physical control of property

    d. long-term use of property

    e. all of the above

True or False?

_____ 1. Under a tenurial system, all land with no private owner automatically belongs to the government.

_____ 2. Under family legislation, part of each spouse's property is deemed to be held in trust for the benefit of the children of the marriage.

_____ 3. A person who owns a life interest in land is not entitled to dispose of that interest by will.

_____ 4. It is possible to have possession of real property (land) without having title to the property.

_____ 5. It is possible to have title to real property without having possession of it.

_____ 6. It is possible to sue a person for theft instead of pursuing a charge under the criminal law.

_____ 7. Upon separation, the spouse with legal title to the family home is entitled to put the house up for sale, as long as he or she provides reasonable move-out notice to the other spouse.

_____ 8. Where a tenant has not paid the rent for three months, the landlord can either give notice of termination of the tenancy or change the locks on the premises doors while the tenant is out.

Short Answer

1. As a law enforcement officer, you answer a call from a homeowner who tells you someone has broken in and is downstairs in his kitchen. When you arrive on the scene, the homeowner greets you at the front door carrying a baseball bat. The invader has fled — luckily, because the homeowner asserts that his home is his castle and that he would have "defended it to the death" had the need arisen.

    a. What if the homeowner had in fact hit the invader with the bat, killing or seriously injuring him or her? What would the legal implications have likely been? Does it make a difference to your answer if the invader had been unarmed and had immediately made it clear that he or she was retreating (albeit carrying a TV)?

b. Going back to the original scenario (the invader got away), you decide you'd better throw some cold water on the homeowner's plans to defend his home to the death. What reasons do you give him?

2. While executing a search warrant at a personal residence, law enforcement personnel seize a quantity of white powder that proves, on analysis, to consist primarily of diacetylmorphine. The owner of the white powder is considering suing under property law for return of the material.

a. Will she succeed? Why or why not?

b. What if the substance, on analysis, turned out to be bicarbonate of soda?

c. What if the substance was bicarbonate of soda and there was no warrant for the search?

CHAPTER 12

Family and Employment Law: The "Relationship" Disciplines

Chapter Objectives

After completing this chapter, you should be able to:

- Understand the basic principles of the law relating to marriage and divorce in Canada.
- Understand the basic principles of the law relating to child custody, access, and support.
- Explain the basic principles of the law relating to child protection in Canada.
- Describe the role of the police in protecting family members at risk on family breakdown.
- Understand the basic principles of employment law in Canada.

Introduction

The two subject areas mentioned in the title to this chapter — family and employment law — may seem unrelated. However, whereas the previous chapter's topics shared property as a common link, family ties and employment arrangements share a basis in the concept of relationship. Both family and employment relationships are entered into voluntarily, with an expectation of permanence and with obligations flowing from each party to the other. Because of the interdependence created by both family and employment bonds, the breakdown of the relationship, in both cases, presents unique problems that require sophisticated solutions. In Canada, these solutions are prescribed by a mixture of common law and statute law.

Principles of Family Law

DUAL JURISDICTION

Canadian family law is characterized by an overlap in legislative jurisdiction. Marriage and divorce are matters of federal responsibility and are governed by the *Divorce Act*.[1] Other aspects of family relationships — notably those that relate to property (discussed in chapter 11), spousal and child support, and child custody and access — are within provincial jurisdiction by virtue of s. 92(13) of the constitution, which gives the provinces the power to legislate property and civil rights in the province. This generally means that if the disputants in a family law matter are legally married, they can choose to pursue issues of support, custody, or access under either provincial or federal legislation. Remedies for unmarried spouses, where they exist, are found exclusively under provincial law. The content of the provincial statutes varies from province to province. For the purposes of this chapter, we will focus on the Ontario *Family Law Act*[2] (FLA).

VALIDITY OF MARRIAGE

The requirements for a valid marriage may be an issue where parties seek to obtain a marriage licence, where one party to a marriage seeks an **annulment** (a court order terminating the marriage as if it had never existed), or where the validity of a marriage is relevant to another legal question (for example, rights of inheritance).

annulment
a legal declaration that a marriage was never valid and never legally existed; it permits remarriage without need for a divorce

Essential Validity

The essential validity of marriage means the capacity of the parties to marry. In Canada, capacity to marry is a matter of exclusive federal legislative jurisdiction. Depending on the defect or deficiency, a marriage could be void, void but capable of ratification, or voidable.

Certain defects or disabilities existing at the time of the marriage render a marriage **void**. A void marriage will be regarded by every court in which the existence of the marriage is an issue as never having taken place and can be treated as such by the parties without the necessity of obtaining an annulment. A marriage will be void if one of the following defects exists at the time of the marriage:

void
null or of no effect; as if never having taken place

- one or both parties have a prior existing marriage, or
- the parties are too closely related (the federal *Marriage (Prohibited Degrees) Act*[3] sets out what kinds of relationships are too close to permit marriage).

A marriage between two people of the same sex is legal, according to recent case law and the *Civil Marriage Act*.[4]

A marriage will be **void but capable of ratification**, by continued cohabitation after the defect or disability no longer exists, if at the time of the marriage

void but capable of ratification
void but capable of becoming valid by certain actions

- the parties were below the common law marriageable age (14 for boys and 12 for girls),
- one of the parties was mentally ill or mentally defective, or

- one of the parties was intoxicated by drugs or alcohol to the point of lacking capacity.

Some defects existing at the time of the marriage render a marriage **voidable**. A voidable marriage will be regarded by every court as a valid subsisting marriage unless and until a decree of annulment has been obtained by one of the parties. The validity of a voidable marriage can be questioned only in annulment proceedings brought by one of the parties to the marriage, and can never be questioned by third parties or after the death of one of the parties to the marriage. A marriage will be voidable where

- one of the parties entered the marriage as a result of duress,
- one of the parties was mistaken about the nature of the ceremony or the identity of the other party, or
- one of the parties is physically incapable of fulfilling his or her matrimonial (sexual) obligations.

voidable
valid but capable of being rendered invalid through annulment proceedings by certain actions

Formal Validity

The formal validity of marriage refers to the formalities and evidentiary requirements for marriage (such as the need to obtain a marriage licence and to be of the age of majority). Formal validity is governed by the law of the place where the marriage was celebrated. In Canada, formal validity is a matter of exclusive provincial legislative jurisdiction. In Ontario, the *Marriage Act*[5] is the relevant legislation.

DIVORCE

The *Divorce Act* sets out only one ground of divorce: **marriage breakdown**, which may be established on the basis of

- one year's separation,
- adultery, or
- cruelty.

marriage breakdown
the only ground for divorce under Canadian law

Parties may apply for a divorce on the basis of one year's separation at any time after separation, but must wait until the one-year period has elapsed before obtaining the divorce. There must be an intention on the part of the parties to live apart. Living apart without the intention to end the marriage (for example, where one party is required to work abroad for a certain period) is insufficient. It is even possible for parties to satisfy the requirement of one year's separation while living under the same roof if the required intention is accompanied by physical separation.

Adultery is voluntary sexual intercourse between a married person and a person of the opposite sex other than the married person's spouse.

Cruelty must be physical or mental cruelty of such a kind as to render intolerable the continued cohabitation of the spouses.

Various provisions in the *Divorce Act* aim to encourage reconciliation where possible and amicable divorce where reconciliation is not possible. Section 9 requires lawyers to draw these provisions to the attention of clients, to discuss the possibility of reconciliation with clients, to advise clients of the advisability of

adultery
voluntary sexual intercourse outside a marriage by one of the partners to the marriage; not a ground for divorce but rather evidence by which marriage breakdown may be proven

cruelty
under divorce law, physical or mental cruelty to a degree that makes continuing a marriage intolerable to one of the parties

negotiating issues of support and custody, and to inform clients of mediation facilities known to the lawyer that might assist the spouses in negotiating support and custody.

SPOUSAL SUPPORT

A party may claim spousal support under the *Divorce Act* if the party is seeking a divorce, or under provincial legislation, which is the *Family Law Act* in Ontario. Under the FLA, spousal support is available to legally married spouses and to people who are not married to each other but who have cohabited continuously for a period of not less than three years, or in a relationship of some permanence, if they are the natural or adoptive parents of a child.

The amount of spousal support that will be awarded depends on many considerations, including

- the need of the dependent spouse,
- the other spouse's ability to pay,
- the economic advantages or disadvantages to the spouses arising from the marriage or its breakdown,
- the financial consequences arising from the care of children, and
- the promotion of self-sufficiency of each spouse where possible.

Where appropriate, spousal support may be time-limited — that is, last only for a defined period after the separation.

CHILD SUPPORT

Under the *Divorce Act*, either or both spouses may be ordered to pay support for any child of the marriage. A child of the marriage is a child of the parties who

- is under the age of 16, or
- is 16 or over and under their charge but unable, by reason of illness, disability, or other cause, to withdraw from their charge or to obtain the necessaries of life.

Also included are any non-biological children for whom a party stands in the place of a parent.

Under Ontario's FLA, every parent has an obligation to provide support for his or her unmarried child who is under the age of 18 or is enrolled in a full-time program of education. The obligation to provide child support does not extend to a child who is 16 or older and who has withdrawn from parental control. "Child" includes a person for whom a parent has demonstrated a "settled intention" to treat as a child of his or her family — for example, a step-child.

The amount of child support payable is determined, in many jurisdictions, by referring to a legislated formula based on the needs of the children and the income of the paying parent.

CUSTODY AND ACCESS

In the case of divorce, either spouse may apply for custody of, or access to, a child of the marriage under the *Divorce Act*, and a person who is not one of the spouses may apply for custody or access in the context of divorce proceedings with leave of the court.

Ontario's *Children's Law Reform Act*[6] (CLRA) provides that a parent of a child or any other person may apply for custody or access. Non-parents may apply for custody but, in a contest with a parent, they are rarely successful unless they are the "psychological parents" of the child and have actually raised the child for some period. Parents are rarely denied access, although in cases of violence, possible abduction, or lack of parenting skills, *supervised* access may be ordered. Non-parents are rarely granted access over the objections of parents unless the non-parents have a very significant relationship with the child — for example, grandparents.

Best Interests of the Child

Custody and access are determined according to what is in the "best interests of the child." All circumstances relevant to the interests of the child are considered. The *Divorce Act* states that the court must ensure that a child has as much contact with each parent as is consistent with the best interests of the child, and specifically cites the willingness of a party seeking custody to facilitate contact with the other parent as a factor to consider when determining the best interests of the child. Because the child's interests are determinative, there is no enforceable "right" on either parent's part to have access to the child, regardless of the desire of the parent to have access or the responsibility to pay support for the child.

The CLRA lists many factors to consider in determining what is in the best interests of the child, including the child's emotional ties with each person claiming custody or access, the views and preferences of the child, and the plans proposed for the care and upbringing of the child. Although neither the *Divorce Act* nor the CLRA contains a primary caregiver presumption, it is often determined that it is in the best interests of the child for the parent who has been the primary caregiver to be awarded custody. And although there is no presumption in favour of mothers, the majority of custodial parents are mothers.

Possible Custodial Arrangements

In Canada, the custodial parent has the right and responsibility to make all decisions relating to the upbringing of the child, subject to any agreements or court orders that limit this right. Parents with joint legal custody share decision-making responsibility. Parents with shared custody (or joint custody) share decision-making responsibility, and each spends substantial amounts of time with the child. Custodial arrangements are diverse, and the ideal is for families to create custody and access arrangements that best serve the interests of the child, modifying the arrangements over time as the family's circumstances and the child's needs and interests change.

LAW ENFORCEMENT ISSUES ON FAMILY BREAKDOWN

As most law enforcement officers know, not all spousal relationships end in an orderly and civilized way. Spousal or child abuse (whether physical or emotional) can precede a breakup or be precipitated by the departure of a spouse. The FLA contains certain provisions — including provincial offence provisions — that recognize this reality and provide for police involvement in certain situations. These situations and the role of the police are dealt with in greater detail in provincial offences courses. Listed below are some situations that may warrant police involvement.

- Particularly where there has been a history of violence or harassment, police may be called on to enforce an order of exclusive possession of the matrimonial home by one of the spouses.

- The FLA provides for the arrest of an "absconding debtor" (a spouse who is not paying court-ordered support and who is suspected of preparing to leave Ontario) in certain circumstances.

- The FLA provides for the arrest (without warrant), on reasonable and probable grounds, of a spouse who has violated an "order restraining harassment" (commonly called a restraining order) issued under the legislation.

Child Protection

Besides the FLA and the *Divorce Act* and their provisions relating to support, custody, and access, other legislation deals with parental responsibility for the welfare of children.

The *Criminal Code*[7] prescribes several offences with which parents may be charged, including infanticide (murder of children), child abandonment, child abduction (a non-custodial parent can be charged with the abduction of his or her own child), sexual offences against children, and child neglect (failure to provide the necessaries of life).

In many jurisdictions, there is also provincial legislation dealing with child protection issues. For example, the Ontario *Child and Family Services Act*[8] provides for the apprehension of a "child in need of protection"; the definition of a child in need of protection includes children whose parents have subjected them to abuse or neglect, have allowed them to be subject to abuse or neglect by others, or who have failed to provide adequate supervision or care.

Employment Law

In essence, employment law is a matter of contract. The employment relationship is based on a contract — express or implied, written or unwritten — between an employer and an employee. In the case of unionized employment, the individual employment contract is replaced in whole or in part by a **collective agreement** — a contract between the union that represents a group of employees and the employer.

collective agreement
an employment contract between a labour union and an employer

However, largely because of the special importance of paid work in employees' lives (employment is, after all, the cornerstone of economic security for a large percentage of Canadians and their dependants), a number of statutes have been passed that influence the employment relationship and limit, to some degree, the freedom of the parties to define the terms of an employment relationship. A discussion of some of the more important employment law issues and the legislation that governs them follows.

DISCRIMINATION IN HIRING AND EMPLOYMENT

All provinces have human rights legislation that prohibits discriminatory hiring. In Ontario, the *Human Rights Code*[9] guarantees equal treatment with respect to employment and provides that that right is violated if an employer advertises a job opening that "directly or indirectly classifies or indicates qualifications by a prohibited ground of discrimination." Each jurisdiction has a slightly different list of prohibited grounds of discrimination, but these typically include

- religious beliefs/creed,
- colour,
- race,
- nationality/national origin/place of origin/ethnic background/citizenship,
- sex/gender (includes pregnancy in some jurisdictions),
- physical or mental disability,
- marital/family status,
- sexual orientation,
- age (many jurisdictions allow employers to require employees to be between age 18 and 65; currently, Ontario is considering abolishing age 65 as the mandatory retirement age), and
- political beliefs/opinions.

Some jurisdictions also prohibit discrimination based on a criminal record. However, in Ontario, for example, an employer is permitted, for certain types of employment, to ask for proof of a "clean record" (free of convictions that have not been pardoned) before making an offer of employment. A typical application to a police service in Ontario contains the question whether the applicant has been convicted of any offences for which a pardon has not been granted. Similarly, where a position reasonably requires that an employee be bondable, questions relating to bondability are permissible, or where driving is part of the job, questions about offences under provincial highway traffic legislation may be permitted.

When interviewing job applicants, it is important for an employer to avoid asking any question that might require an employee to disclose information about any of the above-listed grounds of discrimination.

Once an employee is hired, the obligation not to discriminate against him or her continues. Under human rights legislation, discrimination (either direct or indirect) is not acceptable as a factor in decisions related to promotion, continued employment, or termination. In certain narrow circumstances, discrimination based on personal characteristics is permissible if the employer can prove that the employee lacks a quality (such as a specified degree of physical strength) that would allow him or her to meet a bona fide occupational requirement. However, the courts interpret such requirements narrowly, and employers must be able to provide evidence of the reasonableness of their requirements and performance standards.

EMPLOYMENT STANDARDS

All jurisdictions have legislation in place that attempts to regulate the quality of the work environment by imposing minimum standards for the treatment of employees (in Ontario, the relevant legislation is the *Employment Standards Act*[10]).

Wages

Minimum wages are legislated in all jurisdictions. A province's minimum wage is typically prescribed by regulations under its employment standards legislation. The minimum wage varies across the country, and there may be lower minimum wages for certain occupations (typically where employees, such as servers, receive tips), or for employees under the age of 18.

Hours of Work

Many provinces also legislate the maximum hours of work per week and the minimum periods of rest during shifts for most occupations (professional employees are generally excepted, and there are also exceptions for emergency situations and certain kinds of industries). Finally, where an employee works longer than a standard workweek (again, defined differently depending on the jurisdiction), he or she may be entitled to overtime pay, which is usually calculated as a factor (1.5 or 2.0 times) of the regular wage.

Holidays

Employment standards legislation also prescribes a list of public holidays (sometimes called statutory holidays) that employees are entitled to take off with pay if they fall on a regularly scheduled workday. Certain exceptions apply, and employees who are required to be at work on a public holiday are typically entitled to overtime pay (generally time-and-a-half).

Vacations

Once employees have satisfied a minimum qualification period (typically one year), they are entitled, under employment standards legislation, to take an annual paid vacation. The details of vacation entitlements and the amount of vacation pay vary by jurisdiction, but in general, employers are not allowed to substitute pay in lieu of vacation except in very special circumstances.

Leaves of Absence

Finally, all jurisdictions prescribe, under employment standards legislation, that pregnant employees who have met a minimum qualification period may take several weeks or months of pregnancy leave around the time of birth. This leave is unpaid by the employer (though usually covered by employment insurance), but employees taking it are entitled to have their employment benefits continued during the period of leave and to return to their employment at the end of the leave. The federal government *Employment Insurance Act*[11] sets out the length of insured absences. Ontario is one province that changed its pregnancy leave provisions to coordinate with the federal provisions. Most provinces also offer parental leave for employees of either sex who have recently become parents, either by birth or by adoption. Many provinces offer other statutory leaves for other purposes, including bereavement, jury duty, voting, and family responsibilities.

TERMINATION: STATUTORY AND COMMON LAW RULES

The most contentious legal issue in employment law is that of employment termination. The rights of the parties on the termination of employment are governed both by statute (most commonly under employment standards legislation) and by the common law.

Reasonable Notice

Under the common law, an employee who is terminated without **just cause** is entitled to reasonable notice of termination or to pay in lieu of notice. The reasonableness (sufficiency in terms of duration) of common law notice is decided by the court on the basis of the facts of the case. Relevant facts to be considered when determining the adequacy of common law notice include

just cause
cause for terminating a person's employment that meets a standard specified either under the common law or under a statute

- the duration of the employment before the termination,

- the nature of the work performed (more specialized, professional, or senior-level work tends to warrant longer notice),

- the age and re-employability of the terminated employee,

- the conduct of the parties (abuse of the employment relationship by either party can affect the notice granted), and

- any contractual agreements made between the parties with respect to the issue of notice, as long as these are not in conflict with applicable legislation.

Although courts are loath to characterize it as a "rule" (because of the need to weigh all of the facts in any given case), there is a general trend toward granting approximately one month's notice for every year of service, all other factors being equal. Although employers are less likely to sue on the issue of notice, departing employees are considered to be subject to a similar requirement to give reasonable notice to employers on leaving their employment.

Because not all parties are able or are inclined to sue for notice under the common law, statutory provisions (which vary from province to province) exist to guarantee a minimum period of notice of termination (usually between two and eight weeks, depending on an employee's length of service). Employment contract terms that grant less than the applicable minimum notice period are invalid.

Where an employee can successfully prove that he or she has been wrongfully dismissed (without cause or without proper notice), damages over and above any monetary amount granted in lieu of notice may be granted. These damages are tortlike in their nature and basis and are designed to compensate for such issues as serious maltreatment in the termination process or unusual losses related to the termination. For example, if an employer unnecessarily humiliates or embarrasses an employee in the process of firing him or her such that the employee's reputation is damaged, the employer could be found liable for extra damages beyond the usual notice payment.

Just Cause for Termination

Notice of termination or pay in lieu of notice is not normally required if the employer can prove that an employee has been terminated for just cause. The common law and statutory definitions of just cause can be different; be sure to check your provincial legislation. Some circumstances that can form the basis of termination for just cause include

- dishonesty that is prejudicial to the employer's economic interests or reputation,
- serious insubordination or disobedience,
- chronic lateness or unexcused absenteeism, and
- serious incompetence.

In general, for the conduct to warrant dismissal, the conduct must have occurred more than once, and the employer has to show that progressive discipline (often a series of warnings, or more minor penalties such as suspensions) has preceded the dismissal.

KEY TERMS

adultery	marriage breakdown
annulment	void
collective agreement	void but capable of ratification
cruelty	voidable
just cause	

NOTES

1. *Divorce Act*, RSC 1985, c. D-3.
2. *Family Law Act*, RSO 1990, c. F.3.
3. *Marriage (Prohibited Degrees) Act*, SC 1990, c. 46.
4. *Civil Marriage Act*, SC 2005, c. 33.
5. *Marriage Act*, RSO 1990, c. M.3.
6. *Children's Law Reform Act*, RSO 1990, c. C.12.
7. *Criminal Code*, RSC 1985, c. C-46, as amended.
8. *Child and Family Services Act*, RSO 1990, c. C.11.
9. *Human Rights Code*, RSO 1990, c. H.19.
10. *Employment Standards Act, 2000*, SO 2000, c. 41.
11. *Employment Insurance Act*, SC 1996, c. 23.

EXERCISES

Multiple Choice

1. Unmarried spouses can claim support from each other

    a. under the *Divorce Act*

    b. if they have cohabited for three years

    c. on the basis of a prenuptial agreement

    d. if they can prove adultery or cruelty

    e. any or all of the above

2. Twelve-year-old children can

    a. be awarded support from their parents according to their needs

    b. withdraw unilaterally from parental control

    c. be awarded the right to see as much of each of their parents as is consistent with their best interests

    d. determine for themselves who will have custody of them

    e. a and c

3. Employers are normally required to pay their employees at least the provincial minimum wage, although exceptions apply, which may include the following:

    a. employees who work as servers

    b. employees who are not Canadian citizens

    c. employees who are under the age of 21

    d. employees who are on probation

    e. all of the above

4. An employer is required to give a terminated employee the reasonable notice prescribed under the applicable employment standards legislation unless

    a. the employee and the employer have contracted out of the application of the legislation

    b. the employee is over the age of 65

    c. the employee has been terminated for just cause

    d. the employer has made payment in lieu of notice

    e. c or d

5. What constitutes reasonable notice of termination does not depend on

    a. the duration of employment of the terminated employee

    b. the age of the terminated employee

    c. the employer's financial situation

    d. the conduct of the employer

    e. the re-employability of the terminated employee

True or False?

_____ 1. Whether a parent will be granted access to a child when a marriage breaks down depends on whether that parent has been ordered to contribute to the child's financial support.

_____ 2. Extreme drunkenness of one party at the time a marriage is performed can render a marriage void.

_____ 3. Adultery is a ground for divorce in Canada.

_____ 4. A party to a marriage that has been annulled cannot claim support from the other party.

_____ 5. Two married people who live in the same house can be "separated" for the purpose of divorce law.

_____ 6. Provincial employment standards legislation prescribes maximum notice periods in the event an employee is terminated without cause.

_____ 7. An employee can legally be terminated without cause as long as the employer gives reasonable notice of the termination or makes payment in lieu of notice.

_____ 8. If an employee is charged with a criminal offence, the employer has just cause to terminate him or her.

Short Answer

1. It's 10:30 a.m. on a Saturday. You are a police officer called to the scene of a domestic dispute. A woman has asked that her ex-husband be made to leave her front porch, where he has been standing for 45 minutes continuously ringing the doorbell. When you arrive, the woman shows you a court order granting her temporary exclusive possession of the house, which was the matrimonial home during the marriage. There is no restraining order in force against the ex-husband. The ex-husband tells you that he is not interested in entering the house; he simply wants his ex-wife to send out his daughter, Maxine, age three. He shows you his court document, which grants him unsupervised access to Maxine. According to the order, he is supposed to be able to pick up Maxine on Saturday mornings by 9 a.m., returning her to her mother by 7 p.m. When you ask the woman why she won't let Maxine go with her father, she tells you that her ex-husband has not paid his court-ordered child support for the past four months. The woman also tells you that the ex-husband's constant doorbell ringing is harassment and psychological abuse, and that in light of these she is justified in not letting Maxine go with him.

a. Is the man entitled to take Maxine with him for the day, despite the delinquent support payments?

b. Do you agree with the woman's actions? Why or why not?

c. What advice should you give the ex-husband?

d. What advice should you give the ex-wife?

2. An employer owns an ice-cream store franchise in a busy location. There are between one and three employees working in the store during each of two daily shifts, depending on the expected volume of business. The first shift of the day ends at 5 p.m. The business has nine employees.

   Easter Monday is a beautiful day. Temperatures reach over 15 °C for the first time that spring, and the ice-cream store is very busy. Marcia, a mother of one who has been employed full-time by the store for four years, is working the early shift alone, and is frustrated because business is very heavy. She anxiously awaits the arrival of Stephanie, scheduled to take over for the second shift. By 5:20, Stephanie has not arrived. Marcia calls her employer to say that Stephanie is missing and that she has to leave to be in time to pick up her son from day care by 6:00. The employer tells Marcia she can't leave until Stephanie arrives. At 5:35, Marcia calls again, and is given the same message.

   At 5:45, Marcia, needing to pick up her son, locks the front door of the store, serves the customers still in line, and then closes the store, leaving at 5:50. The next day her employer calls and tells her that she's fired.

   a. Was Marcia entitled to close the business early on such a busy day? Could she be held liable to her employer for loss of revenue? Explain.

   b. Did the employer have just cause to terminate Marcia for leaving against orders? Why or why not?

c. Does the employer have just cause to terminate Stephanie? Why or why
    not?

d. If Marcia was dismissed without just cause, how much notice is she
    entitled to under the Ontario *Employment Standards Act*?

e. How much notice might Marcia be awarded if she sued under common
    law? What factors would be taken into account in determining her
    notice entitlement?

Appendixes

Abbreviations of Case and Statute Reporters

AC	Law Reports: Appeal Cases (England)
ACWS	All Canada Weekly Summaries
AR	Alberta Reports
Admin. LR	Administrative Law Reports
All ER	All England Law Reports
Alta. LR	Alberta Law Reports
Alta. LR (2d)	Alberta Law Reports (Second Series)
App. Cas.	Law Reports: Appeal Cases (England)
BCLR	British Columbia Law Reports
BLR	Business Law Reports
CBR	Canadian Bankruptcy Reports
CBR (NS)	Canadian Bankruptcy Reports (New Series)
CCC	Canadian Criminal Cases
CCC (2d)	Canadian Criminal Cases (Second Series)
CCC (3d)	Canadian Criminal Cases (Third Series)
CCEL	Canadian Cases on Employment Law
CCLI	Canadian Cases on the Law of Insurance
CCLT	Canadian Cases on the Law of Torts
CCSM	Continuing Consolidation of the Statutes of Manitoba
CED (Ont. 3rd)	Canadian Encyclopedic Digest (Ontario Third Edition)
CELR	Canadian Environmental Law Reports
CLR	Construction Law Reports
CPR	Canadian Patent Reporter
CPR (NS)	Canadian Patent Reporter (New Series)

CR	Criminal Reports
CR (3d)	Criminal Reports (Third Series)
CRR	Canadian Rights Reporter
CTC	Canada Tax Cases
CTR	Canada Tax Reports
Can. Abr. (2d)	Canadian Abridgment (Second Edition)
ER	English Reports
ETR	Estates and Trusts Reports
FTR	Federal Trial Reports
Imm. LR	Immigration Law Reporter
KB	Law Reports: King's Bench Division (England)
LAC (3d)	Labour Arbitration Cases (Third Series)
LR	Law Reports (England)
LR Ch.	Law Reports: Chancery Cases (England)
LRCP	Law Reports: Common Pleas (England)
LR Eq.	Law Reports: Equity (England)
LR Exch.	Law Reports: Exchequer (England)
LRHL	Law Reports: House of Lords (England)
LTR	Law Times Reports (England)
MPLR	Municipal and Planning Law Reports
MVR	Motor Vehicle Reports
Man. LR	Manitoba Law Reports
Man. R	Manitoba Reports
Man. R (2d)	Manitoba Reports (Second Series)
NBR	New Brunswick Reports
NBR (2d)	New Brunswick Reports (Second Series)
NR	National Reporter
NSR	Nova Scotia Reports
NSR (2d)	Nova Scotia Reports (Second Series)
Nfld. & PEIR	Newfoundland and Prince Edward Island Reports
OAC	Ontario Appeal Cases
OJ	Ontario Judgements
OMBR	Ontario Municipal Board Reports

OR	Ontario Reports
OR (2d)	Ontario Reports (Second Series)
OR (3d)	Ontario Reports (Third Series)
OWN	Ontario Weekly Notes
RFL	Reports of Family Law
RFL (2d)	Reports of Family Law (Second Series)
RSA	Revised Statutes of Alberta
RSBC	Revised Statutes of British Columbia
RSC	Revised Statutes of Canada
RSM	Revised Statutes of Manitoba
RSN	Revised Statutes of Newfoundland
RSNB	Revised Statutes of New Brunswick
RSNWT	Revised Statutes of Northwest Territories
RSO	Revised Statutes of Ontario
RSPEI	Revised Statutes of Prince Edward Island
RSQ	Revised Statutes of Quebec
RSS	Revised Statutes of Saskatchewan
RSYT	Revised Statutes of Yukon Territory
SA	Statutes of Alberta
SCR	Supreme Court Reports
SBC	Statutes of British Columbia
SC	Statutes of Canada
SM	Statutes of Manitoba
SN	Statutes of Newfoundland
SNB	Statutes of New Brunswick
SNWT	Statutes of Northwest Territories
SO	Statutes of Ontario
SPEI	Statutes of Prince Edward Island
SQ	Statutes of Quebec
SS	Statutes of Saskatchewan
SYT	Statutes of Yukon Territory
Sask. LR	Saskatchewan Law Reports
TLR	Times Law Reports (England)

UCCP	Upper Canada Common Pleas Reports
UCQB	Upper Canada Queen's Bench Reports
WCB	Weekly Criminal Bulletin
WDCP	Weekly Digest of Civil Procedure
WLR	Weekly Law Reports (England)
WWR	Western Weekly Reports
WWR (NS)	Western Weekly Reports (New Series)

Case Brief

Brief

R v. PAUL AND OWEN

PROCEDURAL HISTORY

This is an appeal to the Ontario Court of Appeal from the jury trial decision of Madam Justice Wein, who found the appellants guilty of a number of charges, including attempted murder, robbery, assault with a weapon, and several firearms offences.

FACTS

The appellants assaulted and attempted to rob a customer in a Toronto dry-cleaning store, which took place in the presence of two eyewitnesses. At trial, counsel for one of the appellants tendered the evidence of an expert witness, who on *voir dire* advised the court he was prepared to testify on the subject of "eyewitness testimony." According to the witness, his testimony would focus on the results of an analysis of the identification evidence disclosed during the appellant's preliminary hearing, transcripts of which he had examined. The witness informed the court of the factors present at the time the incidents were alleged to have taken place that would be likely to impair the ability of the eyewitnesses to make an accurate identification of the appellant. Counsel for the Crown did not examine the expert witness about his qualifications, nor challenge his testimony. At the conclusion of the *voir dire*, the trial judge refused to admit the evidence tendered by the expert witness.

ISSUES

1. Did the trial judge err in refusing to admit expert opinion evidence on the issue of eyewitness identification tendered on behalf of the appellant?

2. Did the trial judge employ the proper test in assessing the admissibility of expert witness evidence?

3. What is the test used by courts in determining the admissibility of expert witness evidence in a jury trial, and did the trial judge err in her application of this test?

DECISION

The Court of Appeal dismissed the appeals of both appellants, holding that the trial judge did not err in refusing to admit the testimony of the expert witness proffered by the defence.

RATIO

Expert opinion about unusual theories or techniques is subject to special scrutiny by a trial judge to determine if it is reliable, and its admission is essential for the trier of fact to reach a satisfactory conclusion. The closer the evidence comes to being an opinion about a key issue at trial, the stricter the application of the scrutiny and the more essential its admission must be. The overriding factor to be considered in determining the admissibility of such evidence is whether it is more likely to assist, than hinder, the jury in its fact-finding mission.

Original Judgment

R v. Paul and Owen
Court of Appeal for Ontario
Finlayson, Labrosse, and Austin JJA

FINLAYSON JA: The appellants, Morris Paul and Mack Owen, were tried before the Honourable Madam Justice Wein and a jury on a ten-count indictment charging them with attempted murder, robbery, assault with a weapon and various firearm offences arising out of events which occurred on August 24, 1998 and November 16, 1998. The appellants were convicted of aggravated assault as an included offence of attempted murder and with the other nine offences in the indictment. The appellant Paul was sentenced to seven years in prison and the appellant Owen to five. Both appeal against their convictions.

THE FACTS

The accusations against the appellants were that on August 24, 1998 they accosted Vern Tim in a dry-cleaning store in Toronto and attempted to rob him of $500 in cash. Tim struggled with the man said to be Paul. In the midst of the struggle, his assailant fired three shots from a handgun, one of which lodged close to his heart. The other man, said to be Owen, beat Tim with a metal rod until he and his accomplice were able to make good their escape. The first five counts of the indictment charged attempted murder, robbery, possession of an unregistered firearm, use of a firearm and assault with a weapon arising out of the incident in the dry-cleaning store on August 24, 1998. Three months later, on November 16, 1998, the appellants were arrested together in a car and charged with the offences committed in August.

The case for the Crown with respect to the robbery consisted primarily of three eyewitnesses: the victim Tim, the owner of the store named Sam Loo and a passerby, Robert Passey. Passey was outside of the store where his car was parked. He observed two persons in a skirmish with a third person inside the store. When the assailants came out of the store they got into a red mid-size car parked down the street. He thought there was a third person already in the car. He took the licence number and gave it and a description of the assailants to the police. The vehicle turned out to be rented to Owen's sister, Judy. After the licence number of the car in question was traced, a police officer attended at the address of Judy Owen and saw a red car with the plates described by the witness. It was driven off by Ms. Owen, accompanied by a child. A warrant was issued for the arrest of Owen. The car was located and staked out. When two persons attempted to drive off in it, they were stopped. The driver was Mack Owen and the passenger Paul. In the glove compartment was a loaded Glock 40-calibre pistol. At trial, a firearms expert testified the shells found at the dry-cleaners after the shooting had been fired from this pistol.

At trial the appellants denied they were involved in the robbery in the dry-cleaning store. Owen stated at the time of the robbery he was with his mother, who he had picked up from her workplace. Paul also testified, and denied ever being in the store in question or being aware of its location. However, he did admit that a red Bible found at the scene of the crime and containing a receipt for a money order that he had purchased belonged to him. He explained that he was reading it one day in August on his grand aunt's lawn when a man calling himself Rambo came up to him and asked to look at the Bible. Paul handed it to him and then he went inside the building to assist his cousin. When he returned to the lawn, Rambo and the Bible had disappeared.

ISSUE

The appellants raise one issue: (1) Did the trial judge err in refusing to admit expert opinion evidence from a defence psychologist tendered on the issue of eyewitness identification?

ANALYSIS

Counsel for Owen tendered the evidence of Dr. Alexander Smith, a professor of psychology at the Laurentian University on a *voir dire* relating to the admissibility of "in dock" identification evidence and later as defence evidence on the issue of identification generally. Very briefly, this testimony involved an analysis of the identification evidence as disclosed in the transcripts from the preliminary hearing. Dr. Smith commented on the factors present at the time of the robbery that would impair the witnesses' ability to make an accurate identification, the problem of cross-racial identification, the quality of memory recall for perceived events over different time spans, the influence of "post event information" on memory, the validity of the photographic lineup, the misconceptions of jurors with respect to photographic lineups, the difficulties with "in dock" identifications and police procedures relating to the identification of the two accused.

In the light of the limited argument before this court on the matter, it is evident that this is not the case to engage in a full-scale analysis as to whether the type of evidence proffered by Dr. Smith is admissible in any circumstance. However, I do not intend to leave the subject without raising some warning flags. In my respectful opinion, the courts are overly eager to abdicate their fact-finding responsibilities to "experts" in the field of the behavioural sciences. We are too quick to say that a particular witness possesses special knowledge and experience going beyond that of the trier of fact without engaging in an analysis of the subject-matter of that expertise. I do not want to be taken as denigrating the integrity of Dr. Smith's research or of his expertise in the field of psychology, clearly one of the learned sciences, but simply because a person has lectured and written extensively on a subject that is of interest to him or her does not constitute him or her an expert for the purposes of testifying in a court of law on the subject of that specialty. It seems to me that before we even get to the point of examining the witness's expertise, we must ask ourselves if the subject-matter of his testimony admits of expert testimony. Where is the evidence in this case that there is a recognized body of scientific knowledge that defines rules of human behaviour affecting memory patterns such that any expert in that field can evaluate the reliability of the identification made by a particular witness in a given case?

I would caution courts to scrutinize the nature of the subject-matter of the expert testimony. Any natural or unnatural phenomenon may become the subject of an investigation conducted according to the scientific method. The scientific method requires the formation of a hypothesis, the testing of the hypothesis using reliable methodology, the examination of the results (usually with statistical analysis) and the formation of a conclusion. However, the fact that the testimony recites the application of the scientific method does not necessarily render the original object of study a matter requiring opinion evidence at trial.

In the case in appeal, I think that I can deal with relevance and necessity together because they appear to overlap. This opinion evidence is noteworthy in that, unlike most expert psychological or psychiatric testimony, it is not directed to making the testimony of a particular witness more understandable to the trier of fact and therefore more believable (e.g., an explanation of repressed memory syndrome or battered spouse syndrome). This opinion evidence is directed to instructing the jury that all witnesses have problems in perception and recall with respect to what occurred during any given circumstance that is brief and stressful. Accordingly, Dr. Smith is not testifying to matters that are outside the normal experience of the trier of fact: he is reminding the jury of the normal experience. This is not to say that a reminder as to cross-racial identification is not appropriate in a case where it is an issue. However, the argument that impresses me is that such a reminder from the trial judge is more than adequate, especially when it is incorporated into the well-established warnings in the standard jury charge on the frailties of identification evidence. Writings, such as those of Dr. Smith, are helpful in stimulating an ongoing evaluation of the problem of witness identification, but they should be used to update the judge's charge, not instruct the jury. I think that there is a very real danger that such evidence would "distort the fact-finding process." More than that I am concerned that much of what Dr. Smith and those who support him are saying is that our jury system is not adequate to the task of determining the guilt of an accused person beyond a reasonable doubt where identification evidence is pivotal to the case for the Crown. Much of Dr. Smith's evidence might well give us pause to consider whether our present jury instruction is adequate to the task, but to admit such evidence in the particular case may foster apprehension in the timorous juror and give him or her an excuse for not discharging that juror's duty to the community that he or she has sworn to serve.

To address the specific ground of appeal in this case, I am of the opinion that the manner in which the issue of identification was handled by the court (and by "court" I mean the trial judge and counsel for the Crown and the defence) was a model of fairness. The trial judge was correct in rejecting the proffered expert evidence. Her charge to the jury, following the very full closing arguments of all counsel, was exemplary. She impressed upon the jury the frailties of witness identification evidence generally and then, in considerable detail, she set out the identification problems as they applied to the particular facts of the case.

The trial judge was in a far better position than any witness or counsel to point out the frailties of the identification evidence, and her opinions, which she expressed, would have a very positive effect on the jury. She was also in a position to place these frailties in the context of the case for the Crown as a whole and she did that as well. This was not a "straight" identification case as counsel for the appellants submitted. After reading the complete charge of the trial judge on all of the evidence, I am left with no concern about the soundness of the verdict in this case. I would reject this ground of appeal.

Accordingly, I would dismiss the appeals of both appellants against conviction.

Appeal dismissed.

The Canadian Charter of Rights and Freedoms

Part I of the Constitution Act, 1982

Whereas Canada is founded upon principles that recognize the supremacy of God and the rule of law:

GUARANTEE OF RIGHTS AND FREEDOMS

1. The *Canadian Charter of Rights and Freedoms* guarantees the rights and freedoms set out in it subject only to such reasonable limits prescribed by law as can be demonstrably justified in a free and democratic society.

FUNDAMENTAL FREEDOMS

2. Everyone has the following fundamental freedoms:
   (a) freedom of conscience and religion;
   (b) freedom of thought, belief, opinion and expression, including freedom of the press and other media of communication;
   (c) freedom of peaceful assembly; and
   (d) freedom of association.

DEMOCRATIC RIGHTS

3. Every citizen of Canada has the right to vote in an election of members of the House of Commons or of a legislative assembly and to be qualified for membership therein.

4(1) No House of Commons and no legislative assembly shall continue for longer than five years from the date fixed for the return of the writs at a general election of its members.

(2) In time of real or apprehended war, invasion or insurrection, a House of Commons may be continued by Parliament and a legislative assembly may be continued by the legislature beyond five years if such continuation is not opposed by the votes of more than one-third of the members of the House of Commons or the legislative assembly, as the case may be.

5. There shall be a sitting of Parliament and of each legislature at least once every twelve months.

MOBILITY RIGHTS

6(1) Every citizen of Canada has the right to enter, remain in and leave Canada.

(2) Every citizen of Canada and every person who has the status of a permanent resident of Canada has the right

(a) to move to and take up residence in any province; and

(b) to pursue the gaining of a livelihood in any province.

(3) The rights specified in subsection (2) are subject to

(a) any laws or practices of general application in force in a province other than those that discriminate among persons primarily on the basis of province of present or previous residence; and

(b) any laws providing for reasonable residency requirements as a qualification for the receipt of publicly provided social services.

(4) Subsections (2) and (3) do not preclude any law, program or activity that has as its object the amelioration in a province of conditions of individuals in that province who are socially or economically disadvantaged if the rate of employment in that province is below the rate of employment in Canada.

LEGAL RIGHTS

7. Everyone has the right to life, liberty and security of the person and the right not to be deprived thereof except in accordance with the principles of fundamental justice.

8. Everyone has the right to be secure against unreasonable search or seizure.

9. Everyone has the right not to be arbitrarily detained or imprisoned.

10. Everyone has the right on arrest or detention

(a) to be informed promptly of the reasons therefor;

(b) to retain and instruct counsel without delay and to be informed of that right; and

(c) to have the validity of the detention determined by way of *habeas corpus* and to be released if the detention is not lawful.

11. Any person charged with an offence has the right

(a) to be informed without unreasonable delay of the specific offence;

(b) to be tried within a reasonable time;

(c) not to be compelled to be a witness in proceedings against that person in respect of the offence;

(d) to be presumed innocent until proven guilty according to law in a fair and public hearing by an independent and impartial tribunal;

(e) not to be denied reasonable bail without just cause;

(f) except in the case of an offence under military law tried before a military tribunal, to the benefit of trial by jury where the maximum punishment for the offence is imprisonment for five years or a more severe punishment;

(g) not to be found guilty on account of any act or omission unless, at the time of the act or omission, it constituted an offence under Canadian or international law or was criminal according to the general principles of law recognized by the community of nations;

(h) if finally acquitted of the offence, not to be tried for it again and, if finally found guilty and punished for the offence, not to be tried or punished for it again; and

(i) if found guilty of the offence and if the punishment for the offence has been varied between the time of commission and the time of sentencing, to the benefit of the lesser punishment.

12. Everyone has the right not to be subjected to any cruel and unusual treatment or punishment.

13. A witness who testifies in any proceedings has the right not to have any incriminating evidence so given used to incriminate that witness in any other proceedings, except in a prosecution for perjury or for the giving of contradictory evidence.

14. A party or witness in any proceedings who does not understand or speak the language in which the proceedings are conducted or who is deaf has the right to the assistance of an interpreter.

EQUALITY RIGHTS

15(1) Every individual is equal before and under the law and has the right to the equal protection and equal benefit of the law without discrimination and, in particular, without discrimination based on race, national or ethnic origin, colour, religion, sex, age or mental or physical disability.

(2) Subsection (1) does not preclude any law, program or activity that has as its object the amelioration of conditions of disadvantaged individuals or groups including those that are disadvantaged because of race, national or ethnic origin, colour, religion, sex, age or mental or physical disability.

OFFICIAL LANGUAGES OF CANADA

16(1) English and French are the official languages of Canada and have equality of status and equal rights and privileges as to their use in all institutions of the Parliament and government of Canada.

(2) English and French are the official languages of New Brunswick and have equality of status and equal rights and privileges as to their use in all institutions of the legislature and government of New Brunswick.

(3) Nothing in the Charter limits the authority of Parliament or a legislature to advance the equality of status or use of English and French.

17(1) Everyone has the right to use English or French in any debates and other proceedings of Parliament.

(2) Everyone has the right to use English or French in any debates and other proceedings of the legislature of New Brunswick.

18(1) The statutes, records and journals of Parliament shall be printed and published in English and French and both language versions are equally authoritative.

(2) The statutes, records and journals of the legislature of New Brunswick shall be printed and published in English and French and both language versions are equally authoritative.

19(1) Either English or French may be used by any person in, or in any pleading in or process issuing from, any court established by Parliament.

(2) Either English or French may be used by any person in, or in any pleading in or process issuing from, any court of New Brunswick.

20(1) Any member of the public in Canada has the right to communicate with, and to receive available services from, any head or central office of an institution of the Parliament or government of Canada in English or French, and has the same right with respect to any other office of any such institution where

(a) there is a significant demand for communications with and services from that office in such language; or

(b) due to the nature of the office, it is reasonable that communications with and services from that office be available in both English and French.

(2) Any member of the public in New Brunswick has the right to communicate with, and to receive available services from, any office of an institution of the legislature or government of New Brunswick in English or French.

21. Nothing in sections 16 to 20 abrogates or derogates from any right, privilege or obligation with respect to the English and French languages, or either of them, that exists or is continued by virtue of any other provision of the Constitution of Canada.

22. Nothing in sections 16 to 20 abrogates or derogates from any legal or customary right or privilege acquired or enjoyed either before or after the coming into force of this Charter with respect to any language that is not English or French.

MINORITY LANGUAGE EDUCATIONAL RIGHTS

23(1) Citizens of Canada

(a) whose first language learned and still understood is that of the English or French linguistic minority population of the province in which they reside, or

(b) who have received their primary school instruction in Canada in English or French and reside in a province where the language in which they received that instruction is the language of the English or French linguistic minority population of the province,

have the right to have their children receive primary and secondary school instruction in that language in that province.

(2) Citizens of Canada of whom any child has received or is receiving primary or secondary school instruction in English or French in Canada, have the right to have all their children receive primary and secondary school instruction in the same language.

(3) The right of citizens of Canada under subsections (1) and (2) to have their children receive primary and secondary school instruction in the language of the English or French linguistic minority population of a province

(a) applies wherever in the province the number of children of citizens who have such a right is sufficient to warrant the provision to them out of public funds of minority language instruction; and

(b) includes, where the number of those children so warrants, the right to have them receive that instruction in minority language educational facilities provided out of public funds.

ENFORCEMENT

24(1) Anyone whose rights or freedoms, as guaranteed by this Charter, have been infringed or denied may apply to a court of competent jurisdiction to obtain such remedy as the court considers appropriate and just in the circumstances.

(2) Where, in proceedings under subsection (1), a court concludes that evidence was obtained in a manner that infringed or denied any rights or freedoms guaranteed by this Charter, the evidence shall be excluded if it is established that, having regard to all the circumstances, the admission of it in the proceedings would bring the administration of justice into disrepute.

GENERAL

25. The guarantee in this Charter of certain rights and freedoms shall not be construed so as to abrogate or derogate from any aboriginal, treaty or other rights or freedoms that pertain to the aboriginal peoples of Canada including

(a) any rights or freedoms that have been recognized by the Royal Proclamation of October 7, 1763; and

(b) any rights or freedoms that may be acquired by the aboriginal peoples of Canada by way of land claims settlement.

26. The guarantee in this Charter of certain rights and freedoms shall not be construed as denying the existence of any other rights or freedoms that exist in Canada.

27. This Charter shall be interpreted in a manner consistent with the preservation and enhancement of the multicultural heritage of Canadians.

28. Notwithstanding anything in this Charter, the rights and freedoms referred to in it are guaranteed equally to male and female persons.

29. Nothing in this Charter abrogates or derogates from any rights or privileges guaranteed by or under the Constitution of Canada in respect of denominational, separate or dissentient schools.

30. A reference in this Charter to a province or to the legislative assembly or legislature of a province shall be deemed to include a reference to the Yukon Territory and the Northwest Territories, or to the appropriate legislative authority thereof, as the case may be.

31. Nothing in this Charter extends the legislative powers of any body or authority.

APPLICATION OF CHARTER

32(1) This Charter applies

(a) to the Parliament and government of Canada in respect of all matters within the authority of Parliament including all matters relating to the Yukon Territory and Northwest Territories; and

(b) to the legislature and government of each province in respect of all matters within the authority of the legislature of each province.

(2) Notwithstanding subsection (1), section 15 shall not have effect until three years after this section comes into force.

33(1) Parliament or the legislature of a province may expressly declare in an Act of Parliament or of the legislature, as the case may be, that the Act or a provision thereof shall operate notwithstanding a provision included in section 2 or sections 7 to 15 of this Charter.

(2) An Act or a provision of an Act in respect of which a declaration made under this section is in effect shall have such operation as it would have but for the provision of this Charter referred to in the declaration.

(3) A declaration made under subsection (1) shall cease to have effect five years after it comes into force or on such earlier date as may be specified in the declaration.

(4) Parliament or a legislature of a province may re-enact a declaration made under subsection (1).

(5) Subsection (3) applies in respect of a re-enactment made under subsection (4).

CITATION

34. This Part may be cited as the *Canadian Charter of Rights and Freedoms.*

Glossary of Terms

abet   intentionally encourage the commission of a crime

absolute liability offence   an offence that permits a conviction on proof of the physical elements of the offence (*actus reus*), with no proof of intention to commit the offence (*mens rea*) required

abuse of process   a course of action, on the part of the police or the prosecution that misuses court process or ignores the spirit of that process and interferes with the accused's ability to make full answer and defence; is inconsistent with good public policy or threatens to bring the administration of justice into disrepute

accessory after the fact   a person who, knowing that another person has committed an offence, helps that person to commit a related offence (for example, converting stolen goods) or to escape prosecution

accused   a person against whom a criminal or quasi-criminal charge has been laid, but who has not yet been convicted

acquit   find an accused not guilty of an offence

act   something done or committed

actus reus   Latin for "criminal act"; the objective element of an offence, which may be an act, an omission, or a state of being

adjournment   postponement of a trial

adultery   voluntary sexual intercourse outside a marriage by one of the partners to the marriage; not an independent ground for divorce, but rather evidence by which marriage breakdown may be proven

adverse possession   a legal doctrine by which rights in land or buildings are acquired or are sought to be acquired through possession (sometimes called "squatting") unaccompanied by title

aggravating factor   in the sentencing context, a circumstance of the offence or the offender that supports a more serious punishment (for example, the use of a weapon, or a long criminal record)

aid   knowingly assist the commission of a crime

amend   change a law or rule

annotate   supplement published statutes with references to, and/or summaries of, cases that have interpreted the application of statutory provisions

annulment   a legal declaration that a marriage was never valid and never legally existed; it permits remarriage without need for a divorce

appeal   the review or challenge of a legal decision in a court of higher jurisdiction

appearance notice   a formal document, given to a person charged with a minor offence, that sets out the requirement to attend court for trial at a certain date and time to answer to the charge

appellant   the party that decides to appeal a court's decision to a higher court

arrest   the act of taking a suspect into police custody

assault   under the common law, a threat of injury

attempt   a criminal offence in which the offender took steps toward committing a crime but failed to complete it

authority   a previously decided case that supports a particular position or conclusion about a question of law

authorized by law   conducted under the authority of a statute or with judicial authorization

automatism   involuntary or unconscious behaviour

autrefois acquit   French for "previously acquitted"; a special plea by which the accused alleges that he or she has already been charged, tried, and acquitted of the offence that is currently being charged

autrefois convict   French for "previously convicted"; a special plea by which the accused states that he or she has already been charged, tried, and convicted of the offence that is currently being charged

bail   the release of a person accused of a crime before trial, with or without conditions; also called judicial interim release

bailment   a delivery of physical possession of goods, without transferring ownership, from one person to another

battery   under the common law, a (usually negligent or intentional) act of physical contact

bill   a document created for the purpose of parliamentary review of a proposed statute; usually a statute in draft form that has yet to be adopted as law

binding   in common law, the determinative quality of a legal decision on future decisions (assuming similar facts) if it was decided in a court of superior jurisdiction

breach   the failure of one party to perform a contract or contractual obligations

burden of proof   the requirement that a certain party prove a particular fact at trial

Canadian Charter of Rights and Freedoms   the constitutional document that sets out the rights and freedoms enjoyed by all people of Canada

carelessness   a level of intent (*mens rea*) where a person fails to appreciate a risk that a reasonable person would have foreseen

case brief   a summary of a legal judgment prepared for research purposes

case law   previously decided court cases as described in written reasons for judgment

causation   the element of an offence that involves whether an act or omission of one party resulted directly in the injury to the other party

challenge for cause   the right of either party in a criminal jury trial to require that prospective jurors be questioned about certain aspects of the offence or the accused (for example, race or religion) that may result in bias on the part of the jurors

charge screening device   *see* preliminary inquiry

charging document   a written document, either an information or an indictment, that sets out the charges against a person accused of an offence

citation   an expression, in standard form, of the bibliographical information for locating a case or legislative document

cite   describe or refer to, orally or in writing, a legislative provision or legal decision

civil standard   the level of proof that a party must achieve in a civil trial to be successful — proof on a balance of probabilities

codify   formalize a law or rule by incorporating it (usually in print form) into an existing or new code

cohabitation agreement   a contract entered into before or during cohabitation of unmarried parties that addresses the rights and obligations of the parties during cohabitation or upon separation

collateral contract   a contract that is related to or depends on, but is separate from, another contract

collective agreement   an employment contract between a labour union and an employer

common law   a legal rule or a body of legal principles, established through judicial decisions, that deals with a particular legal issue or subject area

condition   a requirement that limits the freedom of an accused who has been released on bail or on parole

consent   the informed, voluntary approval by one party of the actions of another

consideration   the benefit(s) flowing to each party under a contract

considered   applied or interpreted in a court case; refers to statutory provisions

contractual defect   a legal problem with a contract that can either invalidate a contract or give rise to damages without invalidating the entire contract

contributory negligence   the role that a plaintiff or victim may play in negligently contributing to the cause of, or aggravation of, his or her own injury

conviction   a guilty verdict, where an accused is found, beyond a reasonable doubt, to have committed an offence

counsel   advise another person to be a party to an offence

count   a single charge on a charging document

counteroffer   a new offer that replaces an original offer, often with revised terms

criminal negligence   actions that are defined as criminal under the *Criminal Code* even though they incorporate a level of *mens rea* falling below conscious intent—for example, indifference

criminal standard   the level of proof that the prosecution must provide in a criminal trial to obtain a conviction — proof beyond a reasonable doubt

cruelty   under divorce law, physical or mental cruelty to a degree that makes continuing a marriage intolerable to one of the parties

culpability   guilt or responsibility

culpable intervention   an unexpected action, often by a third party, that contributes to or causes a chain of events

damages   losses suffered as a result of the breach of a contract or the commission of a tort, or compensation awarded for contract or tort losses

defence   the lawyers representing the person accused of an offence in a criminal trial

defences   the arguments that the defence uses to contradict the prosecution's evidence against the accused

deposit   partial payment of a surety

direct intent   a level of intent (*mens rea*) where the accused has a clear intent to commit the offence or to cause certain results

directed verdict   an early verdict of acquittal based on the prosecution's failure to meet its standard of proof

discharge   the release of an accused after a finding of guilt, either with or without conditions

disclosure   the requirement that the prosecution and police provide to the defence any and all evidence relevant to the charges against an accused

distrain   keep and resell the personal property of another; traditionally a landlord's remedy that allowed the taking of a tenant's property as compensation for a default (typically non-payment of rent or property damage), now either banned or strictly constrained in all Canadian jurisdictions

duplicity   a flaw in a charging document where a single count contains two or more alternative offences so that the accused does not know against which offence to defend

duress   a defence that allows the accused to be acquitted if he or she committed the offence under threat of immediate death or bodily harm

duty of care   a legal duty owed by one person to another based on a relationship or on the doctrine of foreseeability

duty to mitigate   a party's duty to minimize his or her damages from breach of contract or from the commission of a tort

easement   a limited property interest (often a right of access) that "attaches" to and is passed on with the land; it can either be a benefit or a burden

election   choice

element   a part of an offence that must be proven

entrapment   a situation where the police lure, draw, or entice a person into committing a crime

equalization payment   a payment ordered from one spouse to another, under family property legislation, that is designed to equalize property holdings on separation

error   a mistake made by the judge (or, less commonly, the jury) that might lead to an appeal

escheat   a reversion of property to the Crown when there is no will or heir to inherit it, or when a corporation that is the legal owner of property is dissolved

estate   an interest in land

evidence   oral or physical proof of the truth of an allegation

evidentiary standard   a basic level of proof; an alleged fact meets the evidentiary standard when there is at least some evidence that the allegation might be true

excluded   (with respect to evidence) barred by a judge's order from being used as evidence at trial, often as a result of a breach of a Charter right in producing the evidence

exclusion clause   a part of a contract that limits the contractual or statutory liability of a party in the event of a breach of the contract

exculpatory   proving innocence; evidence that tends to show that a person did not commit an offence

excuse   a defence that concedes that the accused's actions were wrong but claims that external or internal forces influenced the accused

expectation anticipation of benefits from a contract being fulfilled

expropriation the reclaiming of private land by the government

factual causation the situation where a certain result would not exist if a specific action or event had not occurred (for example, the man would not be dead if the woman had not shot him)

factual mistake an error made about the truth of a fact or the existence of a condition

factum a document used in an appeal that sets out the grounds for the appeal, the facts of the case, and the legal arguments as to why the appeal should succeed or fail

fault responsibility for an action

fine a form of punishment, requiring the payment of money, generally used for quasi-criminal or minor criminal offences

fitness to stand trial the accused's mental competence, at the time of trial, to understand the trial and what is at stake

foreseeability a test to determine whether a reasonable person could expect that a certain result may follow from his or her act; typically, an objective precondition to imposing a duty of care or to imposing liability for a particular class of damages

formal equality a measure of equality based on equality or inequality of opportunity

formalities procedural or formal requirements, such as writing, a seal, or a signature (typically prescribed by statute), that are necessary to make certain kinds of contracts enforceable

frustration a legal doctrine that releases the parties to a contract from their responsibilities under the contract when something (a circumstance or an object, for example) necessary to the performance of the contract no longer exists

full answer and defence a principle of fundamental justice whereby the accused person must be provided with the information and the means to have the opportunity to defend himself or herself against the charges

fundamental justice the basic tenet of the Canadian system of rights and freedoms that requires that all persons investigated for and accused of a crime

receive procedural protections to ensure that they are treated fairly throughout the process

general intent a level of *mens rea* where the accused need not have specifically intended to commit the offence or cause certain results but must have intended to act in a way that resulted in the offence occurring

ground for appeal a reason — generally an error made by the trier of law or of fact — for a party to be allowed to ask a higher court to reconsider the decision of a lower court

headnote an unofficial summary of reasons for decision that may precede the full text of a published case in a commercial case reporter

hearsay evidence information that comes from a source that does not have direct knowledge of the truth of the information — for example, when person A gives evidence about what person B, who is not present, said in the past

"housekeeping" provisions provisions found at the end of some statutes that deal with such administrative issues as the timing of coming into force of individual provisions

hybrid offence a crime that allows the prosecution to elect to proceed by way of summary conviction or by way of indictment

imprisonment incarceration in a prison, the most serious punishment allowable in Canada for persons convicted of offences

inadmissible refers to evidence that was obtained in a manner that breached a Charter right and is disallowed by a trial judge so that the prosecution cannot use it as part of its case against the accused; *see also* excluded

inchoate crime a crime that is incomplete or attempted

included offence a less serious offence that might be proven even when the more serious offence charged is not (for example, assault is included in assault causing bodily harm because assault might be proven even if the prosecution fails to prove that bodily harm resulted from the assault)

inculpatory proving guilt; evidence that tends to show that a person committed an offence

indictable offence   a serious crime that attracts more serious penalties and that is prosecuted using the more formal of two possible sets of criminal procedures

indictment   a form of charging document used for serious (indictable) offences

induce   persuade or bring about

informant   for a document, the person, usually a police officer, who swears the facts in an application for a search warrant or on a charging document

information   for a search warrant — a sworn affidavit that serves as an application for a search warrant; in provincial or youth court — a form of charging document used for less serious offences

instructions   directions given to the jury by the judge at the end of a trial advising it on how to apply the law to the facts of the case

instrument   a formal legal document

insufficiency   a flaw in a charging document that causes it to fail to contain the required information to sustain the charge

intangibles   things or concepts that may be the subject of a property right without having a physical form

intent   the mental element of an offence; *see also mens rea*

intellectual property   intangible property, including copyrights, trademarks, and patents

joinder   where two or more charges or two or more accused persons are tried together in the same trial

judicial interim release   *see* bail

jurisdiction   authority to make law, either by government or by courts

jury   a group of 12 citizens who are chosen to act as the trier of fact in a criminal trial

just cause   cause for terminating a person's employment that meets a standard specified either under the common law or under a statute

justification   a rare defence that negates the objective wrongfulness of an act and exempts the accused from the application of the *Criminal Code*

lapse   the expiry of an offer that has not been accepted by a stipulated acceptance time or on the occurrence of stipulated conditions

leave to appeal   permission to file an appeal; certain decisions can be appealed only if permission is granted by the court hearing the appeal

legal capacity   the ability to enter into an enforceable contract, based on the absence of factors (for example, cognitive impairment) that might impair capacity

legal causation   the situation where one or more actions could have caused a certain result and, for the purposes of a legal suit, the action that was most responsible for the result must be determined

licence   permission to use another's land for a specific purpose; does not give any other rights

marriage breakdown   the only ground for divorce under Canadian law

marriage contract   a contract entered into before or during marriage that addresses the rights and obligations of the parties during the marriage or upon separation

matrimonial home   a dwelling place that meets criteria making it subject to special treatment under family property law

mens rea   Latin for "guilty mind"; the subjective element of an offence that describes the state of mind or required intention of the accused

mental disorder   a disease or condition of the mind under s. 16 of the *Criminal Code* that results in the accused lacking the mental ability to intend to commit a crime

misrepresentation   a representation based, either innocently, negligently, or intentionally, on incorrect information

mistake of fact   a defence to a criminal charge that involves the Crown failing to prove the *mens rea* of the offence

mistrial   a declaration by a judge that the trial of an accused cannot be allowed to continue due to unfairness to the accused, and that a new trial must be conducted

mitigating factor   in sentencing for crimes, a fact or condition relating to either the offence or the offender that decreases the punishment (e.g., an early guilty plea, or remorse)

mitigation   avoidance or minimization of a party's damages from breach of contract or from the commission of a tort

motive   the reason a person committed an offence (for example, jealousy, greed, a wish for vengeance)

negligence   the failure of a person to respect or carry out a duty of care owed to another

net family property   a statutorily defined value of the property owned by one spouse that may be subject to equalization under family property legislation

non est factum   Latin for "I didn't sign/make [this contract]"; a legal doctrine that can be pleaded, based on a narrow set of circumstances, in an attempt to render a contract unenforceable

non–s. 469 offence   a less serious *Criminal Code* offence for which, at a bail hearing, the onus is on the prosecution to show cause why the accused should not be released pending trial

nuisance   a tort law concept generally used to describe something that interferes with another person's use and enjoyment of his or her property

offence   an act or omission that breaks a law and leads to punishment; a crime codified in a statute such as the *Criminal Code*

offence grid   a feature of some annotated versions of the *Criminal Code* that provides, in chart form, a summary of the elements, punishment, and other aspects of different offences

offer   the proposal of a contract or a set of contract terms; an offer is not a contract until it is accepted

omission   a failure to do something that is required by statute or by common law

onus   burden of proof; the necessity for a certain party to prove a certain fact

oral testimony   evidence provided verbally by witnesses

overruled   rejected or contradicted in a decision of a court of higher jurisdiction

parol evidence rule   the rule that the meaning of a contract must be determined without reference to external sources of evidence, such as other documents or oral testimony

particulars   details of a count

party   a person who has involvement in the commission of an offence, whether direct or indirect

passive defence   a defence by which the accused and his or her lawyers simply assert (through cross-

examination or in closing arguments by counsel) that the prosecution has failed to prove the accused's guilt beyond a reasonable doubt

penalty part (of an offence)   the part of a section of the *Criminal Code* that sets out the maximum or minimum punishment, or both, for the particular offence

peremptory challenge   the right of either party to a criminal jury trial to reject a prospective juror without giving a reason

personal property   property without a land or real estate component — physical possessions (chattels)

physical evidence   proof of the truth of an allegation in the form of actual objects (for example, a gun, bloody clothes, photographs)

plea   a statement of a legal position (guilty or not guilty); a legal argument or basis for a claim

plea bargain   an agreement between the defence and the prosecution as to how the accused will plead and what punishment the prosecution will seek

plead   argue or claim

positive (or affirmative) defence   a trial defence where the accused and his or her lawyers actively attempt to refute the evidence of the prosecution and perhaps introduce evidence of their own to clear the accused

possession   rights acquired or conferred through physical occupancy or control

preamble   an introduction, made up of one or more provisions, that sets out the objectives and guiding philosophy of a statute

precedent   a court decision that influences or binds future decisions on the same issue or similar facts

preliminary inquiry   a judicial hearing where the prosecution must demonstrate that it has enough evidence to prove, if uncontested and accepted by the trier of fact, that the accused is guilty of the charges against him or her; also called a charge screening device

presentence report   a document prepared by a probation officer at the request of a judge that provides background on the offender for use in deciding on a sentence for the offender

presumption of innocence   the basis of criminal legal procedure and rules of evidence — that an accused person is considered innocent until proven guilty

primary ground a ground for ordering detention of an accused at a bail hearing for a non–s. 469 offence; based on the judge's belief that the accused is unlikely to appear at trial if released

principal a person who is directly involved in committing an offence

probation a type of sentence that does not involve imprisonment but allows the accused to remain free, subject to conditions

probation order the list of conditions that apply to an accused released on bail or a convicted person released on parole

procedural law law that establishes the process by which substantive issues will be addressed

procedural part (of an offence) the part of a section of the *Criminal Code* that identifies the type of offence created by indicating the procedure by which an offender will be tried — indictable, summary conviction, or hybrid offence

proof beyond a reasonable doubt *see* criminal standard

proof on a balance of probabilities *see* civil standard

prosecution the Crown attorney or attorneys who are given the task of proving an accused guilty of an offence

quash overthrow or void

quasi-criminal similar in nature to offences listed in the *Criminal Code*, but under provincial or municipal jurisdiction

question of fact a ground for appeal that is available only to the defence that is based on the validity of a piece of evidence presented at trial

question of law a ground for appeal that is available to either the defence or the prosecution that is based on the misinterpretation or misapplication of a legal rule at trial

question of mixed law and fact a ground for appeal that is available only to the defence that is based on an error that combines elements of a question of law and a question of fact

ratio decidendi Latin for "reasons for decision," but often used to describe the few words or phrases that form the most essential part of a legal decision for precedent purposes

real property land and affixed dwellings; real estate

reasonable a subjective standard, used in the Charter or common law rules, of what is acceptable to society under the circumstances

reasonable person a hypothetical person on which a standard of behaviour is based for comparison with someone's actual behaviour

reasonable reliance reasonable actions by one party, generally based on representations or actions by the other party, that may result in losses that a court will compensate

reasons for decision the written expression of a legal decision; some decisions include reasons from more than one judge or justice

recklessness a level of intent (*mens rea*) where the accused knows the potential consequences of his or her action and takes an unjustifiable risk despite that knowledge

recognizance a promise — for example, to appear at trial if released on bail

rejection the refusal of an offer

reliance dependence on a promise or contract, including the expenditure of money in dependence on the contract

remedy an award or order provided by the court to redress a legal wrong, such as a tort or breach of contract

remoteness the degree to which the consequences of a contract breach or the commission of a tort results, directly or indirectly, from the breach or the tort

repeal terminate the application of a statute or statutory provision

representation a statement or claim made during contract negotiations that, though not necessarily a term of the contract, may be relied on by a party in deciding whether to enter into the contract

res judicata Latin for "already decided"; a special plea with which the accused argues that the charges against him or her have already been dealt with in a court of law; *see also* autrefois acquit and autrefois convict

rescind to opt, generally with good legal reason, not to carry out one's side of a contract, as if the contract had never been made in the first place

respondent   the party that defends the original trial court decision when it is appealed by another party

restitution   the return of benefits to put contracting parties back into their precontractual position

reverse onus   a situation where, instead of the prosecution being required to prove all aspects of an offence (which is the norm), the accused bears the burden of proving a fact or allegation

revocation   the withdrawal of an offer by its maker

s. 469 offence   a *Criminal Code* offence of such seriousness that, at the bail hearing, the accused has to show cause why he or she should be released (a reverse of the usual onus in bail hearings)

search and seizure   part of investigating offences, where the police inspect people or places and take into custody any physical evidence of crime that is found

search warrant   a written authorization to conduct a search

secondary ground   a ground for ordering detention of an accused at a bail hearing for a non–s. 469 offence; based on the judge's belief that the accused poses a danger to the public

self-defence   a defence that can be used against assault if the force used was no more than was necessary to protect against the assault

sentence   the punishment imposed on a person convicted of an offence

separation agreement   a contract entered into by married persons or cohabitants after separation that addresses the rights and obligations of the parties after separation

show cause   another name for a bail hearing, where the prosecution is required to show cause as to why the accused should not be released before trial

special plea   a statement, other than guilty or not guilty, made by an accused when he or she is required to enter a plea to the charges; *see res judicata*

specific intent   a level of *mens rea* that requires the prosecution to prove that the accused meant to commit the offence or to cause the harm that resulted

specific performance   a court order requiring a party in default to fully perform his or her obligations under a contract

squatter   a person who occupies or controls property to which he or she does not have formal legal title

standard of care   the standard by which discharge of a duty of care is measured, which depends on the relationship between the parties and the circumstances under which the duty arises

standard of proof   the level to which a party must convince the trier of fact of a given allegation; *see also* criminal standard, civil standard, and evidentiary standard

statute law   legal provisions, in codified form, that are developed and adopted by the parliamentary and legislative process

stay of proceedings   a decision by a judge to drop the charges against an accused, usually the result of improper actions (such as entrapment) on the part of the police or the prosecution

strict liability   in the civil law context, liability that depends only on proof of the consequences of an action even though there is no negligence on the part of the tortfeasor

strict liability offence   an offence that depends for conviction only on proof of the physical element of the offence although there is no negligence on the part of the accused

struck down   made null or void; applies to laws that are found to infringe on individual rights and freedoms

substantive equality   a measure of equality based on equality or inequality of outcomes, regardless of opportunity

substantive law   law that addresses the substance or factual content of a legal issue

substantive part (of an offence)   the part of a section of the *Criminal Code* that identifies the actual elements of the offence created

summary conviction offence   a less serious crime that carries a light penalty; the accused is tried in the Ontario Court of Justice without the benefit of a jury or a preliminary hearing

summons   a document that may be delivered to a person accused of a crime requiring that person to be in court at a certain date and time to answer the charges

sureties monetary guarantees that a person will appear at court to answer the charges against him or her; this money is forfeited if the accused does not appear as required

suspect a person the police are actively investigating with regard to an offence but who has not yet been charged

suspended sentence a form of punishment that involves delaying the imposition of the punishment indefinitely if the accused person complies with certain conditions, failing which the punishment is enforced

telewarrant a search warrant that is issued by telephone or other telecommunication method, such as fax

tertiary ground a ground for ordering detention of an accused at a bail hearing for a non–s. 469 offence; based on the judge's belief that there is some justifiable reason necessary for the administration of justice

title ownership based on rights acquired or conferred through legal transactions or instruments

tort literally, a "wrong"; in law, an injury — whether physical, emotional, economic, or otherwise — suffered by a person for which another person may be held liable

tortfeasor literally, "wrongdoer"; a person who commits a tort

trespass the wrongful entry onto or damage to the property of another

trier of fact the person or people who must decide what facts have been proven at a criminal trial (either the judge or the jury)

trier of law the judge, who interprets the law and applies it to the facts as found by the trier of fact at a criminal trial

trust a complex legal doctrine based on the rights of a person in the property of another

unconscionability serious unfairness in a contract; unfairness that no reasonable person would accept and no honest person would propose

undertaking a promise or monetary payment made as security for a recognizance

verdict the decision as to the guilt or innocence of the accused

void null or of no effect; as if never having taken place

void but capable of ratification void but capable of becoming valid by certain actions

voidable valid but capable of being rendered invalid through annulment proceedings by certain actions

waive give up a legal right, such as the right to counsel or the right to silence

wilful blindness a circumstance in which the accused suspected the potential for criminal consequences but closed his or her mind to them

Index